emma
goldman

emma goldman

Sexuality and the Impurity of the State

Bonnie Haaland

BLACK ROSE BOOKS

Montréal/New York
London

BLACK ROSE BOOKS No. W193
Hardcover ISBN 1-895431-65-4
Paperback ISBN 1-895431-64-6

Library of Congress No. 93-70392

Canadian Cataloguing in Publication Data

Haaland, Bonnie
Emma Goldman: sexuality and the impurity of the State

ISBN 1-895431-65-4 (bound) –
ISBN 1-895431-64-6 (pbk.)

1. Goldman, Emma, 1869–1940. 2. Feminism. 3. Women's rights. I. Title.

HX843.7.G65H33 1993   305.42   C93-090103-7

Mailing Address

BLACK ROSE BOOKS
C.P. 1258
Succ. Place du Parc
Montréal, Québec
H2W 2R3 Canada

BLACK ROSE BOOKS
340 Nagel Drive
Cheektowaga, New York
14225 USA

Printed in Canada

A publication of the Institute of Policy Alternatives of Montréal
(IPAM)

Contents

ACKNOWLEDGEMENTS   vi

INTRODUCTION
Sexuality, Reproduction and Anarchism:
Emma Goldman and the Impurity of the State   vii

CHAPTER 1
Kropotkin and Ibsen: Supplying the Theoretical
Foundation for Goldman's Vision of Anarchism   1

CHAPTER 2
Community Versus Society: Goldman's View of the
Supremacy of Instinct   25

CHAPTER 3
The Social Historical Context Surrounding Goldman
and the "Sex Question"   66

CHAPTER 4
Theoretical Perspectives on Sexuality and
Reproduction   99

CHAPTER 5
Goldman and the Sexologists   123

CHAPTER 6
Emancipation, Feminism and Same-Sex
Relationships: Goldman and the Interconnections   144

CHAPTER 7
Conclusion   182

BIBLIOGRAPHY   191

INDEX   199

Acknowledgements

The ideas and support of many people have played an important role in the development of this book. I wish to acknowledge the critical readings and suggestions of Ruth Roach Pierson, Malcolm Levin, Carole Farber, Hesh Troper, Candace Falk and the staff of the Emma Goldman Papers. I also wish to acknowledge the superb word processing skills of Sheri Scott and the able assistance, in the final stages, of Christine Stephens.

Bonnie Haaland
Vancouver, 1993

INTRODUCTION

Sexuality, Reproduction and Anarchism: Emma Goldman and the Impurity of the State

I was initially drawn to the ideas of Emma Goldman because of her views on women's emancipation and the relevance of these views to contemporary feminist debates. Goldman's indictment of the bureaucratic/legislative realm and her rejection of it as a viable location for women's emancipation struck a sympathetic cord in me. I was in agreement with many of the contemporary critiques of the bureaucratic/legislative realm, or what Goldman referred to as the "State," after having experienced many of its alienating and depersonalizing consequences. The development of the public sphere (i.e., the world of politics and business) as one in which men are the creators and representatives makes the already alienating consequences of the public sphere even more severe for women who must work and live in this realm.

On the other hand, I was not comfortable with Goldman's suggestion that women should abandon the public sphere in favour of the realm of their private "instincts," "tastes," or "desires." As contemporary feminist debates about women's difference versus women's equality have illustrated, women's so-called different "nature" (sexual, biological, psychological, etc.) has been the basis upon which women have been separated, excluded, and oppressed.

The discomfort I felt in unequivocally endorsing the private over the public is a discomfort which many contemporary feminist theorists express in their debates over the difference/equality issue. As they have argued in their efforts to reclaim a female "voice" in a patriarchal world, to say that women are different and possess a specific feminine nature, has damaging consequences for women, including the possibility that women's difference may be used as justification for their exclusion, separation and oppression in a "separate sphere." On the other hand, to advocate the equality for women in the bureaucratic/legislative sphere could be perceived to be a tacit endorsement of the norms and values of that sphere. To what extent must women become like men in order to survive in this realm? Does equality mean sameness for men and women? These are questions which contemporary feminists have grappled with in considering the equality side of the difference/equality debate.

For Goldman, there appeared to be little discomfort or tension in her choice—the basis for women's emancipation was through the unfettered expression of their "instincts." According to Goldman, female "instincts" could be most fully expressed outside the organized authority of the public sphere and within the realm which historically has been considered the private sphere. Goldman's view of "instinct," which views sexuality and reproduction as emancipatory possibilities for women, intrigued me, particularly in light of contemporary feminist theorists who suggest that women's bodies—particularly their sexual and reproductive vulnerability—inhibited their opportunities for self-expansion.

I, therefore, come to this book attracted to Goldman's liberatory message for women, yet cautious of the implementation of the message, given the existing power relations between the sexes—relations which, in my mind, would not disappear should Goldman's anarchist vision come into being.

Like some contemporary feminists who endorse an "integrative" approach to the private/public distinction, I believe the separation of spheres to be an artificial one. I also believe that women's historical assignment to life-sustaining roles has been misinterpreted as women's "natural" location; as a result women have been isolated and separated from the realm of public power and decision-making. Like Goldman, however, I believe that the public realm will not necessarily be "purified" by women's entry into it and, correspondingly, that women's condition may not necessarily improve with their entry into the bureaucratic/legislative realm and its professions.

Emma Goldman: A Biographical Sketch

For contemporary feminists, Emma Goldman has become somewhat of a cult figure. Her ideas on women's emancipation, sexual freedom, birth control, voluntary motherhood, homosexual rights, and the oppressive nature of marriage, religion and the State, have struck a sympathetic cord among the ranks of contemporary feminists—particularly those who see sexual liberation and women's liberation as inextricably linked. Since the early 1970s, the legend of Emma Goldman—as "Red Emma," as "the most dangerous woman in America," as an advocate of "free love," as the "Queen of the Anarchists"—has made her the subject of considerable attention within feminist scholarship. Feminist historian, Linda Gordon, argues that Emma Goldman, more than any other person, has been credited with fusing "into a single ideology sex radicalism,"[1] and, according to Goldman biographer, Alice Wexler, with "going further than most radicals in her understanding of the politics of sex."[2] Martha Solomon, a contemporary analyst of Goldman's rhetoric, argues that her "insistence on the significance of issues related to women and the importance of sexuality in human life were hallmarks of her interpretation of anarchism."[3] Solomon's view is shared by anarchist historian, George Woodcock, who considers Goldman's inclusion of the issues of sexuality and feminism to be of significant historical importance to the development of anarchist theory.

Emma Goldman was born in Russia in 1869 to Jewish parents. Abraham Goldman was a shopkeeper, who, despite having two sons, "could not forgive his daughter her sex."[4] As a young child, Goldman was frequently the victim of her father's physical and verbal abuse. His presence created a dark and prison-like atmosphere for young Emma. But despite her father's harshness, Goldman's feelings towards him were "powerfully ambivalent";[5] while she feared and loathed him, she also loved him and wanted his love in return. Taube Goldman, Emma's frequently pregnant and exhausted mother, was distant and detached from her daughter, never forming a mutually sustaining relationship with her. At the age of fifteen, her father insisted that she be married, arguing that girls "do not have to

learn much." Wanting to continue her schooling and travel, Emma
rejected her father's decision. Says her first biographer, Richard
Drinnon:

> Emma's independent views were highly dangerous. The
> Jewish community looked upon the adolescent girl as lit-
> tle more than a chattel and, more specifically, as the
> property of her father....When Abraham Goldman exer-
> cised a father's right by making arrangements to have
> her marry at fifteen, Emma boldly rejected.[6]

Firmly believing in romantic love, Emma maintained that she would
never marry for anything but love.[7]

Shortly after this abortive attempt at an arranged marriage, she
emigrated to the United States to live with her older sister, Helena.
She settled in Rochester, N.Y. and obtained employment as a
seamstress. In 1887, the trial and execution of the Haymarket anarchists[8] took place, drawing Goldman's attention irrevocably to the
anarchist cause. She read about the trial and defense of the Chicago
anarchists in the Rochester press, feeling passionately sympathetic
towards them and their political cause. Goldman's exposure to the
Haymarket affair caused a new world to open up for her.[9] Recalling
her initial dedication to anarchism, Emma stated:

> I had a distinct sensation that something new and
> wonderful had been born in my soul. A great ideal, a
> burning faith, a determination to dedicate myself to the
> memory of my martyred comrades, to make their cause
> my own, to make known to the world their beautiful
> lives and heroic deaths.[10]

In Rochester, Goldman married Jacob Kersner at age eighteen;
he was Jewish, of no particular political persuasion, and was a mate
of her own choosing. The two were divorced one year later.
Goldman recalled that she and Kersner were at "opposite poles" and
had nothing in common, "not even sexual blending."[11] Due to the

urgings of Kersner and her family, Goldman and Kersner were remarried in 1888 and were divorced again shortly after. Abraham and Taube Goldman, then also living in America, forbade their young daughter to enter their home after exhibiting such "loose character" in leaving her husband.

In 1889, at aged twenty, Goldman moved to New York City and joined an anarchist commune where she met Alexander Berkman, who later became her lifelong companion and lover. Her new-found commitment to anarchism and her newly-established relationship with Berkman propelled her into political activism. Goldman and Berkman became involved in the Steelworker's strike in Homestead, Pennsylvania.[12] Berkman planned to shoot Henry Clay Frick, the Carnegie Steel Company chairman, and Goldman raised funds for the purchase of a gun. In 1892 their plan was accomplished. Berkman was caught, convicted of attempted murder, and sentenced to 22 years in prison. After Berkman's imprisonment, Goldman's oratorical career began as she attempted to spread the anarchist message, defending Berkman's deed. In 1893, while still actively engaged as an anarchist propagandist and orator, she was tried and convicted for allegedly inciting riots among the unemployed of New York City. She served one year in prison.

Shortly after her release from prison, in 1895, Goldman left New York to study nursing and midwifery in Vienna where she was exposed to the ideas of Freud, as well as the philosophies and dramatic artistry of Ibsen, Strindberg, Shaw, Hauptmann and Nietzsche.[13] Months later, she returned to New York. In 1899, she returned to Europe from New York with the intention of fulfilling a childhood dream of studying medicine, but found medical school too restrictive and withdrew. There were also objections from her financial sponsor who reminded the young Goldman that he was supporting her medical studies and not her political activism. Goldman responded to a letter from her sponsor by saying: "E. G., the woman and her ideas are inseparable. She does not exist for the amusement of upstarts, nor will she permit anyone to dictate to her. Keep the money."[14]

Upon her return to New York from Europe in 1901, Goldman became a midwife and nurse on New York City's East Side. It was here that her real exposure to the degradation, oppression, and objectification of woman took place as poor women pleaded with her to end their pregnancies and to provide them with reliable birth control methods. Also in 1901, Goldman was drawn into the centre of controversy over the assassination of President William McKinley. Although not connected in any way to McKinley's assassination, she was accused of being an accomplice to the crime and was jailed but later released for lack of evidence.

In 1906, after five years of underground activity following the McKinley assassination, Goldman founded a monthly journal, *Mother Earth*, which developed into a popular vehicle for American radicalism. *Mother Earth* contained articles on civil rights, poems by Oscar Wilde, plays by Ibsen and essays on birth control and sexual egalitarianism.

In 1908, Goldman entered into a relationship with Ben Reitman, a doctor cum vagrant. Their relationship was an intense and emotionally charged one in which the two combined their professional and private lives. In 1910, Reitman and Goldman toured the United States together: he as manager, she as lecturer. Goldman recalled "speaking 120 times in thirty-seven cities, in twenty-five states."[15] She presented her lectures in union halls, churches, Y.M.C.A.'s, theatres and hotels, and universities. Her most unreceptive audience were students at the University of Michigan and she called them "pampered parasites." Finding confrontation exhilarating, Goldman rose to every challenge asserting that the more hostile her audience, the "more caustic" she became.[16]

In 1910, Goldman published her first volume of essays entitled *Anarchism and Other Essays,* which contained treatises on women's emancipation, marriage and love, female prostitution, anarchism, education and "puritanism." In many of her essays, Goldman advocated "free love" and marriage based on mutual affection rather than property relations. Unlike her more proper suffragette opponents, she advocated sexual experimentation (engaging in "varietism" or heterosexual variety), rather than chastity. She followed this principle in her personal associations with men, carrying on a number of sexual/romantic relationships with a variety of fellow anarchists.

In 1914, Goldman published a volume of her lectures on modern drama, *The Social Significance of Modern Drama,* which contained critiques of plays by Shaw, Ibsen, Hauptmann, Brieux, Yeats, and Strindberg and others. Many of her assessments of the social significance of their plays were based on their treatment of such socially and sexually relevant issues as venereal disease, motherhood without marriage, female chastity, "puritan" hypocrisy surrounding sexual behaviour, sex education of the young, and premarital and extra-marital sexual activity. In 1916, Goldman was arrested for giving a public lecture advocating birth control. The following year she was sentenced to two years in prison for conspiring to obstruct the draft. Shortly after, *Mother Earth* ceased publication.

The Russian revolution in 1917 led Goldman to support the "glorious work" of the Bolsheviki.[17] In 1920, she was deported along with Alexander Berkman and other "radicals" to her native Russia,[18] where her subsequent criticisms of the newly created Soviet State and its repressive tactics were to become the subject of years of scholarship, lectures and public debates. In 1921, a disillusioned Goldman left Russia to live in exile in Europe, where she published *My Disillusionment in Russia* in 1923 and *My Further Disillusionment in Russia* in 1924. In 1931, Goldman published an autobiography, *Living My Life,* in which she reconstructed her "persona," one of her most "powerful creations."[19]

Returning to the United States in 1934 by virtue of special permission granted by the U.S. government, Goldman embarked upon a ninety-day lecture tour on drama. From 1936-1939, Goldman worked in England as a propagandist for the Spanish anarchist revolutionaries. Emma Goldman died in Toronto in 1940 and was buried in Chicago near the Haymarket martyrs.

Goldman's views on women's emancipation, sexual freedom and birth control (as well as her so-called "private" life) were subsumed within a larger anarchist framework. By her own account, from the time Goldman entered the anarchist movement in 1889 at the age of twenty, she had no personal life which did not reflect the movement or her activities in it.[20] Goldman's anarchism was not just a *public* theory separate from her personal life. Goldman attempted,

through her writing, particularly her autobiography and her powerfully crafted "persona,"[21] to "create" a perfect fusion of her private
and public lives. According to Wexler, Goldman was aware of the
need for role models within the anarchist movement and believed
that the "way one lived one's life everyday was an individual's most
important political statement."[22] While some feminist analyses of
Goldman have suggested that her deeds and her ideas were inextricably linked,[23] others have illuminated the contradictions between Goldman's private life and her public persona.[24] In relation to
Goldman's major contributions to anarchist thinking—sexual
freedom and feminism—the contradictions between private deeds
and public rhetoric are clearly apparent.

Privately, Goldman acknowledged the contradiction between
her private and public lives—between the independent "sex radical"
and the dependent monogamist. Calling herself the Mary
Wollstonecraft of the twentieth-century, Goldman felt the tension-
filled inconsistency between her public and private roles which, in
many respects, were inseparable yet embodied vastly different sides
of her character. Goldman's strength and courage were exhibited in
numerous settings—in prisons and in lecture halls with hostile
audiences. Her public persona elicited admiration for the strength of
her convictions and the extent to which she would place herself in
danger in order to voice those convictions. The contradiction between the sexual libertarian and the weak child-like lover was not lost
on Goldman. On July 26, 1911, she wrote to her lover Ben Reitman:

> Years ago I read *The Life of Mary Wollstonecraft*. Her weak
> and humiliating love life with Imlay, was the most terrible
> thing to me. Mary Wollstonecraft, the most daring woman
> of her time, the freest and boldest exponent of liberty, of
> free love, the slave of her passion for Imlay. How could
> anyone forgive such weakness? Thus I reasoned many
> years ago. Today? Today E.G., the Wollstonecraft of the 20th
> century even like her great sister, is weak and dependent,
> clinging to the man no matter how worthless and faithless
> he is. What an irony of fate.[25]

There were also contradictions between Goldman's public support of feminist causes and her private life. While Goldman championed the cause of women, lecturing on and writing about women's emancipation through spiritual discovery,[26] sexual freedom, voluntary motherhood, access to reliable birth control, and motherhood without marriage, privately she found relationships with women difficult, often preferring the company of men. Adrienne Rich's theory that women who feel unmothered (as Goldman did) have difficulty in feeling comfortable with other women of equal status,[27] seems to fit Goldman. As one of a very few prominent women in the anarchist movement, Goldman did not "easily identify with other women in the movement or see herself as part of a community of women."[28] Her closest contacts in the anarchist movement were men and she disliked all-women gatherings and associations. Throughout her career in the movement she experienced deep personal rivalry and jealousy toward other feminists—notably Margaret Sanger, Lucy Parsons and Voltairine de Cleyre.[29] Sounding remarkably like Rich in her assessment of Goldman's "uneasiness felt with equals," Wexler comments:

> Her relationship with individual women tended to be uneasy...her closest friendships, as she grew older, were with younger women whose admiration and devotion overcame her sense of rivalry.[30]

These inconsistencies between Goldman's public and personal life, as Wexler points out, were not unique but rather typical of the "contradictory values experienced by many women at this moment of transition from the Victorian to the modern eras..."[31] She outlines the conflict of values that Goldman, and other women, experienced at this time:

> ...The conflict between masochistic nineteenth century values of self-sacrifice, submission, and dependence associated with the ideal of "true womanhood" (or its European equivalents) and the modern values of asser-

tion, self-expression, and independence associated with the "new woman" of the early twentieth century.[32]

Contemporaries such as Charlotte Perkins Gilman, experienced similar inconsistencies and contradictions between their private and public lives.[33] Although representative of a different school of feminism than that of Goldman, Gilman experienced many of the same conflicts.[34] Carol Ruth Berkin explains:

> Her [Charlotte Perkins Gilman's] life bears witness to the difficulties of feminism, not as an ideology or a political commitment, but as a personal experience. Charlotte Perkins Gilman struggled for intellectual and emotional liberation, hampered through much of her life by an internalization of the very split vision of masculine and feminine spheres and destinies that, in her work, she would expose as artificial.[35]

Goldman and her feminist contemporaries were, in Goldman's words, "still rooted in the old soil, though our visions are of the future and our desire is to be free and independent."[36]

While there were contradictions between Goldman's public rhetoric and her private life, it would be unfair to judge her by standards we would not apply to ourselves. At various times in our lives, we all face our inability to live up to our publicly pronounced convictions. Goldman was no better at subordinating her emotions to her rational beliefs than most of us are.

Review of the Literature on Emma Goldman

The existing literature on Emma Goldman is mainly biographical. Alice Wexler's *Emma Goldman: An Intimate Life* (1984) focuses on Goldman's life up to her deportation to Russia in 1919. Wexler provides a comprehensive view of Goldman, illuminating the tension between the private lover and public rhetorician and political activist. Despite the use of the adjective "intimate" in her subtitle, she provides a historical perspective on the contradictions and complexities of Goldman's life. She attempts to understand Goldman in light of "the psychological tensions and conflicts facing women at a moment of rapid historical change."[37] As well, Wexler deepens and enriches the reader's understanding of the complexity of Goldman's character by examining Goldman through the eyes of contemporaries such as Margaret Anderson, editor of the socialist journal *Little Review,* and the civil libertarian, Roger Baldwin. Wexler continues her biographical study of Goldman in *Emma Goldman in Exile: From the Russian Revolution to the Spanish Civil War* (1989), concentrating on Goldman's post-deportation activities in Russia, Spain, England, and France. In volume two, Wexler highlights the complexity of Goldman's character including recurring feelings of isolation and loneliness.

Candace Falk's biography *Love, Anarchy, and Emma Goldman* (1984), like Wexler's, treats as inextricably interrelated the private and public realms of Goldman's life. Also like Wexler, Falk highlights the tension between the private and public Goldman and the glaring contradictions between Goldman's public pronouncements on freedom and her private admissions to being, in Goldman's words, an "abject slave" in her romantic/sexual life. Falk's discovery, in 1975, of Goldman's correspondence with her lover and manager Ben Reitman spurred her to juxtapose Goldman's erotic and romantic dependence on Reitman against her fiercely independent public persona. Her work concentrates on Goldman's relationship with Reitman between 1908 and 1918, using the passionate and explicitly erotic correspondence between Goldman and Reitman as her primary source.

In contrast to the works of Falk and Wexler, the earlier biographical study of Goldman by Alix Kates Shulman, *To the Barricades: The Anarchist Life of Emma Goldman* (1971), is based largely on Goldman's autobiography *Living My Life.* Consequently, Shulman's work does not convey the same element of tension and contradiction between the private and public sides of Goldman's life; nor does Shulman's work historically and socially "situate" Goldman as extensively as do the works of Falk and Wexler.

Richard Drinnon's *Rebel in Paradise: A Biography of Emma Goldman* (1961), the so-called "bench mark" biography of Goldman, concentrates more on Goldman's public persona in the context of her anarchist activities. Although historically detailed, Drinnon's work lacks the intertwining and coalescing of the public and private sides of Goldman's life found in the later biographical studies of Wexler and Falk. Drinnon, typical of many biographers of his time, referred to Goldman as "Emma" while using either surnames or full names when referring to men.

In contrast to these biographical studies of Goldman, Martha Solomon's *Emma Goldman* (1987) examines Goldman as a speaker and writer. Solomon examines Goldman's *Anarchism and Other Essays*, *The Social Significance of Modern Drama*, *Living My Life*, *My Disillusionment in Russia* and *Mother Earth* in order to analyze her literary style and her rhetorical strategies. In focusing on Goldman as a "public" communicator, she leaves unattended the connections and contradictions between Goldman's public rhetoric and her private experience.

The Central Inquiry

This work is not intended to compete with other major works on Goldman. In contrast to previous work which, with the exception of that of Martha Solomon, deals primarily with the *life* of Emma Goldman, this book will focus on the *ideas* of Emma Goldman as they relate to the centrality of sexuality and reproduction within her anarchist theory. It is my intention to provide an analysis of Goldman's ideas on sexuality and reproduction in light of contemporary feminist theories and the so-called "sex debates" of second-wave feminism, which focus on the extent to which women's sexuality can be viewed as a liberatory force. Specifically, Goldman's view of sexuality will be given a critical reading in light of the current feminist debate between those who stress the inherent dangers of sexuality, versus those who argue for sexuality's inherent pleasures and possibilities for self-expansion and personal emancipation. My interpretation of Goldman's views on sexuality and reproduction will be grounded in feminist theories concerning women's difference versus women's equality. To what extent did Goldman view women as "different"; to what extent did Goldman view women as "equal"? These questions will be addressed in the course of interpreting Goldman's ideas on sexuality and reproduction in light of the contemporary difference/equality debates.

Chapter Development

Chapter one will attempt to illuminate the theoretical and philosophical foundations of Goldman's conception of anarchism which, by incorporating sexuality and reproduction, constituted a major contribution to anarchist theory. Goldman stated that her vision of anarchism brought together the communitarianism of Kropotkin and the individuality of Ibsen. Ibsen's conception of the strong individual, his feminist perspective, and his acknowledgement of the significance of sexual and reproductive matters, attracted Goldman to his work. Goldman and Kropotkin, however, held different views on sexuality and reproduction in relation to anarchist theory. Goldman argued with Kropotkin over his insistence that issues related to sexuality and reproduction were outside the scope of anarchist theory. Goldman's construction of sexuality as an "essential" emancipatory force meant that sexuality had to be centrally located in her anarchist theory of freedom.

Having established sexuality's central location in Goldman's vision of anarchism, I will turn in Chapter two to Goldman's construction of "instinct" as it relates to women's so-called sexual and reproductive "nature." This chapter will attempt to situate Goldman's views on women's "nature" and "placement" in the context of feminist theory related to the nature/culture dichotomy and its corollaries (e.g., private/public), as well as the theoretical positions on women's difference versus women's equality. Goldman's views on women's sexuality and reproductive capability, as emancipatory forces, will be examined in light of contemporary feminist theories and those with which she competed during her day.

Chapter three will ground Goldman's construction of sexuality and reproduction, its proper placement, and its emancipatory potential in the social and historical context of Goldman's day. This chapter will discuss popular discourses surrounding women's "nature"; the birth control movement and its inextricable links to race-suicide and eugenics debates; the roles played by the medical profession and organized religion as "moral entrepreneurs" in the debates surrounding women's proper placement, their reproductive autonomy and their social responsibility; the entrenchment of liberalism as a social ideology and its applicability to women and their sexual and reproductive lives; the growth of the legislative/bureaucratic realm (which Goldman referred to as the "State") and how Goldman's views on sexuality and reproduction related to the growing influence of the public realm on peoples' personal and professional lives.

Chapter four will deal with various theoretical positions on sexuality and reproduction. Drawing on a taxonomy of sexual theories and theorists developed by social construction theorist, Jeffrey Weeks, I will attempt to "fit" Goldman's views into Weeks' categories. Weeks' taxonomy will be used to enhance our understanding of Goldman's views on sexuality and reproduction and to illuminate Goldman's thought relative to competing theoretical positions including those of the contemporary "sex debates."

Having established Goldman's view of sexuality in relation to Weeks' taxonomy of theories of sexuality, I will examine in Chapter five the influences of early twentieth-century "sexologists" (i.e., those who attempted to develop a "science" of sexuality) on Goldman's ideas concerning sexuality and reproduction. Specifically, the ideas of Sigmund Freud and Havelock Ellis will be discussed in an attempt to show how "sexology" shaped Goldman's construction of sexuality and reproduction.

Chapter six will focus on Goldman's construction of women's same-sex relationships in light of her broader view of emancipation and feminism. This chapter will also assess the influence of sexology in shaping Goldman's construction of female same-sex relationships.

Chapter seven, the concluding chapter, will highlight the central themes developed in the preceding chapters in an attempt to synthesize my interpretation of Goldman's ideas on sexuality and reproduction.

Defining the Concept of Sexuality

"Sexuality" is an ambiguous concept and, therefore, difficult to define. Social constructionist, Jeffrey Weeks, notes that the dominant meaning of the term "sex" since the early nineteenth century refers to the "physical relations between the sexes."[38] For the purposes of this book, sexuality will be defined as a historical concept, "constructed" through the use of "a host of different biological and mental possibilities—gender identity, bodily differences, reproductive capacities, needs, desires, fantasies"[39] which may or may not be linked together. In this way, sexuality encompasses a broad range of psychic and physical possibilities—biological reproduction being just one. This definition assumes that the capacities of the body and the mind are given meaning through social relations.[40]

Proposed Methodology

My analysis of Goldman's ideas on sexuality and reproduction—ideas expressed in her autobiography, her personal correspondence, her speeches, her collection of essays, her editorial work in *Mother Earth* and her drama criticism—will be developed through a social constructionist perspective. Social constructionist perspectives begin with the assumption that the meaning of all human activity is socially constructed and organized. Social constructionism rejects the view that human phenomena possess an essential "essence," immutable "nature," or "laws" of their own. Instead, social constructionism assumes that the meanings and definitions of all human phenomena are "constructed" by the social structures and discourses of the community or society in which they are played out. As a result, social constructionist perspectives view sexuality as inextricably dependent on and connected to the social order in which it exists. Social constructionism, therefore, rejects the view that sexuality is a unitary biological force, similarly experienced by everyone regardless of race, sexual orientation, religion, class, region, etc. Instead, it assumes that sexuality is a historical construct and, therefore, changeable and unstable. It will be my intention to "deconstruct" Goldman's seemingly unitary views on sexuality and reproduction (which she treated as biological "givens") in order to show how these views were ideologically structured according to particular discourses of Goldman's day. In deconstructing the ideas of Goldman, I intend to identify the discourses and their ideas (or what social constructionists, J. H. Gagnon and William Simon call the "scripts") which mediated between sexual and reproductive functioning, and Goldman's social world.

NOTES

1. Linda Gordon, *Woman's Body, Woman's Right: A Social History of Birth Control in America* (New York: Penguin Books, 1977), p. 213.
2. Alice Wexler, *Emma Goldman: An Intimate Life* (New York: Pantheon Books, 1984), p. 278.
3. Martha Solomon, *Emma Goldman* (Boston: G.K. Hall, 1987), p. 77.
4. Richard Drinnon, *Rebel in Paradise* (Chicago: University of Chicago Press, 1961), p. 5.
5. Wexler, Emma Goldman: *An Intimate Life*, p. 19.
6. Drinnon, *Rebel In Paradise*, p. 10.
7. Emma Goldman, *Living My Life* Vol. I: (New York: Alfred A. Knopf, 1931, Reprint, New York: Dover Publications, 1970), p. 12.
8. Eight alleged anarchists were convicted on a variety of charges stemming from the Haymarket riot. The riot ensued after police arrived to break up a workers' meeting and resulted in the fatal wounding of seven police officers and two civilians.
9. Ibid., p. 10.
10. Ibid.
11. Ibid.
12. The famous steel strike occurred when negotiations between The Amalgamated Association of Iron, Steel, and Tin Workers and Carnegie Steel Company failed. The strike grew bitter and was eventually broken as the national guard was called in to protect non-union workers.
13. The years during Goldman's sojourn in Vienna and subsequent return to New York marked the completion of a number of important works and her exposure to a number of radical ideas, which would become influential in the construction of Goldman's anarchist beliefs. In 1896, the British sexologist, Edward Carpenter wrote *Love's Coming of Age* and, in the following year, Havelock Ellis' *Studies in the Psychology of Sex* was released. In 1898, Goldman's political mentor, Peter Kropotkin, wrote *The State: Its Historic Role*.
14. Goldman, *Living My Life*, p. 268.
15. Emma Goldman, in Shulman, *Red Emma Speaks: Selected Writings and Speeches by Emma Goldman*, compiled and edited by Alix Kates Shulman (New York: Random House, 1972), p. 15.
16. Goldman, *Living My Life*, p. 213.

17. Drinnon, *Rebel in Paradise*, p. 231.
18. This was part of a mass deportation of "radical aliens" initiated by the Feds under the direction of Attorney General A. M. Palmer.
19. Wexler, *Emma Goldman: An Intimate Life*, p. 278.
20. Ibid.
21. Ibid.
22. Ibid.
23. Alix Kates Shulman, "Emma Goldman: 'Anarchist Queen,'" in Dale Spender, ed., *Feminist Theories* (London: The Women's Press, 1983), p. 222.
24. See Wexler's *Emma Goldman: An Intimate Life* and Candace Falk *Love, Anarchy and Emma Goldman* (New York: Holt, Rinehart and Winston, 1984).
25. Goldman, in Wexler, *Emma Goldman: An Intimate Life*, p. 160.
26. Goldman maintained that woman's emancipation began in her "soul."
27. See Adrienne Rich, *Of Woman Born: Motherhood as Experience and Institution* (New York: W. W. Norton and Co., 1976), p. 243.
28. Wexler, *Emma Goldman: An Intimate Life*, p. 95.
29. Ibid.
30. Ibid.
31. Ibid., p. 280.
32. Ibid.
33. Carol Ruth Berkin, "Private Woman, Public Woman: The Contradictions of Charlotte Perkins Gilman," In *Women of America: A History*, edited by Carol Ruth Berkin and Mary Beth Norton. (Boston: Houghton Mifflin Company, 1979), p. 151.
34. Ibid., p. 152.
35. Ibid.
36. Emma Goldman, *Nowhere At Home: Letters from Exile of Emma Goldman and Alexander Berkman*, edited by Richard Drinnon and Anna Marie Drinnon. (New York: Schocken Books, 1975), p. 133.
37. Wexler, *Emma Goldman: An Intimate Life*, p. 147.
38. Jeffrey Weeks, *Sexuality* (London and New York: Tavistock Publications, 1986), p. 13.
39. Ibid.
40. Ibid., p. 14.

CHAPTER 1

Kropotkin and Ibsen: Supplying the Theoretical Foundation For Goldman's Vision of Anarchism

This chapter will examine the major philosophical influences on Goldman's construction of a "theory" of anarchism, in which sexuality and feminism were centrally located. In this discussion, Goldman's construction of anarchist theory will be situated in the context of contemporary feminist critiques of the private/public dichotomy and its corollaries, as they relate to theory construction and the social organization of knowledge.

The contradictions between the principles of anarchism and the principles of patriarchy are great, as well as apparent, yet they proved to be virtually invisible to the "great" thinkers and writers of anarchism whose theories presupposed the seemingly permanent and immoveable institution of the patriarchal family. As sexuality and reproduction were assumed to gain their definition within the confines of the family and were shaped by the pressures which church and State brought to bear upon the family, this "veil of invisibility" was dropped upon the subjects of sexuality and reproduction rendering them, too, invisible and, thus, unattended to. Emma Goldman's feminism enabled her to pull aside that veil and see women's situation in the family, women's relation to reproduction, and women's and men's sexuality as integral elements of life, and thus, also of a theory of anarchism. Goldman's historical importance to the development of anarchist theory is her inclusion of the issues of sexuality and feminism[1]—issues which were considered by many of Goldman's male colleagues as being a source of embarrassment and therefore peripheral, if not irrelevant, to the scope of anarchist theory.

It may be postulated that the fact that Goldman was a woman explains, at least in part, her tendency to see *how* anarchism applies to sexuality and reproduction and *why* it must be included in any credible and thorough theory of anarchism. To reject discussion of sexuality on the grounds that it belongs to the realm of the personal and not the political, as Kropotkin did in his discussions with Goldman, is to create a vision of the world in which public and private never meet. While this view of the antinomy of realms was (and is) prevalent among androcentric thinkers and writers, Goldman's work is important because she included in it so-called "private" details of sexuality and rejected the separation of the private from the public. Emma Goldman's theory of anarchism is not *public* theory detached from private experience. Emma Goldman formulated a theory of anarchism, in which the schism of public and private is absent.

It has been said that positions on reproductive policy are rooted in social or political ideologies.[2] For Plato, a limited population justified his view of elites; for John Stuart Mill, birth control was part of a larger view of individualism and liberalism; for Marx, population issues were related to economic organization.[3] As a result, "population views are strongly felt because they are tied to deeper intellectual or political positions, and the interaction hence becomes reciprocally sustaining."[4] It will be argued that, in the case of Goldman, the view of a reciprocal interplay between her ideas on sexuality and reproduction and her public political commitment to anarchism, is not a complete view of her position on these issues. This view is not complete as it, like so many androcentric accounts of public life, assumes a bifurcation of public and private, placing "intellectual or political positions" on the "public" side of the bifurcation while rendering the personal or private irrelevant. For Goldman, the personal was very much the political, and while ideas on sexuality and reproduction may be rooted in a deeper political or philosophical commitment to anarchism, she believed that these ideas were sustained by and through lived experience. Thus, the "mutually sustaining interaction," in Goldman's view, becomes one involving the interplay of the so-called "public" and "private"—one in which intellectual positions and political commitment exist because of "private" experience and, at the same time, one in which intellectual positions and political commitment bring about the conditions and events of personal experience.

While Goldman's inclusion of sexual and reproductive matters in her theory of anarchism challenged a dichotomous view of public theory versus private experience held by her fellow anarchists, Goldman's construction of a theory of anarchism is not without its inherent contradictions and tensions. Despite Goldman's important contribution of amalgamating matters previously considered to be "private" (i.e., sexuality and reproduction) with so-called "public" theory, she did engage in dichotomous thinking, endorsing many of the corollaries of the private/public bifurcation. As will be discussed more fully in the following chapter, Goldman's view of the supremacy of "instinct" was based on a bifurcated view of instinct and intellect, desire and reason. Goldman also held a dichotomous view of gender; she, however, rejected a philosophy of separate spheres for men and women.

The Bifurcation of Private and Public in Theory Construction

Feminist philosopher, Jean Bethke, Elshtain contends that the schism of reason and desire and its corollary public and private, common in androcentric theories, has lead to the concepts of "public knowledge" and "private desire":

> The presumption that human beings are rational, metaphysically free, prudential calculators of marginal utility—and all think alike in this regard in the public sphere of politics and understanding—is used as a contrast model for the qualities and activities in the private world from which the public sphere is bifurcated theoretically. The public realm and the "public mind" exist as defenses against the private sphere in which desire, conceived as unconscious and arbitrary, is held to rank supreme.[5]

Bethke Elshtain explains that thinkers, such as John Locke, presumed that knowledge situated in the public sphere is "the same knowledge shared by all."[6] Social philosopher, Roberto Unger, in *Knowledge and Politics,* elaborates upon this bifurcation, commonly found in androcentric thinking:

> Men differ by what they desire, but they are capable of knowing the world in the same way. Particular desires felt by the individual are arbitrary from the standpoint of understanding.[7]

In Unger's exposition (statement) of the bifurcation of reason and desire, we are able to infer that knowledge becomes synonymous with the public realm. Thus, we are also able to infer that activities situated in the private realm (e.g., sexuality and reproduction) are considered random, arbitrary, and irrelevant and are excluded from the realm of theory or knowledge.

According to sociologist, Dorothy Smith, this bifurcation of the private and public creates a "bifurcation of consciousness."[8] Smith argues that the realm of public "theory" possesses a number of distinguishing characteristics; it is objectivistic, abstract, atemporal, extralocal and endogenous. It is one in which a "case" or "account" is viewed independent of its particular context; one in which "subjects" are to be studied, theorized upon, and documented as "objects-in-themselves" in order that they may be "known." According to Smith, the objectivistic approach to theory construction, common to androcentric thinking, entails the separation of the private realm of experience from the public realm of "theory." This separation of the public theory and private experience, or "bifurcation of consciousness," in Smith's view "institutionalizes the rupture between concept and phenomenal base."[9] By bifurcating the subject and removing the individual from a private, local, or "phenomenal base" into a public, theoretical realm, the subject can be "known" as a "phenomenon"—the subject becomes objectified through a process which Smith calls "the known": "In the context we are concerned with here a highly complex socially organized practice mediates the relation of knower and known."[10] This mediation of the relationship between the knower and the known is based on a dichotomous model of human existence, containing dichotomies such as public/private, extralocal/local, atemporal/temporal, abstract/concrete, and objective/subjective, which are largely rejected by feminist thinkers.

In her theory of anarchism, Goldman included feminist issues related to sexuality and reproduction—issues considered to be private, local, temporal, concrete and subjective by her anarchist predecessors and, therefore, outside the scope of anarchist "theory." Anarchist historian, George Woodcock states, that:

> Kropotkin was not very much interested in the movement for sexual liberation or even in feminism. Proudhon was if anything an anti-feminist. But Emma [Goldman] really first brought these currents to the front within the anarchist movement, and I think the anarchist movement was completely changed by that.[11]

Her inclusion of these issues marked a paradigm shift in anarchist theory—a shift away from androcentric public theory to what contemporary feminists refer to as an "integrative" form of theory construction.

The Influence of Kropotkin and Ibsen: A Synthesis of Community and Individuality

Emma Goldman's conception of anarchism, while based largely on her lived experiences,[12] was modelled theoretically on the work principally of two individuals—Peter Kropotkin and Henrik Ibsen.[13] To the limited extent that Goldman placed importance upon theory, Kropotkin and Ibsen provided Goldman with the major theoretical and philosophical underpinnings of her theory of anarchism.

Among anarchist communists who followed Kropotkin, Goldman was during her life accused of focusing too much on individualistic, sexual, and "instinctive" issues and too little on the structural or social elements of the anarchist vision.[14] However, Goldman's all-encompassing vision included both "external" dynamics related to the structure, economics and organization of anarchism, as well as "internal" psychological dynamics related to the human personality. Both internal and external elements were important in Goldman's theoretical model of anarchism. Goldman stressed that anarchism does not "involve a choice between Kropotkin and Ibsen; it embraces both."[15]

Alice Wexler has assessed Goldman's vision and the reaction to it from those inside, as well as outside the anarchist movement, as follows:

> Her own radical vision, broader and more encompassing than that of almost anyone else on the left, had shocked, inspired, and educated thousands, both inside and outside the anarchist movement.[16]

The key to understanding Goldman's theoretical model of anarchism is an appreciation of her view of the interdependence of "social organization and individual 'well being.'" Kropotkin's contribution to Goldman's vision was his model of social organization. Ibsen inspired Goldman's theory-building with his vision of the free and strong individual, unfettered by social constraint and limitation. Ibsen's character Dr. Stockmann, in *An Enemy of the People,* exemplified this vision, a vision which Goldman embraced both in theory and in personal practice.

Goldman attempted to conquer through her theory-building, the age-old enigma of the individual and society.[17] Rejecting the view that emphasis on the individual meant bourgeois thinking, incapable of being fused with the group, Goldman attempted to conjoin the individual and the society in what she perceived to be a mutually complementary and interdependent fashion. Her use of the works of Ibsen and Kropotkin stood for a rejection of the position that anarchism must reflect an either/or philosophy—a philosophy which stood for the primacy of either the organization *or* the individual. Goldman was "keenly aware"[18] of the excesses of both mass organization and individuality and argued that the theories of Ibsen and Kropotkin, conjoined, addressed these excesses. According to Richard Drinnon:

> She [Goldman] was as keenly aware as Ibsen of the
> tragedy of the modern individual and mass organization;
> she was as apprehensive as Kropotkin of the power-ob-
> sessed, socially irresponsible individual. Caught between
> these two positions, she tried to fuse them into a higher
> synthesis...[19]

Goldman's synthesis of "internal" and "external" dynamics rejected the enigma of the individual and the organization. Goldman embraced the work of Kropotkin and Ibsen arguing that individuality requires organization and, in a reciprocal fashion, that organization requires individuality. At the Anarchist Congress of 1907 held in Amsterdam,[20] she spoke out in favour of a synthesis of the ideas of Kropotkin and Ibsen. These ideas were contained in a paper written with and delivered by fellow anarchist, Max Baginsky, at the Congress and published as "The Relation of Anarchism to Organization," in the October 1907 issue of *Mother Earth*. Goldman and Baginsky's first proposition (the proposition that individuality requires a particular organizational structure) was meant to correct "a mistaken notion that organization does not foster individual freedom; that, on the contrary, it means the decay of individuality."[21] Using the vocabulary and evolution-bound model of Kropotkin, they described the development of the human personality as a "mutual" process involving "co-operative effort with other individualities."[22] "In reality," Goldman and Baginsky stated, "the true function of organization is to aid the development and growth of personality."[23] More fully, Goldman and Baginsky stated their argument using metaphors:

> Just as the animal cells, by mutual co-operation, express
> their latent powers in the formation of the complete or-
> ganism, so does the individuality, by co-operative effort
> with other individualities, attain its highest form of
> development. An organization, in its true sense, cannot
> result from the combination of mere non-entities. It must be
> composed of self-conscious, intelligent individualities.[24]

Goldman and Baginsky's second and corresponding proposition (that organization requires individuality) represented the notion, portrayed by Ibsen, of "the psychological struggle that culminates in the revolution of the human soul, the revolt of individuality."[25] In their address to the Anarchist Congress they supported a view of the strong individual by claiming that "the greater the number of strong, self-conscious personalities in an organization, the less danger of stagnation and the more intense its life-element."[26]

The Influence of Kropotkin Upon Goldman's Theory of Anarchism

Wexler has observed that, while Goldman may have been privately critical of Kropotkin, publicly she identified him as her principal teacher.[27] Although Kropotkin and Goldman did have their differences of opinion, particularly over the inclusion of the subject of sexuality in anarchist theory, Goldman spoke of Kropotkin, personally and philosophically, in a glowing manner, describing him as anarchism's "clearest thinker and theoretician."[28] Woodcock has labelled Kropotkin as "the last of the great anarchist theoreticians."[29] Kropotkin's contribution to anarchist theory included such classics as (in English translation) *The State: Its Historic Role* (1898), *Fields, Factories and Workshops* (1899), *Memories of a Revolutionist* (1899), *Mutual Aid* (1902), *The Conquest of Bread* (1906), *Modern Science and Anarchism* (1912) and *Ethics: Origin and Development* (1924).

In her autobiography, Goldman describes Kropotkin as "one of the greatest minds and most unique personalities of the nineteenth century."[30] Goldman praised Kropotkin's ability to blend mental activity and manual effort[31] although, privately, according to biographer, Alice Wexler, she was critical of what she called Kropotkin's "book life" and his limited "knowledge of the world or people."[32]

Recalling her first meeting with Kropotkin, Goldman wrote:

My visit with Peter Kropotkin convinced me that true greatness is always coupled with simplicity. He was the personification of both the lucidity and brilliance of mind combined with his warm-heartedness into the harmonious whole of a fascinating and gracious personality.[33]

George Woodcock echoes Goldman's assessment of the quality of Kropotkin's character, calling him "a man of unimpeachable honesty, kind and conscious of the needs of others, generous and hospitable, courageous and uncomfortably devoted to sincerity."[34] Kropotkin's "well-balanced goodness"[35] made him a man of great popularity and personal likeability, inside and outside anarchist circles. Woodcock explains that Kropotkin opened his home in rural England to visitors and guests—geographers, anarchists, English radicals and intellectuals such as Shaw, Frank Harris and Ford Madox Ford. Woodcock writes:

> To the anarchists he became the great prophetic savant of the movement, to be asked for advice and articles, to be welcomed when he made a rare appearance at a public meeting...[36]

Outside the movement, Kropotkin was accepted and respected by the educated British public, his articles appearing in *The Times* and his works *Mutual Aid* and *Memoirs of a Revolutionist* gaining popular support.[37] To the British elite, Kropotkin was "an honoured symbol of Russian resistance to autocracy."[38]

Kropotkin, the Concept of Mutual Aid and the Role of Women

In *Mutual Aid*, Kropotkin writes:

> Sociability is as much a law of nature as mutual struggle. Of course it would be extremely difficult to estimate, however roughly, the relative numerical importance of both these series of facts. But if we resort to an indirect test, and ask Nature: "Who are the fittest: those who are

continually at war with each other, or those who support
one another?", we at once see that those animals which
acquire habits of mutual aid are undoubtedly the fittest.[39]

Kropotkin challenged the popular Darwinian view of competitive struggle as the "natural" outcome of group life. The anarchist
concept, as articulated by Kropotkin, rejected competition as "the
natural law" and inserted in its place the "instinct of human
sociability."[40] The choice of vocabulary and articulation of the concept of "mutual aid" is very much grounded in a particular view of
"nature" and evolution.

Kropotkin held the view that "nature" was inherently good and
that human instinct as well as animal instinct contained an element
of moral virtue. Where Marx based his theories on historical
materialism, Kropotkin based his world view on "the anarchist
moral imperative," and attention to human values:

> The anarchists, including Kropotkin, were comfortable
> with the very concept of ethics and morality whereas for
> the Marxists this is a wholly fallacious category, a super-
> structural blind. For the anarchists there was a realm of
> absolute human values.[41]

Goldman, although critical of what she considered to be
"moralist" positions,[42] supported the notion of the anarchist moral
imperative, articulating the essence of anarchism through the use of
concepts such as "values," "morality" and "ethics." In *My Disillusionment in Russia* (1923), for instance, Goldman articulated her position
that the reordering of a society cannot be accomplished according to
economic principles alone, but instead must include a system of
ethics through which relations between and among individuals
would be mediated. Unlike many of her Marxist contemporaries,
Goldman echoed Kropotkin's advocacy for the inclusion of human
ethics into a design for the transformation of society.[43]

Economic reform, redistribution of income and services and superstructural change were not the sole ingredients of social transfor-

mation, according to Goldman. For her, the "materialist" view of history was flawed as it represented a truncated view of human life—a view which did not recognize the "inner" life of individuals and how this inner life, if projected in concert with a core of moral values, could transform a society. In other words, social reform was more than economic reform; social reform encompassed "mental and spiritual regeneration."[44] The positive value that she put on human instinct is part of Kropotkin's legacy to Goldman and can be seen as integral to her position on sexuality and reproduction. Goldman and Kropotkin shared the strongly held centrally-positioned belief that the State was the enemy of human freedom. In many of her writings, Goldman echoes Kropotkin's vision of human society in the future as being free of restrictions and limitations—life according to this view ought to be a carefree expression of impulses and instincts without the repressive and restrictive limitations of State or institutionalized social structures. As Kropotkin formulated this vision:

> The ideal basis of society would be myriad number of free constructs or agreements between individuals and groups, freely made. Feeling comes into play as the irrational elements in nature, the poetry of nature, that which defies delamination [separation or deconstruction] or definitiveness.[45]

Despite his recognition of the value of what he called "individuality,"[46] Kropotkin was clear in his view that the individual must mesh with the group. Since, according to Kropotkin, the instinct of sociability was "biologically-mandated,"[47] the gratification of individual impulses was realized through social activity. The need to be social in one's individual efforts highlights Kropotkin's conception of the "social" creating the individual, rather than the atomistic view of the individual creating his/her social world. Kropotkin states "that a society is a natural phenomenon existing anterior to the appearance of man, and that man is naturally adapted to observe its laws without the need of artificial regulation."[48]

Belief in the human characteristic of "sociability," upon which Kropotkin constructed his view of anarchism, caused him to consider the group first, the individual second. Kropotkin suggested that even the intellectual faculty was "eminently social."[49] Goldman's orientation, although emphatically "social" in its nature,[50] was, at the same time, one which emphasized individuality. The emphasis and focus which Kropotkin and Goldman place on "the social" versus "the individual" are major points of difference in the two anarchists' theories.

Although Goldman found Kropotkin to be a source of inspiration and theoretical lucidity, there are a number of instances in which Goldman's conception of anarchism departs radically from that of Kropotkin. The first and perhaps the most obvious departure relates to Goldman's emphasis on women and, correspondingly, Kropotkin's seeming blindness to the presence and perspective of women. Kropotkin's most famous treatise, *Mutual Aid*, renders an account of women as being virtually invisible members of the group, mentioning them only peripherally in the context of a description of the logistics of "mutual aid." Kropotkin in *The Conquest of Bread* states:

> ...No one has a right to force the housewife to take her potatoes from the communal kitchen ready cooked if she prefers to cook them herself in her own pot on her own fire; and, above all, we should wish each one to be free to take his own meals with his family.[51]

Kropotkin discusses the family in the context of mutual aid while skimming over the apparent contradictions between the power imbalances within the family and his theoretic rejection of social institutions which restrict human freedom and expression. Is one to infer that by not supplying a critique of the patriarchal family, Kropotkin extends his view of a "biologically-mandated" instinct of sociability to the roles of men and women within the family? If so, one sees an obvious contradiction between the potential for women's expressiveness and their "instinct" or "nature."

George Woodcock argues that the major flaw of *Mutual Aid* is Kropotkin's failure to "acknowledge the tyrannies of custom and habit" as he did those of "government and regulation."[52] Woodcock explains:

>...Kropotkin shows that he is willing to accept moral compulsion, whether it is the rule of custom in a primitive tribe or that of public opinion in an anarchist society, without admitting how far this force negates the freedom of the individual.[53]

Goldman, although greatly aware of the presence of women in "anarchist society," fails, like Kropotkin, to recognize the "custom or habit" of patriarchy as being a potential force limiting individual freedom.

Goldman, Kropotkin and the "Sex Question"

According to Goldman, Kropotkin viewed her emphasis on marriage, sexuality and reproduction as excessive and peripheral to the major concerns of anarchism.[54] Goldman maintained that these matters were at the heart of anarchism.

While Kropotkin viewed the "laws" of State to be counter to the nature of human instinct, he did not apply this analysis to gender relations. Goldman openly confronted Kropotkin over his views on sexuality. On a visit to Peter Kropotkin's London home in 1895, Goldman and Kropotkin discussed Goldman's lecture tour in California. Goldman, thirty-six years later in her autobiography, recalls Kropotkin's reaction to her work on the anarchist paper *Free Society*, published in 1895 in San Francisco and later in Chicago:

>The paper is doing splendid work...but it would do more if it would not waste so much space discussing sex... when she [woman] is his equal intellectually and shares his social ideals, she will be as free as he.[55]

Goldman recalls "pacing the room in growing agitation, each strenuously upholding his side of the argument,"[56] afterwhich Goldman recalls responding to Kropotkin: "All right, dear comrade, when I have reached your age, the sex question may no longer be of importance to me. But it is *now*, and it is a tremendous factor for thousands, millions even, of young people."[57] According to Goldman, Kropotkin yielded to her position stating: "Fancy, I didn't think that.... Perhaps you are right, after all."[58]

Goldman's personal approach to sexuality, consistent with her view of anarchism, was one of openness and freedom. Goldman, in a letter to Ben Reitmann in 1910, reported that this caused Kropotkin to levy the criticism that she was "too loose":

> One thing more about Kropotkin, he does not like me—thinks me too "loose." I guess I have never made much fuss over him, have gone my own way and developed on independent lines. Like all old teachers, he looks askance at the younger element that leave the old path.[59]

Drinnon interprets Kropotkin's indifference to the "sex question" and the opposition facing Goldman's efforts to promote the theme of sexuality within the anarchist movement as being representative of a "broad stream of puritanism" which ran through the movement—a belief that vital needs be subordinated to "the great end of the revolution."[60] There was, according to Drinnon, "a kind of devaluation of sex...sex is what? No more than having a glass of water when you are thirsty. This kind of ascetism was to her [Goldman] always anathema."[61] George Woodcock echoes Drinnon's assessment of the "puritanism" inherent in the values of anarchists such as Kropotkin:

> Her [Goldman's] personal relationship with Kropotkin is, as I say, rather guarded, because Kropotkin like many of the older anarchists was a very puritanical man at heart. And he found her life, her continued series of love affairs, her advocacy of free love and so forth rather disconcert-

ing. He felt that it was a little irrelevant to the mainstream of the anarchist movement.[62]

Kates Alix Shulman adds that Kropotkin was probably uncomfortable with "sexual questions," as were many of Goldman's colleagues in the anarchist movement.[63] Goldman often was an embarrassment to her friends in the movement because of her "outspoken stand on sex."[64] Shulman elaborates:

> Of course anarchists did pay lip service to sexual freedom, but in those days for a lot of them what it meant was availability of women who were not their wives—and still they demanded sexual fidelity of the women who were their wives.[65]

While Kropotkin stressed structural dynamics in his conception of anarchism, Goldman, although recognizing the importance of an appropriately structured system of mutual agreements and voluntary associations, insisted that a comprehensive theory of anarchism must recognize individual autonomy and individual "tastes and desires."[66] Goldman's emphasis on sexuality as a central component of individual "tastes and desires," and Kropotkin's emphasis on the economic, social, and structural elements of anarchism, brought about the ideological and practical schism between the two thinkers. On her side, Goldman expressed the concern that individual sexuality was at the core of anarchist philosophy, while Kropotkin, on his, emphasized the structural factors of anarchist organization and criticized Goldman for emphasizing sexuality. Goldman, in Wexler's view, distinguished herself from her fellow anarchist through her emphasis on sexuality.[67] Wexler writes:

> Goldman's outspokenness on sexual issues and her unconventional love life shocked many of her own comrades as well as those outside the movement. If these reservations reflected the conservatism even of many anarchists, there were other, more serious criticisms as well.[68]

Infusing the belief that "individual instinct is a thing of value in
the world"[69] into Kropotkin's framework of mutual agreements and
voluntary association, Goldman, in her essay "Anarchism: What It
Really Stands For," argued for economic arrangements consisting of
"voluntary production and distribution associations" in which individuals would work in "harmony with their tastes and desires."[70]

Ibsen's Influence on Goldman's Thinking

> While she endorsed Kropotkin's belief that mutual aid
> and co-operation were essential to the success of anar-
> chism, Goldman insisted on the primacy of the individual
> and praised Ibsen's portrayal of the internal psychologi-
> cal factors that produced a personal revolution against
> societal constraints.[71]

Whereas Kropotkin provided a theory of mutual co-operation, Ibsen
supplied Goldman with a theory of individual freedom. Conjoined,
Goldman argued, the two formed a complete theory of anarchism; a
theory which treated as complementary "internal" and "external"
forces.[72]

Henrik Ibsen (1828-1906), the poet, playwright and political
moralist, provided Goldman with inspiration related to the irrepres-
sibility of the human spirit—inspiration that would sustain both her
political theories and her private life. The first issue of Goldman's pe-
riodical *Mother Earth*, in March 1906, contained a review of *Letters of
Henrik Ibsen* (1906) in which Goldman describes Ibsen as a "solitary
soul" who hates the State and whose aim is the revolutionizing of
brains.[73]

Ibsen addressed the concerns and answered the questions posed
by Goldman, which Kropotkin left unaddressed and unanswered.
These concerns and issues included the position of women in society
and the role of sexuality as an expression of individuality. Through
the joining of the theories of Kropotkin and Ibsen, Goldman was tactically able to introduce the key concerns of sexuality and female
emancipation into her overall theory, using Ibsen's ideas on in-

dividuality as her conduit. Under the umbrella "individual expression," sexuality assumed a central position in Goldman's amalgama-
tion of the views of Kropotkin and Ibsen. While Kropotkin believed
Goldman concentrated too much on sex, considering it to be outside
the boundaries of anarchist theory, Ibsen placed individual expression, including sexual expression, at the core of his thought. Goldman
echoed Ibsen's theme of the importance of individual expression. In
her 1940 essay, "The Individual, Society and the State," Goldman
writes: "The very essence of individuality is expression..."[74]

Ibsen, who began his career as an apothecary's apprentice in
Norway, originally had published in Norgwegian such dramatic
works as *Peer Gynt* (1867), *Pillars of Society* (1877), *A Doll's House*
(1879), *Ghosts* (1881), *The Wild Duck* (1884), *Romersholm* (1886), *The
Lady from the Sea* (1888), *Hedda Gabler* (1890), *The Master Builder* (1892),
Little Eyolf (1894) and *John Gabriel Borkman* (1896). Of his plays, *A
Doll's House, An Enemy of the People,* and *Ghosts* bore great significance in Goldman's writings; in her essays, autobiography and
editorial work she makes frequent reference to the Ibsenite characters Nora (*A Doll's House*), Dr. Stockmann (*An Enemy of the People*) and
Mrs. Alving (*Ghosts*). In Goldman's work of dramatic criticism, *The
Social Significance of Modern Drama,* she "critiques" these three plays,
as well as Ibsen's *Pillars of Society.*

Goldman deduced clear and precise meanings from each of the
plays, whether they represented Ibsen's conception of the "social
lie," "provincialism," or "duty." To Goldman, Ibsen was "the hater of
all social shams"[75] and his message was clear—it was a message
which exalted the triumph of human spirit over the confinements of
the group and social custom. It was a message which, understand-
ably, did not sit well among some in Kropotkinite circles.[76]

Richard Drinnon suggests that Goldman's treatment of the
work of Ibsen was typical of her general approach in which she
would make a point forcefully, without exploring the inconsistencies or complexities of the artist's work.[77] Drinnon writes:

> Unfortunately, Ibsen's meaning in all his works was "as
> clear as daylight" to Emma. This was simply another

limitation of her approach, for Ibsen, of course, placed
some rather formidable obstacles in the path of those
who would understand his work.[78]

For example, Drinnon continues, Ibsen's *Wild Duck* tended to blur
his position on the "social lie,"[79] so clearly set out in *A Doll's House* or
Ghosts. "Significantly," Drinnon writes, "Emma did not choose to
discuss *The Wild Duck* in her book.... Indeed, Ibsen's position on this
question ['the social lie'] was less daylight clear than Emma
thought."[80] Martha Solomon's assessment of Goldman's treatment
of Ibsen is congruent with that of Drinnon. Goldman tended, in
Solomon's view, to "gloss over elements in the plot that do not cor-
respond with her philosophy."[81]

Ibsen's Feminism

Ibsen's *A Doll's House* was his most significant statement on
women's condition. To Goldman, the character "Nora," at the conclusion of the play, heralded the coming triumph of the female spirit,
the triumph of women over the confinement and limitation of their
social condition. Goldman, in *The Social Significance of Modern Drama*
(1914), quoted passages from *A Doll's House*, relevant to her vision of
feminism, and to her view of Ibsen's "social significance," in which
Nora asserts that, above all, she is a human being (as opposed to
simply a wife and mother). Responding to her husband, Helmer,
who insists that she is before all else a wife and a mother, Nora exhorts: "That I no longer believe. I think that before all else I am a
human being just as much as you are...."[82]

For Goldman, Ibsen's *A Doll's House* represented a straightfor-
ward example of the "social lie" and tyranny of "duty," as she typically searched for a homily in each play. In Goldman's view, the
homily to be drawn from *A Doll's House* was Nora's closing of the
door of her doll's house, as a result of which, she "opens wide the
gate of life for woman and proclaims the revolutionary message that
only perfect freedom and communion make a true bond between
man and woman."[83]

In her essay, "Marriage and Love," Goldman uses Ibsen's characters Nora, and Mrs. Alving (*Ghosts*), as examples to illustrate and, presumably strengthen, the argument that love and marriage have nothing in common.[84] Goldman states that Ibsen was "probably the first" to realize that men and women tended to remain strangers in marriage, due to an "insurmountable wall of superstition, custom, and habit" which separates them.[85] Using the character of Nora as a case in point, Goldman wrote:

> Nora leaves her husband, not...because she is tired of her responsibilities or feels the need of woman's rights, but because she had come to know that for eight years she had lived with a stranger and borne him children. Can there be anything more humiliating, more degrading than a life-long proximity between two strangers?.... We have not yet outgrown the theologic myth that woman has no soul, that she is a mere appendix to man, made out of his rib just for the convenience of the gentleman who was so strong that he was afraid of his shadow.[86]

In "Marriage and Love," Goldman defends the concept of "free motherhood"—motherhood unfettered by customs, laws, and compulsion, based on love and parenthood of "free choice."[87] Ibsen's character Mrs. Alving, in *Ghosts,* is used by Goldman in her essay to illustrate the process through which mothers become "free mothers." Goldman wrote:

> Ibsen must have had a vision of a free mother, when, with a master stroke, he portrayed Mrs. Alving. She was the ideal mother because she had outgrown marriage and all its horrors, because she had broken her chains, and set her spirit free to soar until it returned a personality, regenerated and strong. Alas, it was too late to rescue her life's joy, her Oswald [Mrs. Alving's son]; but not too late to realize that love in freedom in the only condition of a beautiful life.[88]

Goldman, in describing the situations of Nora and Mrs. Alving, emphasized the *process* through which women gain or regain their individuality. The process, typical of her view of anarchism and Ibsen's view of freedom,[89] is one which involves a struggle of the individual spirit, resulting in a strong, sturdy, and fine human character.[90] Through the use of the Ibsenite characters Nora and Mrs. Alving, Goldman demonstrates her view of the process through which women's emancipation is achieved. Women's freedom is accomplished through an individual and psychological process for which some women "have paid with blood and tears for their spiritual awakening."[91]

Emancipation would not be achieved, as Goldman so forcefully argues in "The Tragedy of Woman's Emancipation," through turning women's attention outward, to the reform of the State. Emancipation for women, according to Goldman, did not occur at the ballot box but instead, in Ibsenite fashion, through "spiritual awakening."

Ibsen on Liberty and Individuality: Influences Upon Goldman

In Goldman's essay "What I Believe," she articulates the "process" of anarchism, stating that:

> "What I believe" is a process rather than a finality. Finalities are for the gods and governments, not for the human intellect.[92]

In articulating her view of "anarchism as process," Goldman strengthens her claim, using Ibsen's view of freedom—a view which concentrates on the struggle for freedom, not as an end, but as the means through which the strong and autonomous individual character is developed. Goldman wrote:

> In the battle for freedom, as Ibsen has so well pointed out, it is the struggle for, not so much the attainment of, liberty, that develops all that is strongest, sturdiest and finest in human character.[93]

Goldman uses Ibsen himself as an example of how the human spirit expresses itself in spite of government, and not because of it,[94] stating that "Ibsen's psychological analysis of human life, could never have been induced by government any more than the spirit which causes a man to save a drowning child...."[95]

Arthur Symons in *Universal Review*, April 1889, stated that "the demand of Ibsen is for the liberty of the individual, the 'revolutionizing of people's minds.'"[96] The "revolutionizing of people's minds" would, according to Ibsen, take place along side a revolution against the State. In a letter to George Brandes, Ibsen wrote:

> The State is the curse of the individual. How has the national strength of Prussia been purchased? By the sinking of the individual in a political and geographical formula.... The State must go! That will be a revolution which will find me on its side. Undermine the idea of the State, set up in its place spontaneous action, and the idea that spiritual relationship is the only thing that makes for unity, and you will start the elements of a liberty which will be something worth possessing.[97]

Ibsen's view of the destructive, alienating and soul-diminishing qualities of the State was shared by Goldman and articulated in essays such as "Anarchism: What It Really Stands For," "The Individual Society and the State," "The Tragedy of Women's Emancipation" and "Marriage and Love."

Ibsen's view of the significance of the "struggle" for liberty was incorporated into Goldman's personal affairs, as well as her political theory. In a letter to Ben Reitman written on July 18, 1911, Goldman adapts Ibsen's view of the struggle for liberty to her own love life. Goldman wrote to Reitman: "After all, I am like Ibsen. It is the struggle for rather than the attainment of liberty which is worthwhile."[98]

In conclusion, Goldman's theory of anarchism can be distinguished from previous theories of anarchism by the inclusion of the issues of sexuality and feminism. In constructing a theory of anarchism, Goldman rejected the long-standing bifurcation of private and public held by her anarchist predecessors in Kropotkin, Michael Bakunin and Pierre Joseph Proudhon. Since women were assigned to the so-called "private" sphere, issues of feminism and sexuality were viewed by these theorists as private or personal, outside the scope of what they perceived to be "public" theory. Goldman's inclusion of these issues, subsumed within her overall theory of anarchism, meant that anarchism was not to be a theory only for men in the public sphere, it was to be a theory for women (and men) whose public and private lives were not sharply bifurcated.

In creating a theory of anarchism, Goldman amalgamated the ideas of her principal teacher Kropotkin with the views of (to Goldman) the more personally-inspiring Ibsen. In doing so, Goldman attempted to marry the notions of community and individuality as mutually complementary rather than contradictory ideals. Under the umbrella of Ibsen's view of individuality, Goldman focused on sexuality as an expression of what she considered to be "individual tastes and desires," introducing the ideas of Freud and Havelock Ellis (to be discussed in a later chapter) into anarchist thinking. Ibsen's view of individuality acted as a conduit through which Goldman could incorporate her views on feminism and sexuality into what had previously been a tradition of androcentric communist anarchism.

NOTES

1. George Woodcock, "Emma Goldman: A Life of Anarchy," CBC transcripts, 1983.
2. Bernard Berelson, "Population Policy: Personal Notes," *Population Studies* 24, (July 1971): 173-192.
3. Ibid., p. 175.
4. Ibid.
5. Jean Bethke Elshtain, *Public Man, Private Women*, (Princeton, N.J.: Princeton University Press, 1981), p. 118.
6. Ibid.
7. Roberto Unger, *Knowledge and Politics*, (New York: Free Press, 1975), p. 50
8. Dorothy E. Smith, "The Social Construction of Documentary Reality," *Sociological Inquiry*, 44, no. 4 (1974): pp. 257-268.
9. Ibid., p. 257.
10. Ibid.
11. Woodcock, "Emma Goldman: A Life of Anarchy," p. 11.

12. Alice Wexler, *Emma Goldman: An Intimate Life*, (New York: Pantheon Books, 1984), p. 90.
13. Emma Goldman, *Living My Life*, Vol. I, (New York: Alfred A. Knopf, 1931, reprint, New York: Dover Publications, 1970), pp. 402-403.
14. Wexler, *Emma Goldman: An Intimate Life*, p. 102.
15. Goldman, *Living My Life*, Vol. I, p. 402.
16. Wexler, *Emma Goldman: An Intimate Life*, p. 275.
17. Richard Drinnon, *Rebel in Paradise*, (Chicago: University of Chicago Press, 1961), p. 106.
18. Ibid., p. 107.
19. Ibid.
20. The proceedings of the Congress were printed in *Congresse anarchiste tenu a Amsterdam*, août 1907 (Paris: La Publication sociale, 1908).
21. Emma Goldman and Max Baginsky, "The Relation of Anarchism to Organization," *Mother Earth*, II (October, 1907), p. 310.
22. Ibid.
23. Ibid.
24. Ibid.
25. Goldman, *Living My Life*, p. 402.
26. Goldman and Baginsky, "The Relation of Anarchism to Organization," p. 312.
27. Wexler, *Emma Goldman: An Intimate Life*, p. 48.
28. Goldman, *Living My Life*, p. 168.
29. George Woodcock, *Anarchism: A History of Libertarian Ideas and Movements*, (New York: World Publishing Co., 1962), p. 186.
30. Goldman, *Living My Life*, p. 168.
31. Ibid., pp. 168-169.
32. Wexler, *Emma Goldman: An Intimate Life*, p. 48.
33. Goldman, *Living My Life*, p. 169.
34. Woodcock, *Anarchism: A History of Libertarian Ideas and Movements*, p. 206.
35. Ibid.
36. Ibid., p. 196.
37. Ibid.
38. Ibid.
39. Peter Kropotkin, *Mutual Aid*, (London: William Heinemann, 1903), pp. 5-6.
40. Stephen Osofsky, *Peter Kropotkin*, (Boston: Twayne Publishers, 1979), p. 87.
41. Ibid., p. 61.
42. Wexler, *Emma Goldman: An Intimate Life*, p. 97.
43. Ibid.
44. Ibid.
45. Kropotkin, in Osofsky, *Peter Kropotkin*, p. 114.
46. Woodcock, *Anarchism: A History of Libertarian Ideas and Movements*, p. 191.
47. Osofsky, *Peter Kropotkin*, p. 92.
48. Kropotkin, in Osofsky, *Peter Kropotkin*, p. 201.
49. Ibid., p. 200.
50. Goldman, *Living My Life*, p. 402.
51. Peter Kropotkin, *The Conquest for Bread*, (London: Chapman and Hall, 1906), p. 94.
52. Woodcock, *Anarchism: A History of Libertarian Ideas and Movements*, p. 202.
53. Ibid.
54. Emma Goldman, *My Disillusionment in Russia*, 1922, reprint (New York: Thomas Y. Crowell, 1970), p. 253.
55. Ibid., p. 253.
56. Ibid.
57. Ibid.
58. Ibid.
59. Quoted in Candace Falk, *Love, Anarchy and Emma Goldman*, (New York: Holt, Rinehart and Winston, 1984), p. 137.
60. Richard Drinnon, "Emma Goldman: A Life of Anarchy," CBC transcripts, 1983, p. 23.

61. Ibid., p. 24.
62. Woodcock, quoted in "Emma Goldman: A Life of Anarchy," p. 13.
63. Shulman, quoted in "Emma Goldman: A Life of Anarchy," p. 11.
64. Ibid., p. 23.
65. Ibid.
66. Emma Goldman, *Anarchism and Other Essays* (New York: Mother Earth Publishing Association, 1910), p. 62.
67. Wexler, *Emma Goldman: An Intimate Life,*, p. 280.
68. Ibid.
69. Goldman, *Anarchism*, p. 58.
70. Ibid.
71. Martha Solomon, *Emma Goldman* (Boston: G. K. Hall, 1987), pp. 22-23.
72. Ibid., pp. 402-403.
73. Goldman, *Mother Earth*, Vol. I, 1906-1907 (New York: Greenwood Reprint Corporation, 1968), p. 61.
74. Goldman, in Shulman, *Red Emma Speaks*, p. 88.
75. Solomon, *Emma Goldman*, p. 160.
76. Goldman, *Living My Life*, p. 402.
77. Drinnon, *Rebel in Paradise*, p. 160.
78. Ibid.
79. Ibsen used "social lie" to mean the hypocrisy of keeping up appearances for the sake of public opinion.
80. Ibid.
81. Solomon, *Emma Goldman*, p. 105.
82. Solomon, *Emma Goldman*, p. 12.
83. Ibid., p. 105.
84. Goldman, in Shulman, *Red Emma Speaks*, p. 158.
85. Ibid., p. 160.
86. Ibid.
87. Ibid., p. 166.
88. Ibid., p. 167.
89. Ibid., p. 35.
90. Ibid.
91. Ibid., p. 167.
92. Goldman, in Shulman, *Red Emma Speaks*, p. 35.
93. Ibid.
94. Ibid., p. 37.
95. Ibid.
96. Arthur Symons, "Henrik Ibsen," *Universal Review* (April 1889) in Michael Egan, ed., *Ibsen: The Critical Heritage* (London and Boston: Routledge and Kegan Paul, 1985), p. 100.
97. Ibsen, in Egan, *Ibsen: The Critical Heritage*, p. 80.
98. Falk, *Love, Anarchy and Emma Goldman*, p. 151.

CHAPTER 2

Community Versus Society: Goldman's View of the Supremacy of Instinct

Christopher Lasch noted that during the period in which Emma Goldman wrote and lectured, American radicalism was embedded in a particular notion of freedom which "signified the escape of the soul from a prison of its own devising, the triumph, to put the matter crudely, of instinct over intellect."[1] This chapter will situate Goldman's view of the supremacy of "instinct" in the context of contemporary feminist critiques of the nature/culture dichotomy, and of its corollary dichotomies instinct/intellect, community/ society, woman/man, private/public etc., and the difference/equality debates.

According to her first biographer, Richard Drinnon, Goldman's vision of anarchism, although highly individualistic and "instinctive" in its orientation, was also constructed upon the principle of community.[2] In *Anarchism and Other Essays* Goldman stated:

A certain atmosphere of "belonging," the consciousness of being "at one" with the people and environment, is more essential to one's feeling of home. This holds good in relation to one's family, the smaller local circles, as well as the larger phase of the life and activities commonly called one's country.... Peter Kropotkin has shown what wonderful results this unique force of man's individuality has achieved when strengthened by co-operation with other individualities.... He demonstrated that only mutual aid and voluntary co-operation—not the omnipotent, all-devastating state—can create the basis for a free individual and associational life.[3]

The value which Goldman assigned to the concept of community and her animosity toward the State were not original with her. Ferdinand Tönnies (1855-1936) had already articulated similar views in *Gemeinschaft und Gesellschaft*, in 1887. This work provided seminal ideas for many of the "founders" of modern sociology including Max Weber, Emile Durkheim, Georg Simmel and Karl Mannheim.[4]

In Drinnon's analysis, Goldman saw that "a distinction needed to be made between relatively inflexible abstract organizations such as the state and the more primary, flexible organizations such as communities."[5] Tönnies was the first to make a distinction between "Gemeinschaft" (community) and "Gesellschaft" (society). In *Gemeinschaft und Gesellschaft* Tönnies laments the modern drift from the small, face-to-face human associations to the large, impersonal organizations. Norms and sanctions based on kinship and family found in "Gemeinschaft" are replaced by the social control mechanisms of the state (i.e., the penal code and police power) located in "Gesellschaft."

Tönnies maintained that the drift towards and the domination by "Gesellschaft" would pose a serious threat to the culture if "none of its [Gemeinschaft's] seeds remain alive and again bring forth the essence and idea of Gemeinschaft."[6] Goldman's biographer, Drinnon, states that "in a sense, Emma's lifework was directed to keeping such scattered seeds alive and thereby to [in Tönnies' words] 'fostering a new culture amidst the decaying one.'"[7]

To some extent, the view that Goldman's work attempts to keep Gemeinschaft's "seeds alive" is problematic. Goldman's view of anarchism, abolishing regulation of human activity by church and State and establishing "a new social order based on liberty unrestricted by man-made law,"[8] is consistent with Tönnies' view of concord or informal agreement as the type of social organization which typifies Gemeinschaft. Gemeinschaft's realms of the private, primary and personal in contrast to the public "Gesellschaft" are characterized by a commonality of blood, place and mind. A unity of human will is grounded in familial ties and kinship relations as well as a commonality of location or community of physical life. In addition, a "Gemeinschaft of mind," or common will, brings about a reciprocal understanding between and among members of community—a norm of reciprocity which governs social and economic relations. While Goldman speaks of "individual instinct," Tönnies speaks of "natural will"—"the psychological equivalent of the human body":[9]

> The Gemeinschaft, which is understood best as a metaphysical union of bodies and blood, possesses by nature a will and force of life of its own.[10]

While Goldman's vision of anarchism is similar to Tönnies' vision of Gemeinschaft, in terms of the reciprocity and mutuality of social relations, the primacy of primary relationships and the predominance of group sentiment or concord, the patriarchal mandate in Gemeinschaft presents problems for Goldman. Tönnies' vision of community, which Goldman attempts to perpetuate, assumes sex-typed roles, a sexual division of labour and a gendered specificity of wills (i.e., natural will versus rational will; rational will being assigned to the male, public-dominated "Gesellschaft"):

> Although all individuals participate as social members in both forms of social organizations so that, for example, the Gemeinschaft encloses men as much as women in the communal collective experience of life; nevertheless, there are critical differences for the sexes at the biological and psychological levels of analysis that have consequences for the division of labour.[11]

Goldman, in contrast, sought to "do away with the absurd notion of the dualism of the sexes, or that man and woman represent two antagonistic worlds."[12]

As was the case in Kropotkin's work, the assumptions of patriarchy in Tönnies' "Gemeinschaft" create a tension of "unmanageability" when anarchism and Gemeinschaft are presented as models for Goldman's view of an anarchist community. The "dualism of the sexes," which both Kropotkin and Tönnies assume to be "natural" and "biologically-mandated," conflicts with Goldman's vision of anarchism. Tönnies, as well as Kropotkin, viewed patriarchy to be a given, and did not "acknowledge the tyrannies of custom and habit."[13] To suggest the appropriateness of patriarchy as an organizing principle would appear to a feminist to be a gross violation of anarchist tenets. Given that the rejection of man-made laws and restrictive repressive institutions is central to anarchist theory, patriarchy would appear to violate the basic theory of anarchism. Although it was Goldman who introduced women's perspective, sexuality, and reproduction into anarchist thinking she, too, failed explicitly to address the "custom" or "habit" of patriarchy as a force existing in Gemeinschaft or anarchist community.

Goldman clearly rejected the view that men and women represented antagonistic worlds; she considered the State, government and church to be the major sources of this antagonism. Ignoring the possibility that anarchism might possess "customs and habits" (e.g., patriarchy) which would "negate the freedom of the individual [woman],"[14] Goldman viewed the anarchist principle of community or Gemeinschaft in an accepting and uncritical fashion.

Goldman and Nature/Culture Dichotomy

Jeffrey Weeks notes in *Sexuality and Its Discontents* that during the latter decades of the nineteenth century, "theories of sex" and "theories of society" were created in "a complementary and equally influential fashion."[15] Weeks observed that Auguste Comte, Karl Marx, Herbert Spencer, Emile Durkheim, and many others were attempting to uncover the "laws of society" while the sexologists were attempting to reveal the foundations of our "animal nature." The science of society and the science of sex came, according to Weeks, to rely on one another:

> The science of sex was a necessary adjunct to the science
> of society; each came to rely implicitly but absolutely on

the other. A dichotomy between "sex" and "society" was written into the very terms of the debate.[16]

The dichotomy of "sex" and "society," according to Weeks, sets up an apparent antagonism between apparently separate realms.[17] The realm of "sex" includes such concepts as nature, individuality, and identity while the realm of "society" is associated with, in Week's assessment, the domain of cultural norms, social laws and "(sometimes) history." Weeks continues:

> The sex/society divide evokes and replays all the other great distinctions which attempt to explain the boundaries of animality and humanity: nature/culture, individual/society, freedom/regulation.[18]

Placing Goldman's model of anarchism into a larger theoretical context and history, one is able to observe the extent to which "anarchy" represents one side of what L.J. Jordanova regards as a long-standing conceptual bifurcation of what Weber called "ideal types." This bifurcation, varied in title yet similar in content, includes dichotomies such as Gemeinschaft/Gesellschaft, nature/culture, organic solidarity/mechanical solidarity, and private/public:

> Each polarity has its own history, but it also develops related meanings to other dichotomies. For instance, the pairs church and state, town and country, also contain allusions to gender differences, and to nature and culture. Transformations between sets of dichotomies are performed all the time. Thus, man/woman is only one couple in a common matrix, and this reinforces the point that it cannot be seen as isolated or autonomous.[19]

Functions and roles have been assigned to these dichotomies vis-à-vis gender relations and, therefore, are relevant to the subjects of sexuality and reproduction. Jordanova has represented these dichotomies in the following manner:[20]

nature	*culture*
woman	*man*
physical	*mental*
mothering	*thinking*
feeling and superstition	*abstract knowledge and thought*
country	*city*
darkness	*light*
nature	*science and civilization*

Another common expression of this dichotomy is constructed upon the ideal types, desire and reason, which are situated within the dichotomous locales of private and public. The public realm is depicted as one dominated by the laws of the State and the rules of reason while the private realm is depicted as governed by "sense impressions and desires." As mentioned in the preceding chapter, Roberto Unger is a social philosopher who gives expression to this dichotomous construction:

> In our public mode of being we speak the common language of reason, and live under laws of the state, the constraints of the market, and the customs of the different social bodies to which we belong. In our private incarnation, however, we are at the mercy of our sense impressions and desires.[21]

Goldman, in contrast, did not see being "at the mercy of our sense impressions and desires" as problematic. In her view, becoming aware of and getting in touch with one's senses and desires should become a transformatory force in the construction of anarchism.

In her advocacy of anarchism, Goldman also employed a series of dichotomies, particularly the following:

anarchism as "a free:	*"the State, organized*
individual and	*authority, or*
associational	*statutory*
life"[22]	*law "[23]*

"individuality"[24]	*"individualism" as governed by "social and economic laissez-faire"*[25]
nature, instinct[26]	*intellectual activity and regulation, control by employer, profession and state*[27]
sexual expression	*sexual repression by church, State and "puritan" values.*
women as heterosexual/ emotional partners and mothers[28]	*women as "professional automatons"—single and childless*[29]
rejection of "the dualism of the sexes"—ideally both sexes inhabit equally the[30] *same domain*	*dualism of the sexes—the realm of the "state" primarily the domain of men; ideally not the domain of either sex*[31]

The evolution which Tönnies, Durkheim, Weber and others viewed as inevitable, was one which lifted the social order out of the realm of desire into the realm of reason, the State and civil society.[32] Goldman had experienced the growing bureaucratization of society in American life. By 1916, a bureaucratic orientation defined America's discourse as its government expanded and with it its files, procedures and precedents.[33] Goldman also witnessed the excesses of state intervention in Russia from 1919-1921; this reinforced her ideal that "human values"—individual instincts—must be the primary organizing principles of group life. In Goldman's view, the oppressive nature of the state imposed itself upon the "tastes and desires" of those under its purview, thus forcing individuals to abandon their "nature" in favour of "culture."

Institutionalized religion and "puritanism" were also central targets for Goldman's attack upon oppression. Human sexuality and reproduction were constrained, in Goldman's view, by norms of behaviour grounded in religious, moral or civil doctrine rather than governed by "natural" or "instinctual" criteria. The farther individuals moved away from "nature" towards "culture" and the "State," the more repressed and sublimated their desires would become. Consistent with Jordanova's model, Goldman places issues of sexuality and reproduction on the "nature/instinct" side of the line. According to Goldman, decentralized, loosely-organized, voluntary associations of the anarchic form of social organization should rest firmly on the first principle of the dichotomy—nature. In this way "external" activities associated with the public realm would be reorganized and brought into harmony with "internal" factors of desire and instinct, thus merging the private and public. Goldman viewed both male and female "instinct" as that which was based in "natural" impulses and urges, unfettered by the superimposition of "culture" (i.e., religion, law, state). Thus, Goldman subscribed to the nature/culture dichotomy but not to a mapping of the male/female dichotomy onto it.[34]

Feminist Criticism of the Nature/Culture Dichotomy

While Goldman, with the exception of her rejection of sexual dualism, followed the conventional sociological wisdom (i.e., dichotomizing spheres and assigning particular characteristics and moral value to each), a substantial body of feminist criticism rejects the dichotomous distinction between nature and culture, desire and reason, private and public, etc.

In 1938, Virginia Woolf in *Three Guineas* juxtaposes the "nullity," "immorality," "hypocrisy," and "servility" of the private house and the "possessiveness," "jealousy," "pugnacity," and "greed" of the public world. She rejected the desirability of each on the grounds that the private sphere shuts women up "like slaves in a harem,"[35] while the public sphere forces women to circle "like caterpillars head to tail, round and round the mulberry tree, the sacred tree, of property."[36] Woolf contended that in the performance of public duties and their behavioural demands, human beings become truncated versions of humanity. Speaking of public office-holders, she wrote:

...If people are highly successful in their professions they lose their senses. Sight goes. They have no time to look at pictures. Sound goes. They have no time to listen to music. Speech goes. They have no time for conversation. They lose their sense of proportion—the relations between one thing and another. Humanity goes.[37]

The very separation of private and public was for Woolf an artificial distinction—one which is brought about through the patriarchal organization of both spheres. In contrast to the dichotomy of reason and desire and its corollaries of private and public, Woolf envisioned the "capacity of the human spirit to overflow boundaries and make unity out of multiplicity."[38]

Jean Elshtain also questions the dichotomy of private desire and public knowledge in her work *Public Man, Private Women* when she states:

One could quite plausibly argue that human beings differ from one another less by what they desire and need—as we all desire and need love, recognition, intimacy, sexual satisfaction or some resonant sublimated equivalent, mutual sharing based on moral "instincts," avenues for self-creativity, and other outgrowths of the desiring part of the human personality—than by what they "understand" in an abstract, formal sense, but may neither need or desire.[39]

According to Marilyn French, Elshtain suggests that women are trained for private virtue, men for public power, and this contributes to the separation between the two sexes and the realms by creating irrational thinking and behaviour.[40] According to Elshtain, there are a great many determinants of the degree to which we "know," some being differences in level of industrial development and literacy rates, as well as gender differences. She claims that our so-called "desires" may not be solely private and arbitrary while our "knowledge" may not be publicly shared.[41]

One school of feminist criticism of the nature/culture dichotomy also includes women's specificity as a basis for social transformation. Barbara Ehrenreich and Deirdre English reiterate a long tradition of so-called "maternal feminism" when they suggest that the values women preserve must "expand out of the confines of the private life and become the organizing principles of society.... And the 'womanly' values of community and caring must rise to the centre as the only human principles."[42] Another school of feminist thought views women's reproductive capability as the basis for a transformed social organization. Patricia Hughes writes:

> For feminists, birth, not death, and creation, not destruction, are at the centre of human existence. Feminists intend to change women's condition in a substantial way by transforming that which has been at the root of women's oppression, the ability to reproduce, into the foundation of revolutionary activity which will result in life and creation becoming the organizing force of society.[43]

The idea of women's specificity as a transformatory force has not gone unchallenged by other feminists. As Rosalind Sydie points out, "...the recognition of women's special qualities and insights could be celebrated as the necessary corrective to the extremes of male imagination and ambition without any profound alteration in the day-to-day realities of patriarchy."[44]

Dorothy Dinnerstein (1977) and Nancy Chodorow (1978) and others argue that "exclusive mothering" may simply perpetuate the nature/culture dichotomy which is embedded in patriarchy. Marilyn French explains:

> Dinnerstein hypothesizes that men's pervasive fear of women—a fear she believes is shared by women—arises from the fact that women do most of the early mothering, that we emerge into consciousness facing a woman who appears huge, all-powerful, and awe-ful, in control of all our pleasures, all of our pains. Although as we grow, we

bury this sense of her and, indeed, belittle her, the sense is triggered when we encounter a mature woman in a position of authority or control.... As they [men] reject the control of a woman because it seems overpowering, they also come to reject and devalue "feminine" qualities in general.[45]

An integrative approach has been suggested by some contemporary feminist critics who reject the dichotomies of nature/culture, private/public, desire/reason, etc., but do *not* discount women's specificity although they do not consider it to be the sole basis of social transformation. As Rosalind Sydie suggests:

> Feminists today have the benefit of hindsight as a result of critical exposures of patriarchal ideology represented by the work of Tönnies. The main task is to carve a path through the theoretical and practical temptation to retain dichotomy and hierarchy in order to produce the integrative, human society. In this task women's specificity must not be discounted, at the same time it must not be made the singular principle for social transformation.[46]

Marilyn French, following the private virtue/public power distinction of Jean Elshtain, suggests that the concepts of "virtue" and "power" must be viewed as inter-dependent rather than mutually exclusive:

> The exclusion of women from the public world is at once symbolic of its character and a reason for its character.... To disconnect virtue from power is to ensure that virtue will be powerless, and licenses power to be without virtue.[47]

Goldman and the Impurity of the State

Like many contemporary feminists, Goldman struggles to transcend the public/private divide. Freedom, in Goldman's view, is the ability to express one's desires—sexual desires being among the most fundamental of all natural instincts.[48] Thus, to reject the so-called "reason" of State and civil society, is to reject a pattern of social organization which places social good over individual well-being.

Goldman's distrust and rejection of the "State," explains her objections to her suffragist sisters who strove to be equal participants in civic society. The "State" was, in Goldman's assessment, fundamentally impure and beyond purification despite the well-intentioned efforts of some female reformers. Women who viewed themselves as "moral custodians" attempted to improve upon the institutions through participation in the public sphere.[49] As Sheila Jeffreys explains:

> In the period after 1900 the concerns of those feminists who had earlier worked with social purity seem to have been integrated into the propaganda of the suffrage campaign, which was renewed with unparalleled vigour after 1906. It is possible that feminists were able to pursue their aims of an equal moral standard and the control of male sexuality for the protection of women, through the pursuit of the vote, which was seen as a symbolic achievement through which women's other wrongs might be righted.[50]

While devaluing the "symbolic achievement" of the vote, Goldman critiqued the social institutions which defined and confined women on moral grounds, unlike her male anarchist counterparts who viewed the "sex question" as an unimportant one. However, unlike the suffragists, Goldman's critique of "culture," and the social institutions therein, was not one which recommended the infusion of women on the grounds that the impurities of the State would be purified. Goldman perceived these female reformers to be moral custodians who, instead of improving the conditions of women, were acting on moral imperatives to enslave women further. Under the omnipotent and ubiquitous State, women would become more oppressed, not less. Goldman told an audience that:

...I'm not opposed to the woman having the vote. There
is no reason why she shouldn't have just as much chance
to make a fool of herself with it as men have made of
themselves in the last hundred years. I am here to express
my sympathy for the women who are suffering heroic
things in England for something they believe in. But the
vote is not worth having, that's all.[51]

Goldman believed that obtaining the vote, the symbolic cornerstone
of participation in public life, was a worthless ambition because of
the vote's inevitable corruption by the State. To have and use the
vote was to become further entrenched in the realm of State and
bureaucracy, where one's focus would be directed away from the
"peace and harmony" of inner life towards the "corruption and
alienation of civil society."[52]

In her famous essay on woman's emancipation, Goldman sees
woman's freedom and independence coming from the "private" or
"nature" sides of the private/public, nature/culture dichotomies. Emphatically Goldman insists that "her development, her freedom, her
independence, must come from and through herself" rather than
through the public mechanism, the ballot.

If women are to be free, Goldman contends, they must,
paradoxically, emancipate themselves from emancipation by rejecting public realm participation as a form of emancipation. The triumph of instinct over intellect, of desire over reason, is the true
emancipatory force which liberates women. External emancipation
(e.g., gaining the right to vote or to participate in the professions of
the public sphere) has made woman an "artificial being," divorced
from her own inner qualities:

Merely external emancipation has made modern woman
an artificial being, who reminds one of the products of
French arboriculture with its arabesque trees and
shrubs...anything except the forms which would be
reached by the expression of her own inner qualities.
Such artificially grown plants of the female sex are to be

found in large numbers, especially in the so-called intellectual sphere of our life.[53]

Goldman argued that women's participation in the intellectual sphere of civil society imposed "artificial" modes of behaviour and beliefs which have "isolated woman and have robbed her of the fountain of springs of that happiness."[54]

The "emancipation" which brought women into public sphere activity as teachers, doctors, lawyers, architects and engineers did not equip them with the "necessary strength to compete with man."[55] As a result, Goldman continues, woman "is compelled to exhaust all her energy, use up her vitality and strain every nerve in order to reach the market value."[56]

Goldman states that in very few cases are women able to achieve professional equality with their male counterparts; if and when they do achieve equal recognition, either in the form of remuneration or confidence conferred on them by their male colleagues, they "generally do so at the expense of their physical and psychical well-being."[57] These professional women—teachers, physicians, lawyers, engineers, etc.—possess, in Goldman's words, "a dignified, proper appearance while their inner life is growing empty and dead."[58]

Goldman's rejection of women's involvement in the public sphere can be placed into contemporary debates over women's apparent "equality" versus "difference." Ruth Pierson and Alison Prentice (1982) have set out the arguments and the attendant problems associated with the demand for equality, the acceptance or celebration of difference, and "the co-existence of the demand for equality with the acceptance or celebration of difference."[59]

Pierson and Prentice suggest that in order for women to be as "autonomous and self-determining" as men, they must be able to participate in the public realm.[60] An attendant problem of this goal, according to the authors, is one which could lead to a further "atomizing" of society:

The self-sufficient woman, living alone, unencumbered by intimate ties to or responsibilities to other human beings, however, is not necessarily a feminist goal. Feminists insist, rather, that women have a human need equal to men's for affection and emotional support but that for satisfaction of this need women should not have to make a greater sacrifice of autonomy than men.[61]

Goldman envisioned the "self-sufficient woman, living alone, unencumbered by intimate ties"[62] to be denying her true "nature" while engaging in a world of "narrowness and stiffness." Not trusting or valuing the mechanisms of the public sphere, Goldman suggested that "external emancipation" (i.e., public sphere activity) has made women artificial beings.[63] Accordingly, Goldman suggested that women retreat from the public realm and, particularly, from the "so-called intellectual sphere"[64] to the realm of nature and instinct. Goldman, then, does not attempt to reconcile the conflict between the "private" and the "public," insisting instead that the private must be unreservedly embraced and the public unequivocally rejected. Women's "equality" in the public sphere, according to Goldman, was not only highly unlikely, but was also highly undesirable.[65] In this way, Goldman places women's choices into "rigid categories and dichotomies, positing irreconcilable conflict between two solutions."[66] Goldman suggests that women's "difference" is best expressed in the realm of the private and the instinctual, while women's "equality" as expressed through public realm activity is a hollow and artificial goal.

Contemporary feminist debates on the so-called dilemma of "equality" versus "difference," which Goldman faced earlier in this century, are increasingly "integrative"[67] in their approach. As Pierson and Prentice state:

> We argue that it is possible and desirable to pursue both goals ["equality" and "difference"] at once, despite their apparent contradiction...it [feminism] must go further and insist on the full complexity of human lives and possibilities.... In this sense, liberty joins equality as a watchword for the movement.[68]

However, most recently, Joan Wallach Scott has argued for a
"deconstructive" political strategy to the difference/equality debate,
rejecting the view that the world must be constructed in binary
terms.[69] Scott argues that the "critical" feminist position must involve two moves:

> ...The first, systematic criticism of the operations of
> categorical difference, exposure of the kinds of ex-
> clusions and inclusions—the hierarchies—it constructs,
> and a refusal of their ultimate "truth." A refusal, how-
> ever, not in the name of an equality that implies sameness
> or identity but rather...of an equality that rests on dif-
> ferences—differences that confound, disrupt, and render
> ambiguous the meaning of any fixed binary opposition.[70]

Goldman and Woman's "Nature"

Goldman believed that this highly-prized recognition and
achievement in the realm of civil society would have damaging effects on the "nature" of women and, particularly, her sexual and
reproductive urges. This form of "public" emancipation seduces
women away from the true source of emancipation—her own instincts. In Goldman's assessment, this "artificial" form of emancipation is a "slow process of dulling and stifling woman's nature, her
love instinct, and her mother instinct."[71]

Although Goldman rejected the notion of "compulsory motherhood" and advocated in its place "voluntary motherhood," her
views on the subject of motherhood were embedded in traditional
notions of women's biological fulfilment. The biologically-determined, organic model of human behaviour of the nineteenth century remained to be a powerful influence on views concerning
sexuality and reproduction in the early decades of the twentieth century.[72] The Swedish "maternalist" Ellen Key, whose views were contemporary with Goldman's, shared many of the same
preoccupations with the supreme importance of childhood and the
"right to motherhood" independent of marriage.[73] Key, like

Goldman, deplored the condition in which women were reduced to reproductive drudges and argued for women's entitlement to a limited number of offspring. Also like Goldman, Key was highly critical of those women who were disinclined to become mothers or what she considered to be the "new woman's" disinclination for motherhood.[74] Goldman and Key shared a common view of gender essentialism and eugenics in which women's self-fulfilment was brought about through motherhood as she, at the same time, "performed her self-sacrificing duty to the evolutionary betterment of the race."[75]

Despite Goldman's unorthodox views on such issues as sexual varietism, her position on motherhood was not only in keeping with biologically deterministic views, but was consistent with those of the late Victorian sexologists, whose work she applauded and admired. While Goldman praised the sexologists (i.e., Sigmund Freud, Havelock Ellis and Edward Carpenter) for bringing sexuality "out of the closet" and granting it its rightful place in public discussion, she also uncritically shared their view of the "naturalness" of motherhood. Carroll Smith-Rosenberg notes that while Havelock Ellis, one of the most widely read British sexologists, was "liberal and psychologically sensitive," he remained a man of his times.[76] Ellis conceptualized male/female relations in light of the nineteenth century's organic model of human behaviour and believed that motherhood was women's greatest contribution to the human race.[77]

Like Ellis, Goldman saw motherhood as providing a source of "natural" fulfilment for women and, like Ellis, she expressed grave concern over modern movements which purported to advocate "equality" for women. Smith-Rosenberg notes that "feminism, lesbianism, equality for women, all emerge in Ellis's writings as problematic phenomena."[78] Goldman's belief that women *need* to give and receive love, preferably with a man as well as a child, was consistent with a prevailing gender ideology which defined women's nature as based in a need to nurture a child and to have a heterosexual relationship. Sex and love, for Goldman, were gender-specific experiences in which women and men do not share common emotions and sensations. In many ways reflecting the conventional view of her day which situated women in a "relational" manner (i.e., in relation to men and children), Goldman suggested that women's "nature," affectively and sexually, was different from that of men. Her view of the "relational" nature of women is clearly set out in a letter she wrote to Alexander Berkman in 1925 in which she expounded upon the tragedy of "all of us modern women":

> It is a fact that we ["modern women"] are removed only by a very short period of our transitions, the transitions of being cared for, protected, secured, and above all, the time when women could look forward to an old age of children, a home and someone to brighten their lives... most modern women begin to feel the utter emptiness of their existence, the lack of a man whom they love and who loves them, the comradeship and companionship that grows out of such a relation, the home, a child.[79]

In another letter to Berkman earlier in the same year, Goldman wrote that she is "consumed by longing for love and affection for some human being of my own" and argues, again, that women and men differ in the degree to which each requires love and affection. Goldman wrote:

> I therefore agree fully with you that both men and women need some person who really cares. The woman needs it more and finds it impossible to meet anyone when she has reached a certain age. That is her tragedy.[80]

Russian feminist, Alexandra Kollontai (1983-1952), whose ideas were more or less contemporaneous with those of Goldman, argued that while "love" is important, "love is only one aspect of the life, and must not be allowed to overshadow the other facets of the relationships between individual and collective."[81] Kollontai explains that communist morality encourages "many and varied" bonds among and between people; instead of "all for the loved one'," communist and between people; instead of "all for the loved one'," communist morality "demands all for the collective."[82] "Love" was placed into a broader context by Kollontai than by Goldman to include beyond love for one's sexual partner and one's child also love for one's comrades and children who are not one's own.[83] The tragedy of modern women, according to Goldman, is due to the fact that women "are still rooted in the old soil, though our visions are of the future and our desire is to be free and independent."[84] The tragedy is greater for women who "have no creative abilities"[85] because, according to Goldman, "they, even more than the others, can express themselves only in love and devotion for the man and the child, or for both in the man."[86] Comparing the "ordinary" woman to the "modern" woman, Goldman reveals her view of work and love and how each relates to the two types of women.[87]

Speaking of Fritzie, a fellow worker, secretarial assistant for *Mother Earth* and mutual friend of Goldman and Berkman, Goldman wrote to Berkman:

> Of course, no work fills one's life, one needs love and companionship at all times. But while some of us can forget themselves a little in the work we are doing, or want to do, Fritzie and others like her find little comfort in the work they are doing....[88]

Goldman's view of women's maternal "nature" is clearly set out in a letter to Max Nettlau, dated February 8, 1935. In it, Goldman strongly endorsed "voluntary motherhood":

> ...I wish to say that I have yet to meet the woman who wants to have many children. That doesn't mean that I ever for a moment denied the fact that most women want to have a child, although that, too, has been exaggerated by the male. I have known quite a number of women, feminine to the last degree, who nevertheless lack that supposed-to-be inborn trait of motherhood or longing for the child. There is no doubt the exception.... Well,

granted that every woman wants to become a mother. But unless she is densely ignorant with an exaggerated trait of passivity, she wants only as many children as she can decide to have, and I am sure the Spanish women makes no exception....[89]

Correspondence between Berkman and Goldman provided a candid portrayal of Goldman's position on "women's nature." In a letter to Goldman dated May 20, 1929, Alexander Berkman articulated his views on feeling and reason, and correspondingly, the biological, mental, and psychic differences between men and women:

People live according to their feelings, not with their reason, generally speaking. And even those who try to harmonize feeling and reason can seldom understand each other, and least of all, if they belong to different sexes...people are differing in general, and man and woman particularly so....I think man and woman are not only biologically but also mentally and physically so different that understanding in certain matters is out of the question.[90]

Four days later Goldman responded to Berkman, agreeing with his assessment that feeling, not reason, governs people's lives:

...You are right a thousand times, dearest Sash, that people, even the most devoted friends, know little and understand little of each other. And that talk does not help to bring them to a better understanding. There is more truth than fiction in the German saying, "Wenn Du es nicht fuhlst, wirst Du es nie errathen." [If you do not feel a thing, you will never guess its meaning.] The trouble is, my dear, that you are not very chutko [knowing] in certain things, certainly not in relation to the women who have been in your life.[91]

This correspondence between Berkman and Goldman clearly reveals Goldman's view of women's "sexual nature." Just as women's general "nature" is distinct and different from that of men, so is female sexuality. Berkman and Goldman shared the view that sex bore greater significance and played a larger role in "love" for women than for men. Berkman, in 1931, wrote to Goldman:

> ...I do believe that with women sex plays a far greater role in love than with men, *generally* speaking. By sex here I mean everything, affection, love, passion, all together.[92]

Three days later, on December 25, 1931, Goldman responded to Berkman stating:

> Nor do I disagree in what you say about sex in women as a more dominant force than in men.[93]

Goldman had expressed her views on female sexuality to Frank Harris in 1925. Responding to Harris' *My Life and Loves* (1922) and *Contemporary Portraits* (1915), Goldman argued that Harris has devoted much time to discussing the physical aspects of sex and too little time on the psychological aspects:

> ...I do not consider the mere physical fact sufficient to convey the tremendous effect it [sex] has upon human emotions and sensations. Perhaps it is because to woman sex has a far greater effect than to man. It creates a storm in her being and lingers on when the man is satisfied and at ease.[94]

The view that sex is a more "dominant," all-encompassing force for women than for men, was also articulated by Goldman in a 1935 letter to Dr. Samuel Schmalhausen, author of *Woman's Coming of Age* (1931). In it, Goldman praised him for his assessment of the differential effect of the sex act on men and women:

I am delighted to know that one of your own sex is so
understanding of the different effect of the sex act on the
male and female. Singularly enough I have maintained,
since my intellectual awakening, the same thought.
Namely, that the sex act of the man lasts from the moment of its dominant motivation to its climax. After that
the brute has done his share. The brute can go to sleep.
Not so the woman. The climax of the embrace, far from
leaving her relaxed or stupefied as it does the man, raises
all her sensibilities to the highest pitch. All her yearning
for love, affection, tenderness becomes more vibrant and
carries her to ecstatic heights. At that moment she needs
the understanding of and communion with her mate
perhaps more than the physical. But the brute is asleep
and she remains in her own world far removed from
him.[95]

Advancing her argument, Goldman contended that the conflict between the sexes that exists, regardless of a woman's emancipation, is
due "to the differences in quality of the sex embrace."[96]

Goldman and Women's Place in the "Private" and "Public" Realms

Goldman's placement of woman on the instinctual side of the
instinct/intellect dichotomy does not simply represent a statement of
her belief that woman's "natural" abilities are best suited to biologically-mandated activities and not to intellectual or civic activities. As
feminist scholars have long noted, this distinction has served to perpetuate the oppression of women on the grounds that it is "natural"
to locate women in the private sphere:

...Feminists recognize that the fact and meaning of
reproduction and mothering must be incorporated into
the pursuit of a more humane society because the
dualism that divides reproduction from production,
private from public life, and male from female, is a means

by which the alienation and domination of women has been effected and perpetuated.[97]

Goldman's placement of women on the side of desire and instinct is representative of her placement of *all* human beings—male and female—on that side of the divide and of her rejection of the "public" sphere as a possible climate for inner growth and true emancipation. However, Goldman did not believe that women were disqualified to make the leap to the public sphere because of their biological nature. Nor did she endorse the philosophy of "separate spheres" for men and women. Simply stated, placing both men and women on the "nature" side of the nature/culture dichotomy, Goldman asserted the primacy of instinct over intellect.

Goldman's animosity towards many of her liberal reformer sisters and their reciprocal displeasure with Goldman and her ideas[98] was, to a large extent, due to the extent to which liberals perceived public sphere participation as the road to women's emancipation.[99] Liberal women reformers of Goldman's day concentrated their efforts on attaining female suffrage, greater access to higher education, and increased participation in the labour force.[100] Goldman's rejection of the goals as a means to greater independence for women was based upon her rejection of the State and its impurities—impurities that could not be purified by the injection of female participants. Goldman's rejection of female suffrage, higher education and careerism was not, as many liberal female reformers thought, based on a rejection of women as equal partners with men in the public sphere or a claim that women were not "fit" for public life. Rather, Goldman rejected these feminist goals because she believed that public or "State" life was "unfit" for women and not worthy of their participation.

In a similar light, Goldman viewed access to higher education, and increased participation of women in professional public sphere activity, to be a false prescription for female emancipation. The outright rejection of female suffrage, higher education and "careerism" as indisputable ideals of women's emancipation resulted in her opponents labelling Goldman a "man's woman."[101]

The Progressive women reformers, who campaigned for the
higher participation of women in post-secondary education, met
with conservative opposition and thus their harsh reaction to
Goldman, as a "man's woman," was very much influenced by the
conservative campaign to discredit their achievements. As Smith-
Rosenberg points out:

> By the 1920s, charges of lesbianism had become a com-
> mon way to discredit woman professionals, reformers,
> and educators—and the feminist political reform, and
> educational institutions they had founded.[102]

Ironically, Goldman's objections to female higher education and
careerism bore a striking resemblance to the objections raised by
American conservatives who based their arguments on the na-
ture/culture dichotomy. As Smith-Rosenberg explains their position:

> Put most succinctly, man was the creator and repre-
> sentative of culture, woman of nature. To educate woman
> would violate each of these binary opposites and make
> woman, not man, the mediating figure.[103]

Also, women's higher education elicited negative reaction from the
business community. Rayna Rapp and Ellen Ross argue that in the
years following the First World War, business leaders feared that the
increase in the number of professional, career-oriented women
would have a negative effect upon domestic consumption.[104] A campaign to redomesticate women would ensure a greater market for
American consumer goods.[105]

Goldman's objections to female professionalism, however, were
based on a metaphysical argument rather than on an economic one.
She stressed the importance of the "inner life," of the nurturance of
the soul, and criticized the "narrowness of the existing conception of
woman's independence and emancipation."[106] This narrowness of
vision, said Goldman, was based upon a collection of fears—the fear
that love will limit her freedom and independence; the dread of

loving a man who is not her social equal; the "horror" that love and motherhood will detract from her profession. Collectively these fears, dreads and horrors make the modern emancipated woman a "compulsory vestal, before whom life, with its great clarifying sorrows and its deep, entrancing joys, rolls on without touching or gripping her soul."[107]

Goldman also disagreed with reformers who struggled for the inclusion of women in institutions of higher learning and believed that greater female participation in post-secondary education would liberate women from household drudgery and poorly paid labour. Goldman viewed higher education as a hollow aspiration, which actually served to further entrap women and men. She asserted that education is the means through which the myth of individualism is indoctrinated:

> Individualism is...the exploitation of the masses by the classes by means of legal trickery, spiritual debasement and systematic indoctrination of the servile spirit, which process is known as "education."[108]

During the period in which Goldman wrote and published "The Tragedy of Woman's Emancipation" (1911), participation rates of women in higher education were climbing. An increasing percentage of these women were choosing to pursue a career to the exclusion of marriage and family. Smith-Rosenberg reports that between 1889 and 1908, 55 percent of Bryn Mawr women graduates did not marry and 62 percent entered graduate school. Of those women who married, 54 percent chose to continue their career and remain economically autonomous. Most striking was the percentage of Bryn Mawr graduates who did *not* have paying jobs—only 10 percent.[109] After 1910, however, these figures began to reverse, as the campaigns to redomesticate women gained force. Smith-Rosenberg: "Many factors contributed to this trend; but the campaign against 'masculine straight-forwardness' and independence played its part."[110]

It is easy to appreciate the passion with which Progressive women reformers rejected Goldman's arguments. Superficially, Goldman's

objections were perceived to be anti-female, questioning women's
right to participate in public sphere activities. While the reformers
viewed higher education to be a transformative and emancipatory experience for women, their vision of emancipation was, in some
respects, one which subscribed to the view that "knowledge" was
gained through public sphere activity. That is, their vision was
premised on the belief, or assumption, that emancipation through
"knowledge" was a public realm activity, occurring only after one has
taken the leap from instinct to intellect. They perceived knowledge to
be separate from the private realm of women—divorced from desire,
instinct, mothering and marriage. From this perspective, one can appreciate Goldman's objections to the Progressive women reformers'
battle for emancipation through education. To reject the realm of nature or desire and to assume that worthwhile knowledge was only at-
tainable in the realm of culture or intellect, was to adopt a patriarchal
"culture" in which instinct was devalued. Goldman not only perceived women's placement in "culture" as short-changing women,
but, more specifically, as contributing to the creation of "professional
automatons."[111] In her famous statement about the professional
woman as automaton, Goldman emphasizes the need for a fuller and
richer experience for women—experience she cannot have within the
limiting and soul-diminishing climate of professional life:

> The tragedy of the self-supporting or economically free
> woman does not lie in too many, but in too few experien-
> ces. True, she surpasses her sister of past generations in
> knowledge of the world and human nature; it is just be-
> cause of this she feels deeply the lack of life's essence,
> which alone can enrich the human soul, and without
> which the majority of women have become mere profes-
> sional automatons.[112]

Goldman's antagonism towards the progressive exponents of
women's rights was extended to include a critique of the reformers'
"puritan" views of sexuality and male/female relations. In Goldman's
view their world view was "puritan" because of its lack of endorse-

ment of sexual experimentation (e.g., varietism) and its emphasis on the "protection" of women from male exploitation. Contemporary debates within feminism focus on many of the same issues—the liberatory potential of female sexuality[113] versus the dangers of so-called "sexual liberation" in a male-dominated culture.[114] Contemporary "pro-sex" feminist Aritha Van Herk, in "Laying the Body on the Line (The Feminist Makes a Pass, or Figurations in a Feminist's Erotics)," sides with a view typical of that of Goldman—a view which endorses the "incalculable delights" of sexual expression:

> ...All my intellectual and emotional and political distaste for my sex's colonization does not prevent me from enjoying myself....I refuse my pleasure to be censored: every phrase I write or skin I caress (my own and others) is an excursion in the ardour of discovering incalculable delights, those pleasures that will not be deemed correct or incorrect...[115]

In many respects, the differences of view expressed by Goldman and the female reformers met with the same intensity and irreconcilability as the contemporary pro-life/pro-choice debate. Each side saw its conception of woman's nature as the correct one; each side was not willing to grant concessions to the other; each side seems to hold a fixed and immoveable vision of the goals and aspirations of women. The progressive women reformers sought to make the public sphere more accessible to women. Practical and pragmatic in their vision, they lobbied the State to gain entry into institutions and to improve them through their participation. Goldman's approach was more philosophical and less pragmatic, eschewing incremental change in favour of fundamental reform. Reform for the progressive women reformers meant opening up key institutions (e.g., education) to women. Goldman, in contrast, argued for a transformation in women's souls.

Goldman, as if addressing her entire essay "The Tragedy of Woman's Emancipation" to the exponents of women's rights, compares and contrasts emancipation in the realm of desire and instinct with emancipation in the realm of public sphere activity. According to Goldman, the exponents of women's rights turn their backs on their innate instincts in favour of "artificial stiffness and its narrow respectabilities." She points out to the women's rights exponents that "there seemed to be a deeper relationship between the old-fashioned mother and hostess, ever on the alert for the happiness of her little ones, and the truly new woman, than between the latter and her average emancipated sister."[116] Goldman describes the reaction of the women's rights exponents to her observation: "The disciples of emancipation pure and simple declared me a heathen, fit only for the stake."[117]

Continuing to compare the "old" and "new" woman, Goldman asserted that many of "our grandmothers had more blood in their veins" and a "greater amount of naturalness, kind-heartedness and simplicity, than the majority of our emancipated professional women who fill the colleges, halls of learning and offices."[118] Goldman's attack on the "professional women who fill the colleges, halls of learning and offices" is primarily an attack upon the sphere in which these women choose to conduct their lives rather than a direct attack on the women themselves.

While her opponents interpreted Goldman's objections as regressive and having the potential effect of setting back women's achievements in the public sphere, Goldman claimed that her position did not represent "a wish to return to the past, nor does it condemn woman to her old sphere, the kitchen and nursery."[119] What precisely was Goldman's position on female emancipation if not a position which assigned women to a traditional realm with traditional goals and aspirations (i.e., marriage and family)? How is one able to differentiate, as apparently her opponents could not, between Goldman's view on the "proper sphere" for women and that of the conservative position which *did* "condemn woman to...the kitchen and the nursery?"[120]

Goldman's Rejection of Sexual Dualism

As stated above, Emma Goldman rejected the "absurd notion of the dualism of the sexes, or that man and woman represent two antagonist worlds."[121] In this she not only went against the grain of Western philosophy and social organization, but also introduced a revolutionary conception of gender relations and associational life. Goldman placed both men and women in the domain where feminine traits have traditionally prevailed—in the domain of instinct and desire, where both sexes could express their instincts naturally. Goldman also rejected the taken-for-granted philosophical proposition that because men and women possess different instincts, they belong in *separate spheres.* Elinor Lenz and Barbara Myerhoff in *The Feminization of America* (1985) explain this in the following way:

> Dualism and polarization have marked much of our history, replacing the natural wholeness and unity of life and humankind with separate, disconnected entities, alien to each other and to themselves. The principles of rational analysis and cognitive absolutism of opposites that have dominated Western culture perceive the world in terms of opposites that exist in a state of mutual suspicion and hostility:...proletariat versus bourgeoisie, scientist versus humanist, masculine versus feminine (or yang versus yin). The sensibility that divides the world into opposition inevitably ranks them after dividing them, then sets itself up a superior—in value judgments, clarity and order.[122]

Rejecting the dichotomy of reproduction and production, Goldman makes, given their historical context, next-to-revolutionary claims. These claims are that women's freedom is closely allied with men's freedom and that children need to be nurtured by both men and women.[123] Goldman's vision of gender relations, in which sexual dualism is rejected, represents a radical and revolutionary potential for future generations. Both men and women, according to her vision, would be responsible for the care and nurturance of children. Goldman states:

> But woman's freedom is closely allied with man's freedom, and many of my so-called emancipated sisters

seem to overlook the fact that a child born in freedom needs the love and devotion of each human being about [her or] him, man as well as woman. Unfortunately, it is this narrow conception of human relations [dualism of the sexes] that has brought about a great tragedy in the lives of the modern man and woman.[124]

Goldman envisioned a society in which men would be freed from the mind-numbing, soul-destroying conditions found in the public sphere and be free to assume responsibility as care-givers alongside women. Women, in turn, would not be burdened with sole responsibility for the care of children; nor would they be compelled to "compete" with men in the "public" realm. Thus, men and women would jointly inhabit the realm which had previously been assigned exclusively to women. With this view, Goldman seems to have anticipated the views of more recent feminists, such as Gayle Rubin who has suggested that if children were raised by parents of both sexes, human social relationships would be richer and sexual power and the Oedipus complex would disappear.[125] To the extent that Goldman argued for dual parenting, with both women and men being placed in the realm of community, kinship and family, she offered a revolutionary alternative to the dualism that divides men and women and the responsibility for the giving of care. Some contemporary feminists believe that feminism must call for a "revolution in kinship" in which men would supply the same nurturance as do women.[126] Goldman, in 1911, called for the inclusion of men in the task of care-giving. To this extent, Goldman did call for a dismantling of sexual dualism and the gender ideology in which it was embedded. The implications of this dismantling would have significant influences on family structure as well as gender identity of future generations.

While Goldman explicitly calls for the rejection of "the dualism of the sexes,"[127] she implicitly argues in support of the dichotomy which one present-day feminist identifies as "the means by which the alienation and domination of women has been effected and perpetuated."[128] Goldman does argue for woman's specificity being grounded in "her nature"[129]—a nature which Goldman saw as requiring for fulfilment "life's greatest treasure, love for a man, or her most glorious privilege, the right to give birth to a child."[130]

As feminist scholars have long suggested, women's specificity has been inseparable from women's oppression.[131] However, as Rosalind Sydie has suggested, feminists recognize that the meaning of motherhood must be incorporated into the pursuit of a more humane society since the dualism that divides is the means through which women have been alienated and dominated.[132]

Angela Miles, in "Ideological Hegemony in Political Discourse: Women's Specificity and Equality," argues that, like nineteenth-century beliefs about "true womanhood," contemporary right-wing debates are associated with defining womanhood and assigning a proper sphere for "womanly" activities. Miles states that "this forces us to recognize that the definition and meaning of womanhood is now a key political question."[133] While Goldman did not engage in the assignment of separate spheres for women and men, arguing in support of a single sphere or realm in which *all* would live according to one's tastes and desires, she *did* articulate a view of "the definition and meaning of womanhood."[134] As has been previously mentioned, Goldman based her theory of anarchism on freedom of expression—freedom to explore and express individual tastes and desires. In spite of her view of freedom, she grounds women's definition and meaning, not within a general and wide range of possibilities and potentialities, but in specific and narrow options—that of heterosexual love and childbearing.[135]

Goldman's view of women's "maternalism" is based on a view of women's specificity—a view of women's "nature."[136] While contemporary feminist views, such as those of Angela Miles, suggest that "life, love and trust must be reclaimed by new and free women,"[137] Goldman never advocated women rejecting these values (i.e., life, love and trust), in favour of claiming a place in the "public" sphere.

As Goldman rejected claiming a place for women in the "public" sphere, she dismissed the possibility that women's tastes and desires might also be actualized through "professional" life, as they would through the love for a man and the birth of a child. In rejecting the "artificiality and narrowness" of the public sphere, Goldman rejected the possibility that woman's fulfilment might rest on activities which were situated in the public sphere—intellectual or educational activities, or commitment to a "career." If activities such as intellectual or educational pursuits could be experienced by some women as individually fulfilling, why did Goldman reject them? Because, when pursued as professions and careers, they gained their definition from and were regulated by the oppressive control of "the State." Goldman's rejection of such activities when carried out in service to the State, under institutional control and at the expense of the emotional, sexual dimension of human life, speaks to the degree to which Goldman opposed the bifurcation of "mental" from "physical," "knowledge" from "feeling," "theory from practice" and, thus, to the degree to which she opposed a truncated womanhood. Goldman's horror at the artificiality of professional women stemmed from her theory of anarchism which, by definition, rejects the form and substance of those activities falling under the wide purview of what she considered to be "the State." Hers was a unique form of "integrative feminism" that affirmed women's specificity at the same time as it sought women's freedom to develop their full human potential, only *not* within the State-dominated realm, as, given its oppressive, regulatory character, fulfilment under its domination was impossible. In contrast, contemporary feminist conceptions of "integrative feminism" employ the affirmation of women's specificity in their "revisioning" of the world in such a way as to seek its extension into the public realm or what Goldman called "the State." In this way, women would bring their values into what Goldman considered to be the realm of "the State," having the effect of redefining and restructuring the institutions there within. Miles explains:

> ...This affirmation of female-associated values makes possible the emergence of an over-arching feminist perspective which can encompass both women's specificity and equality in a "revisioning" of the world that challen-

ges the very terms of male-defined political discourse rather than simply claiming women's place within it.[138]

Goldman differed from many of the "maternal" feminists of her day who believed women's higher morality, stemming from their maternal nature, could improve the conditions of the impure State. Instead, she believed that the State was beyond purification and that claims of women's moral virtue only served to enslave them further.

Goldman believed her emphasis on women's sexuality, instinct, nature, and inner regeneration to be revolutionary and "antipuritan." She championed the glorification of "healthy" heterosexuality by such "sex radicals" as Sigmund Freud and Havelock Ellis. In her autobiography, Goldman recalled the impact Freud had upon her conceptualization of the significance of sexuality. Feeling as if she had been "led out of a dark cellar into broad daylight," Goldman came to grasp the "full significance of sex repression and its effect on human thought and action."[139] In *Living My Life*, she articulated the degree to which she regarded sexuality as fundamental to life itself:

> ...I knew from my own experience that sex expression is as vital a force in human life as food and air. Therefore, it was not mere theory that led me at an early stage of my development to discuss sex as frankly as I did other topics and to live my life without fear of the opinions of others.[140]

Goldman was twenty-nine when she made the above statement. Her vision of the importance of "sex expression" was one in which personal experience and theoretical or "expert" endorsement (i.e., Freud) conjoined and congealed. If she felt personally fortified by Freud's endorsement of her own convictions on the value of sex expression, Goldman uncompromisingly laid *true* emancipation at the door of human nature or instinct. If the door was to be opened, one had to "cut loose from the weight of prejudices, traditions, and customs" and begin a process of "inner regeneration."[141] If the door was

to remain closed, woman's future would be one in which her true
nature was perverted by social custom and tradition, truncated from
such fundamental experiences as "sex expression" and giving birth
to a child. As Goldman asserted:

> Until woman has learned to defy them all, to stand firmly
> on her own ground and to insist upon her own un-
> restricted freedom, to listen to the voice of her nature,
> whether it call for life's greatest treasure, love for a man,
> or her most glorious privilege, the right to give birth to a
> child, she cannot call herself emancipated.[142]

The "emancipated" woman who remained celibate either by
choice or social circumstance not only denied herself "life's greatest
treasure" and her "most glorious privilege" but, also ran the risk of
psychological decay. Adopting the negative construction of single
women as unfulfilled, and neurotic, that was developed in her day,
Goldman claimed that women who remained "unnaturally" celibate
would suffer "neurasthenia, impotence, depression, and a great
variety of nervous complaints involving diminished power of work,
limited enjoyment of life, sleeplessness, and preoccupations with
sexual desires and imaginings."[143] Goldman continued her indictment of celibacy by declaring that women's "intellectual inferiority…is due to the inhibition of thought imposed upon them for
the purpose of sexual repression."[144]

The view that intellectual "inferiority" of women stemmed from
the "inhibition of thought" brought about by sexual repression was,
according to Goldman, the belief of Freud.[145] Her support of the
ideas of Freud caused her to uncritically accept his view that women
were, in fact, intellectually inferior. Embracing the sexology of Ellis
and Edward Carpenter influenced Goldman's perception of
"women's nature," which firmly embedded women in maternality
and heterosexuality, rejecting the option of singleness and lesbian
relationships.

Despite Goldman's opposition to the medical establishment's
views on such issues as the dissemination of birth control, she

shared its perception of the human organism as a closed system of energy. Ironically, Goldman's description of the damaging effects of sexual repression sounded much like the medical model of the female organism used by physicians to legitimize sexual intercourse and to discourage female pursuits that might take women away from the therapeutic contributions of the semen.[146] The medical model of the body as a "closed system" treated the body as an organism possessing an interdependent and finite supply of energy— energy that if disproportionately consumed in one area of the body would go lacking in another. For example, the medical profession made a case against the extended education of women on the grounds that the extra energy needed for intellectual pursuits would draw energy away from reproductive efforts.[147] Similar, although in all likelihood not intentionally so, was Goldman's description of the damaging effects of sexual repression on the female intellect. While the medical profession argued that too much intellectual or mental activity would have a harmful effect on sexual and reproductive functioning, Goldman argued that the lack of sexual expression or sexual repression would have harmful effects upon women's mental or intellectual functioning.

Summary

Overall, the objections Goldman posed to the female reformers of the public sphere were reflective of her view of anarchism and indicative of her contempt for the realm of church and State as emancipatory forces. Sounding, at times, traditional and conservative in her pronouncements about the "love for a man" and the "glorious privilege of childbirth," Goldman, at the same time, in essays such as "Marriage and Love" denounces socially perfunctory marriage and childbirth as alienating and soul-destroying.

While Beauvoir referred to the public sphere as the "imposing structure built by males,"[148] Goldman did not reject the existing political and economic structure, or women's involvement in it, on the grounds that it was built by men. Goldman's rejection of the dualism of the sexes and the realms of State and government was in no way a rejection of men or masculine ways. Although men were the "creators" of this realm and acted upon the State just as they were acted upon *by* the State, Goldman levies no responsibility on men for creating and perpetuating a structure as "impure" and corrupt as she envisioned it to be. Her emphasis, instead, was upon the State existing as an "a priori" institution, constantly exerting pressure upon the individual man to conform and comply with State regulation.[149] In this sense, Goldman's critique of the State as "conservative, static" and "intolerant of change"[150] was one in which man is viewed as the *victim* of oppression and not the *creator* of an oppressive institution. Man's status as "victim" was the reason that Goldman saw American women—not men—as the most "ardent workers for social reconstruction." In Goldman's view, middle-class and professional man, lifeless and downtrodden under the control of State life, "has been made an almost complete automaton by our commercial life."[151] Goldman added that "he lacks red blood, without which active interest in an idea is impossible."[152]

Unlike other feminist authors such as Virginia Woolf, who thoroughly and cogently critiqued patriarchal institutions, Goldman did *not* treat as synonymous "men" and the "public realm" and, therefore, made no strong condemnations of men. Instead she made an argument for conciliation and union between the sexes and criticized those who might be cautious of forming relationships because of perceived inequalities inherent in male/female relations: "A true conception of the relation of the sexes will not admit of conqueror and conquered...."[153]

As well, Goldman argues that "complete and true" emancipation of woman "will have to do away with the ridiculous notion that to be loved, to be sweetheart and mother, is synonymous with being slave and subordinate."[154]

Sounding more like a romance novelist than a social activist, Goldman's effusive and melodramatic depiction of love leaves one with the impression that, in the final analysis, all grievances between the sexes should be forgotten and forgiven. However, in this particular instance, it is women who must forget and forgive and it is

women who must do away with "ridiculous notions" and "petti-
ness." As if to say "love conquers all," Goldman pontificates:

> Pettiness separates; breath unites. Let us be broad and
> big. Let us not overlook vital things because of the bulk
> of trifles confronting us. A true conception of the relation
> of the sexes...knows of but one great thing: to give of
> one's self richer, deeper, better. That alone can fill the
> emptiness, and transform the tragedy of woman's eman-
> cipation into joy, limitless joy.[155]

Alice Wexler's understanding of Goldman's emphasis on the
supremacy of instinct or inner freedom is one which suggests that
Goldman herself may have experienced an inescapable "inner
bondage" (e.g., to Reitman) which may explain "both her attraction
to an ideology of total freedom such as anarchism and her great sensitivity to domination in all it guises."[156] Candace Falk, in a slightly
different interpretation to that of Wexler, argues that Goldman, fear-
ing her own deficiencies, "offered an extreme interpretation of the
anarchist doctrine that all that was negative in society could be attributed to government and institutional forces, while human nature was inherently benign."[157]

It is likely that Goldman's view of the supremacy of instinct, accompanied by her antipathy for the "public" realm, is largely a
product of her tendency to dichotomize—to simplistically and
sharply separate in a hyperbolic and overstated manner the so-
called "good" from "bad." Goldman's method of analysis, whether it
be in the area of dramatic criticism or political speech-making, es-
chewed the middle ground, favouring instead the uncompromising
positions of bold extremes. As a result, Goldman's view of "instinct,"
as set in opposition to the public "State," ignores the extent to which
our so-called "instincts" are constructed and shaped by forces contained within the public sphere. Goldman's view of "instinct" places
human beings in opposition to the social and cultural forces which
have shaped them.

NOTES

1. Christopher Lasch, *The New Radicalism in America 1889-1920* (Philadelphia: Temple University Press, 1981), p. 142.
2. Richard Drinnon, *Rebel in Paradise* (Chicago: University of Chicago Press, 1961), p. 111.
3. Emma Goldman, *Red Emma Speaks: Selected Writings and Speeches by Emma Goldman*, compiled and edited by Alix Kates Shulman (New York: Random House, 1972), pp. 94-95.
4. Robert Nisbet, *The Sociological Tradition* (New York: Basic Books, 1966), p. 73.; Drinnon, *Rebel in Paradise*, p. 111.
5. Drinnon, *Rebel in Paradise*, p. 111.
6. Ferdinand Tönnies, *Gemeinschaft and Gesellschaft (Community and Society)*, translated and edited by Charles P. Loomis (New York: Harper and Row, 1965), p. 157.
7. Drinnon, *Rebel in Paradise*, p. 111, n. 4. Drinnon referred to Goldman as "Emma" but not to Tönnies as "Ferdinand."
8. Emma Goldman, *Living My Life* (New York: Alfred A. Knopf, 1970), p. 50.
9. Tönnies, *Gemeinschaft and Gesellschaft*, p. 103.
10. Ibid., p. 177.
11. Rosalind Sydie, "The Value of Reproduction: A Partial Re-examination of Tönnies' Gemeinschaft and Gesellschaft," *Atlantis*, 13 (Fall 1987), p. 140.
12. Goldman, *Red Emma Speaks*, p. 142.
13. George Woodcock, *Anarchism: A History of Libertarian Ideas and Movements* (New York: World Publishing Co., 1962), p. 202.
14. Ibid.
15. Jeffrey Weeks, *Sexuality and Its Discontents* (London: Routledge and Kegan Paul, 1985), p. 64.
16. Ibid.
17. Ibid., p. 97.
18. Ibid.
19. Ludmilla Jordanova, "Natural Facts: A Historical Perspective on Science and Reality," in *Nature, Culture and Gender*, edited by Carol MacCormack and Marilyn Strathern (Cambridge University Press, 1980), p. 43.
20. Ibid., p. 50.
21. Roberto Unger, *Knowledge and Politics* (New York: Free Press, 1975), p. 59.
22. Goldman, *Red Emma Speaks*, p. 95.
23. Goldman, *Anarchism*, p. 23.
24. Goldman, *Red Emma Speaks*, p. 88.
25. Ibid., p. 89.
26. Ibid., p. 136.
27. Ibid., pp. 134-35.
28. Ibid., p. 140.
29. Ibid., p. 137.
30. Ibid., pp. 138, 142.
31. Ibid., p. 138.
32. Robert Nisbet, *The Sociological Tradition*, p. 73.
33. Robert Weibe, *The Search for Order* (New York: Hill and Wang, 1967), p. 295.
34. Goldman's conception of individuality, which played an integral role in her theory, was located on something similar to the "Gemeinschaft" side of Ferdinand Tönnies' Gemeinschaft/Gesellschaft distinction. Goldman's conception of anarchism is very much a prefiguration of a Tönnies-like conception of organic community.
35. Virginia Woolf, *Three Guineas* (London: The Hogarth Press, 1952), p. 135.
36. Ibid.
37. Ibid., p. 131.
38. Ibid., p. 259.

39. Jean Bethke Elshtain, *Public Man, Private Woman* (Princeton, N.J.: Princeton University Press, 1981), p. 120.
40. Marilyn French, *Beyond Power: On Women, Men and Morals* (London: Abacus, 1986), p. 582.
41 Elshtain, *Public Man, Private Woman*, p. 120.
42. Barbara Ehrenreich and Deirdre English, *For Her Own Good* (Garden City N.Y.: Doubleday Anchor, 1979), p. 324.
43. Patricia Hughes, "Fighting the Good Fight: Separation of Integration" in *Feminism in Canada*, edited by Angela Finn and Geraldine Miles (Montreal: Black Rose Books, 1982), p. 287.
44. Sydie, "The Value of Reproduction: A Partial Re-examination of Tönnies' Gemeinschaft and Gesellschaft," p. 145
45. French, *Beyond Power: On Women, Men and Morals*, p. 581.
46. Sydie, "The Value of Reproduction: A Partial Re-examination of Tönnies' Gemeinschaft and Gesellschaft," p. 147.
47. French, *Beyond Power: On Women, Men and Morals*, p. 582.
48. Goldman, *Living My Life*, p. 225.
49. Sheila Jeffreys, *The Spinster and Her Enemies: Feminism and Sexuality 1880-1930* (London: Pandora, 1985), pp. 6-26.
50. Ibid., p. 26.
51. Goldman, quoted in Candace Falk, *Anarchy and Emma Goldman* (New York: Holt, Rinehart and Winston, 1984), p. 125.
52 Jordanova, *Nature, Culture and Gender*, p. 43.
53 Goldman, *Red Emma Speaks*, p. 134.
54. Ibid.
55. Ibid.
56. Ibid.
57. Ibid.
58. Ibid., p. 136.
59. Ruth Pierson and Alison Prentice, "Feminism and the Writing and Teaching of History," in Angela Miles and Geraldine Finn, eds., *Feminism: From Pressure to Politics* (Montreal: Black Rose Books, 1982), p. 107.
60. Ibid., p. 106.
61. Ibid., pp. 106-107.
62. Ibid.
63. Goldman, *Red Emma Speaks*, p. 134.
64. Ibid.
65. Ibid., p. 135.
66. Pierson and Prentice, "Feminism and the Writing and Teaching of History," p. 107.
67. Angela Miles, "Ideological Hegemony in Political Discourse: Women's Specificity and Equality" in Angela Miles and Geraldine Finn, eds., *Feminism in Canada* (Montreal: Black Rose Books, 1982).
68. Pierson and Prentice, "Feminism and the Writing and Teaching of History," pp. 107-108.
69. Joan Wallach Scott, *Gender and the Politics of History* (New York: Columbia University Press, 1988), p. 176.
70. Ibid, pp. 176-177.
71. Goldman, *Red Emma Speaks*, p. 136.
72. Carroll Smith-Rosenberg, *Disorderly Conduct* (New York and Oxford: University Press, 1985), p. 277.
73. Ruth Roach Pierson, "Ellen Key: Maternalism and Pacifism," in Katherine Arnup, Andrée Lévèsque, and Ruth Roach Pierson, eds., *Delivering Motherhood: Maternal Ideologies and Practices in the 19th and 20th Centuries* (London and New York: Routledge, 1990), p. 271.
74. Ibid., p. 272.
75. Ibid., p. 273.
76. Smith-Rosenberg, *Disorderly Conduct*, p. 277.
77. Ibid., pp. 277-278.

78. Ibid., p. 279.
79. Emma Goldman, *Nowhere At Home: Letters from Exile of Emma Goldman and Alexander Berkman*, edited by Richard Drinnon and Anna-Marie Drinnon (New York: Schocken Books, 1975), p. 131.
80. Ibid., p. 83.
81. Alexandra Kollontai, in Alix Holt, ed., *Selected Writings of Alexandra Kollontai* (New York: W. W. Norton, 1977), p. 230.
82. Ibid., p. 231.
83. Ibid., p. 144.
84. Goldman, *Nowhere At Home*, p. 133.
85. Ibid.
86. Ibid.
87. Ibid., p. 134.
88. Ibid.
89. Ibid.
90. Alexander Berkman, in *Nowhere At Home*, p. 153.
91. Goldman, in *Nowhere At Home*, p. 156.
92. Berkman, in *Nowhere At Home*, p. 167.
93. Goldman, in *Nowhere At Home*, p. 168.
94. Ibid., p. 129.
95. Goldman, in *Nowhere At Home*, p. 183.
96. Ibid.
97. Sydie, "The Value of Reproduction: A Partial Re-examination of Tönnies' Gemeinschaft and Gesellschaft," p. 138.
98. Goldman, *Living My Life*, pp. 556-57; Wexler, *Emma Goldman: An Intimate Life* (New York: Pantheon Book, 1984), pp. 94-95, 196-197.
99. Wexler, *Emma Goldman: An Intimate Life*, pp. 94-95.
100. Goldman, *Living My Life*, p. 556; Wexler, *Emma Goldman: An Intimate Life*, p. 197.
101. Goldman, *Living My Life*, p. 557; Goldman, *Red Emma Speaks*, pp. 134-137.
102. Smith-Rosenberg, *Disorderly Conduct*, p. 281.
103. Ibid., p. 258.
104. Rayna Rapp and Ellen Ross, "Sex and Society: A Research Note from Social History and Anthropology," in *Powers of Desire: The Politics of Sexuality*, edited by Christine Stansell, Ann Snitow and Sharon Thompson (New York: Monthly Review Press, 1981), pp. 51-72.
105. Smith-Rosenberg, *Disorderly Conduct*, p. 282.
106. Goldman, *Red Emma Speaks*, p. 136.
107. Ibid.
108. Ibid., p. 89.
109. Smith-Rosenberg, *Disorderly Conduct*, p. 281.
110. Ibid.
111. Goldman, *Red Emma Speaks*, p. 137.
112. Ibid.
113. Alice Echols, "The Taming of the Id: Feminist Sexual Politics, 1968-83," in *Pleasure and Danger: Exploring Female Sexuality*, edited by Carole S. Vance (Boston and London: Routledge and Kegan Paul, 1984), pp. 50-72.
114. Carol Ellen DuBois and Linda Gordon, "Seeking Ecstasy on the Battlefield: Danger and Pleasure in Nineteenth Century Feminist Thought," *Feminist Studies*, 9 (Spring 1983), pp. 31-49.
115. Aritha van Herk, "Laying the Body on the Line," *Border Crossings*, 9 (Fall 1990), p. 86.
116. Goldman, *Red Emma Speaks*, p. 141.
117. Ibid.
118. Ibid., pp. 141-42.
119. Ibid.
120. Ibid.
121. Ibid., p. 123.
122. Elinor Lenz and Barbara Myerhoff, *The Feminization of America* (Los Angeles: Jeremy P. Tarcher Inc., 1985), p. 230.

123. Goldman, *Red Emma Speaks*, p. 138.
124. Ibid.
125. Gayle Rubin in Marilyn French, *Beyond Power: On Women, Men, and Morals* (London: Abacus, 1986), p. 582.
126. Rubin, in French, *Beyond Power*, p. 582.
127. Goldman, *Red Emma Speaks*, p. 142.
128. Sydie, "The Value of Reproduction: A Partial Re-examination of Tönnies' Gemeinschaft and Gesellschaft," p. 138.
129. Goldman, *Red Emma Speaks*, p. 140.
130. Ibid.
131. Angela Miles, "Ideological Hegemony in Political Discourse: Women's Specificity and Equality."
132. Sydie, "The Value of Reproduction: A Partial Re-examination of Tönnies' Gemeinschaft and Gesellschaft," p. 138.
133. Miles, "Ideological Hegemony in Political Discourse: Women's Specificity and Equality," p. 277.
134. Ibid.
135. Goldman, *Red Emma Speaks*, p. 140.
136. Ibid.
137. Miles, "Ideological Hegemony in Political Discourse: Women's Specificity and Equality," p. 277.
138. Ibid., p. 275.
139. Goldman, *Living My Life*, p. 173.
140. Goldman, *Living My Life*, p. 225.
141. Goldman, *Red Emma Speaks*, p. 142.
142. Ibid. p. 140.
143. Goldman, in Martha Solomon, *Emma Goldman* (Boston: Twayne Publishers, 1987), p. 69.
144. Ibid.
145. Goldman, *Anarchism*, p. 178.
146. Carroll Smith-Rosenberg and Charles Rosenberg, "The Female Animal: Medical and Biological Views of Woman and Her Role in Nineteenth Century America," *The Journal of American History*, 60 (March 1974), pp. 332-356.
147. Ibid.
148. Simone de Beauvoir, in Lenz and Myerhoff, *The Feminization of America*, p. 228.

149. Candace Falk, *Love, Anarchy and Emma Goldman* (New York: Holt, Rinehart and Winston, 1984), p. 126.
150. Goldman, *Red Emma Speaks*, p. 92.
151. Goldman, in Falk, *Love, Anarchy and Emma Goldman*, p. 126.
152. Ibid.
153. Goldman, *Red Emma Speaks*, p. 142.
154. Ibid.
155. Ibid.
156. Wexler, *Emma Goldman: An Intimate Life*, p. 279.
157. Falk, *Love, Anarchy and Emma Goldman*, p. 522.

CHAPTER 3

The Social Historical Context Surrounding Goldman and the "Sex Question"

This chapter will contextualize Goldman's ideas on sexuality and reproduction within the social and historical forces of her day. Of particular importance in this discussion will be the social theories of the time, theories on the construction of womanhood, the role of the medical profession and the role of the State/legislative realm.

One of Goldman's biographers, Alix Kates Shulman, characterized the America of the early twentieth century as vital and brash:

> The twentieth century, and its first United States president, Theodore Roosevelt, brought a new spirit to the land. It was a spirit of progress, reform, and modernity. Telephones, telegraphs, automobiles, electric lights, suddenly began to be commonplace, giving the new era a special look and sound and feel. A new gusto and vitality stirred the nation.[1]

The sense of promise and reform gave new meaning to the word "new" as, during the early decades, the "Progressive Era" gained its foothold.[2] The American nation was being permeated by "new" beliefs, "new" people and "new" products—the "New Theology" was being preached by theologians; "New Nationalism" and "New Politics" were being espoused on political platforms; "New Drama," "New Poetry," "New Criticism" and "New Painting" were being discussed by dramatists, critics, artists and writers; magazines were launched with names like the "New Republic" and the "New Democracy"; the "New Woman" was being presented as one who would pursue goals outside of the traditional domestic sphere; a

"New Morality" was being exposed which challenged rigid dictates concerning woman's "proper place"; a "New Psychology," that of Sigmund Freud, was being discussed in the popular media.[3]

Despite the national spirit or cult of "newness," few of these ideas or phenomena were "new" to Emma Goldman. Shulman explains:

> Only, for Emma, little that went on there seemed especially new. The twentieth century's New Woman practising the New Morality and demanding the right to vote, was less daring than Emma had been most of her life. The New Psychology of Sigmund Freud that everyone was suddenly discussing had been familiar to Emma since 1895, when she attended Freud's lectures in Vienna. The New Drama of Shaw, Ibsen and Strindberg Emma had discovered on her own back in 1895.[4]

In the midst of pervasive "newness"—both ideational and material—Emma Goldman preached and lived a "new" philosophy which conjoined "internal" and "external" forces as a recipe for individual freedom. As the British anarchist, Hippolyte Havel remarked, "Emma Goldman does not merely preach the *new* [italics mine] philosophy; she also persists in living it—and that is the one supreme, unforgivable crime."[5] Emma's conception of "new" and that of American culture were, however, vastly different. As Shulman notes, "Emma had always been so far in the vanguard that she seemed to one journalist to be 'about eight thousand years ahead of her age'."[6]

Theories on the Construction of Womanhood

Despite the early twentieth century American fascination with "new" philosophy, art, drama, theology and consumer products, old assumptions continued to serve as the basis for "constructing" the popular view of womanhood. Medical theory, starting at least as early as the mid-nineteenth century, held that the uterus governed and defined the entire female organism. According to Mary Poovey:

> The prominence of the uterus in representations of the
> female body points to the assumption held by almost all
> medical men that women, more than men, were
> governed and defined by their reproductive capacity.
> "The character and position" of women—indeed their
> value—were conceptualized as direct consequences to
> their reproductive function.[7]

Biological determinism and reductionism grounded the theories of
even such sexual "progressives" and "liberationists" as Havelock
Ellis. Goldman was situated within, and, as will later be discussed, to
some extent contributed to a gender ideology which defined women
according to their biological or reproductive characteristics.

The medical model of the female body, prevalent during the
early twentieth century, was essentially Victorian.[8] Bearing great
similarities to Emile Durkheim's model of the "needs of the organism," the medical model of the female "organism" "conveyed a
degree of biological determinism for women which far exceeded
that for men."[9] As mentioned in the previous chapter, vitalist
theories, with notions such as "spermatic economy,"[10] viewed the
body as a closed system possessing a finite energy source. If energy was demanded in one area of the body (e.g., the brain), it
would be diverted from another area (e.g., the reproductive organs).

The theory of the limited energy capacity of the human body
was based on the assumption of the interdependence of its parts.
The basic tenets of the Victorian medical model included, besides the
notion of a closed energy system, a hierarchy of bodily functions, a
polarity of female/body and male/mind, and female fragility.[11] The
ovaries and the brain were hierarchically distinguished, competing
for a limited supply of energy:

> A young woman...who consumed her vital force in intel-
> lectual activities was necessarily diverting these energies
> from the achievement of true womanhood. She would
> become weak and nervous, perhaps sterile...capable of

bearing only sickly and neurotic children...The brain and ovary could not develop at the same time.[12]

More specifically, forms of birth control were emphatically and simplistically denounced as being "unnatural" and deleterious to a woman's mental and physical well-being. The "sex act," by which heterosexual intercourse was meant, was not to be tampered with and the male semen was imbued with therapeutic power:

> Sex, like all aspects of human bodily activity, involved an exchange of nervous energy; without the discharge of such accumulated energies in the male orgasm and the soothing presence of male semen "bathing the female reproductive organs," the female partner could never... find true fulfilment.[13]

Physicians spoke out against the "insidious influence" birth control had on the female, basing their opposition in the belief that the seminal fluid had a healthy effect on the female.[14]

The Role of the Medical Profession

It is not difficult to understand the male medical profession's opposition to birth control considering the extent to which masculine fluids were considered healthy and therapeutic to women. This view of the "sanctity" of sperm carried a number of implications for many of the issues Goldman addressed in her activism and her writing. First and most fundamentally, the medical profession's bias in favour of male anatomy and physiology, suggesting that sexually men can "treat" or "heal" women, simply highlights the degree to which male-centred values and interests were entrenched in the so-called "medical model." As was characteristic of the medical model, the relationship of sperm to ovum implied a hierarchical order—a relationship of greatness to weakness.

Goldman's vision of male/female relationships rejected a dualistic conception of the sexes, arguing, instead, for a free and nonhierarchical association based on the expression of "natural" instincts. The dualistic conception of man and woman which Goldman denounced and which was an integral component of the dominant world view of both society and the medical profession's world view, firmly located women on the "body" side of the body/mind dichotomy. Because women were seen as possessing a biological destiny, the male medical profession saw it as its function to mediate the relationship between woman's body and her destiny. The rejection of the entry of sperm into a woman's body, through prolonging educational goals, postponing or rejecting marriage, or practising celibacy or birth control, was to tamper or interfere with woman's destiny.

Moreover, the medical establishment, acting as the guardians of women's health and sexuality, argued against contraceptive devices on the grounds that they reduced women's sexual satisfaction. Sperm was not only healthy or therapeutic for women, but as well, added to their sexual enjoyment, provided it was ejaculated under the right conditions.

In pamphlets such as "Why and How the Poor Should Not Have Many Children," distributed in the birth control campaign of 1915 and 1916,[15] Goldman advocated the use of pessaries, womb veils and suppositories as means of female birth control. The four-page pamphlet, which may have been written with the help of Goldman's physician friend and fellow pro-contraceptionist, William J. Robinson,[16] set out rules for the safe use of the condom as well as suggestions for homemade contraceptive methods—suppositories, douches, and cotton balls dipped in borated vaseline.

Not surprisingly, Goldman's ideas and actions met opposition from the medical establishment. The possible self-determination and individuation of women through the use of contraception, extended education or the postponement or absence of marriage were seen as running counter to woman's biological nature. Greater autonomy or self-sufficiency was purportedly damaging to her reproductive capacity.

George Kosmak, a noted gynecologist of Goldman's time, made universal condemnations of medical-outsiders such as Goldman, who fought for and participated in the dissemination of birth control information. Kosmak, jealously guarding the medical establishment's monopoly of power and vested interest, asked:

> Shall we permit the prescribing of contraceptive measures and drugs, many of which are potentially dangerous, by non-medical persons, when we have so jealously guarded our legal rights as physicians against Christian Scientists, osteopaths, chiropractors, naturopaths and others who have attempted to invade the field of medical practice by a short cut without sufficient preliminary training such as is considered essential for the equipment of every medical man?[17]

Kosmak accused the "contraceptionists" of being affiliated with quackery and anarchism, condemning them on the grounds that they were not "scientific" and, thus, did not have a right to participate in the alteration of social values let alone the field of physiology.[18] Regarding the ideology of mainstream medical practitioners and that of the "irregulars" of the birth control movement, Linda Gordon states: "The sexual ideology of both groups was formed by professional interests and business pressures."[19]

Kosmak, acting like a "craft unionist,"[20] protected his profession from those who sought to invade his professional jurisdiction and, who, without suitable "authority," might enter into the medical profession's stewardship of moral and social issues.

The issue of birth control which Goldman and others considered key to women's self-determination was an issue which was inextricably connected to other issues and other social policies. For this reason, it was impossible to treat the birth control issue as a single-issue cause, as its roots and connections were intertwined with a broad range of social issues such as education and employment policy. While Goldman made explicit the link between the need for birth control and issues such as "puritan" hypocrisy, women's emancipation and the education of the young, the medical profession was less explicit and more patronizingly protective of the social values which engulfed the issue of birth control. The extent to which one's stance on the birth control issue reflected a fuller, more all-encompassing world view was made abundantly clear when one examined a particular group's (e.g., the medical establishment) position on the issue.

Birth control has fundamental implications for the status of women and, therefore, one's stance on the issue is likely to be rooted in views regarding women's ideal position in society, her physiological, intellectual and sexual constitution, her moral or ethical proclivities, her aspirations and whether they are biologically mandated or socially mandated, her relationships with a partner and her relationship to the larger group (e.g., the family, the community). During the early years of this century, views regarding the nature of man, his aspirations, his social and individual needs, his physiological and sexual needs, his moral and ethical tendencies were also influential in determining one's position on birth control. To the common extent that male interests were placed above female interests, the issue of birth control, although perceived to be a "women's issue," was viewed from the perspective of masculine interests. This meant that the model of "woman as complement" set in place a host of values which, in most instances, led to a rejection of birth control on the grounds that women's use of contraception was not complementary to male nature and desire. Through more circuitous arguments, it was purported that birth control was not in keeping with woman's nature and desire as its use blocked male fluids from reaching the depths of the female reproductive organs. The issue of birth control was not only rooted in beliefs about the "nature" of the sexes, but involved issues of an economic nature—employment patterns, training and education. How will employment in the public sphere and education in training and post-secondary institutions be affected by women's lower fertility? Fundamental social values which assumed a public/private schism entered into a response to this question—the value of woman's participation in the private sphere versus the public sphere and the value of preserving the workplace as a male domain.

One's position on birth control, in addition, had implications for, and was influenced by, one's values pertaining to the size and functioning of the family, the social utility of prostitution, sex education for the young, premarital sexual activity, female chastity, "illegitimate" childbirth, sexual fidelity and infidelity, and the centrality of pregnancy to women's experience.

By the early twentieth century, as has been previously noted, the medical establishment began to supplant the church as the major authority on sexual morality in general, and as the protectorate of the sexual integrity of the "saintly half," in particular. As Robert Latou Dickinson, a former president of the American Gynecological Society, theologized in his 1908 article entitled "Marital Maladjustment: The Business of Preventive Gynaecology" and published in the *Long Island Medical Journal*:

> Our high function as confessors and advisers of the saintly half of the race, and the imperative need, at times, of one step within the Holy of Holies is impossible without intimate speech, gentle, reverent, direct.[21]

The role of sexual moral education had shifted from the pulpit to the physician's examining table. The medical profession played a key role in mediating the relevance of social values to its citizens. Linda Gordon writes:

> Their concern was to establish the validity of their vision of the world, and their right to debate social issues. They shared by and large a vision of science and medicine as the mentors of social advance.[22]

Linda Gordon has noted that doctors did very little to advance the cause of birth control.[23] The medical practitioners made little effort to advance contraceptive technology, and did very little to educate women about sexual and reproductive matters. Instead, Gordon reports, they played a key role in "developing and maintaining fears and mystification."[24]

While individual physicians did perform abortions and provide birth control to individual patients who "found themselves in difficult situations," publicly physicians as a group attacked birth control on a number of grounds. Goldman witnessed personally the variety of justifications—philosophical, physiological and moral—used by physicians to deny birth control to their patients.

In *Living My Life*, Goldman recalled her helplessness in the face of her poverty-ridden patients' pleas for some means of birth control. She wrote: "I refused to perform abortions and I knew no methods to prevent conception."[25]

Speaking to a number of physicians about her patients' unwanted pregnancies, Goldman received a variety of "medical" opinions based, in many cases, on moral or class justifications. One doctor, by the name of White, addressed Goldman's concerns using a class-based explanation: "The poor have only themselves to blame; they indulge their appetites too much."[26] Dr. Julius Hoffman explained to Goldman that children were the only joy the poor had and, another medical opinion, that of Dr. Solotaroff, held out "hope of changes in the near future when woman would become more intelligent and independent."[27] Dr. Solotaroff, using the discourse of vitalist theory, assured Goldman that "when she uses her brains more, her procreative organs will function less."[28] Not surprisingly, Goldman came away from these conversations despairing of her limited ability to help: "I sought some immediate solution for their [her patients'] purgatory, but I could find nothing of use."[29]

Gordon argues that through the society of the nineteenth century:

> ...an overwhelming concern with sex, specifically with the difficult but urgent necessity of checking the anarchic sex drive, was reflected in the narrowing of previously general moral terms—such as virtues, propriety, decency, modesty, delicacy, purity—to exclusively sexual meaning.[30]

The conservative values of sexual morality upheld by the doctors as "moral" and physiologically and reproductively sound, created an unusual marriage between morality and physiology. That which was moral (e.g., female chastity) was, by the doctor's definition, physiologically safe or healthy; that which was immoral (e.g., the use of pessaries or prolonged sexual abstinence) was by definition physiologically unsafe or unhealthy. These conservative values were rooted in the double standard of sexual conduct for men and women, the hierarchical differentiation of men and women on physiological and intellectual grounds, the desirability of female chastity and male sexual varietism and the religious sense of the "sanctity" of family life. Linda Gordon summarizes the sexual values of the medical "moral entrepreneurs" in the following manner:

> ...That the major function of women and sexual intercourse both was reproduction of the species; that the male sex drive is naturally greater than the female, an imbalance unfortunately but probably inevitably absorbed by prostitution; that female chastity is necessary to protect the family and its descent; that female chastity must be enforced with severe social and legal sanctions, among which fear of pregnancy functioned effectively and naturally.[31]

The Role of Religion

According to Goldman, religion, along with the State, represented the major sources of oppression in capitalist society. As illustrated in her essay "The Hypocrisy of Puritanism" (1911), religion's moral claims were particularly irksome for Goldman as she viewed morality and hypocrisy as inextricably linked.

The prominence of religion as a socializing and disciplinary agent of American society during the late nineteenth century and early twentieth century placed Goldman up against a powerful opponent. While Goldman was championing fuller sexual expression, religious moralists viewed sexuality as primarily dangerous.[32] According to David Kennedy's *Birth Control in America*, it wasn't until 1929 that the Federal Council of Churches of Christ softened their position on the danger of sexuality, arguing that although sex could be "destructive," "we must start with the assumption that sex is indeed a creative force."[33]

The religion of the early twentieth century was, as one doctor wrote, "an unrecognized branch of higher physiology"[34] in which morality became increasingly defined by *sexual* morality.[35] As custodians of general morality, and increasingly sexual morality, the churches resisted what Margaret Sanger called "the most revolutionary practice in the history of sexual morals,"[36]—birth control. Despite American popular opinion favouring the use of birth control, the churches lagged behind or rejected the views of their members. Kennedy writes:

> The American churches...only cautiously and belatedly gave birth control their official attention. The Roman Catholic church, objecting to contraception on strict doctrinal grounds, often carried its dissent into overt action to thwart the birth control movement. But the Protestant churches, too, until well into the 1930s... refused to sanction contraception and often argued against it with a vigor equal to Rome's.[37]

To the religious institutions of the late nineteenth century and early twentieth century, fuller expression of sexuality was seen as regression to egotism—as a destructive and anti-social phenomenon.[38] For Goldman, religion represented a force determined to keep sexuality in darkness, inseparable from hypocrisy and oppression.

Social Theories of the Time

Race-Suicide, Eugenics and Birth Control: Goldman's Place Within the Discourses

Inextricably connected to the view that women were defined and governed by their uterus was the opinion that the uterus represented a powerful tool for the salvation (or destruction) of the human race. During the first two decades of the twentieth century eugenics, and its immediate predecessor the race-suicide theory,[39] presented themselves as powerful discourses within which "social purity, sex reform, racial hygiene and scientific advance could all find a home..."[40]

The race-suicide debate, which lasted from 1905 to 1910,[41] and subsequent developments in the field of eugenics, taking place primarily between 1910 and the early 1930s,[42] were used to justify opposition to birth control in America. The birth control movement came to its fullest expression during the second and third decades of the century. During this period, in 1916, Goldman was arrested for giving a public lecture on the topic of birth control. Just two years prior to Goldman's arrest, Margaret Sanger, the touted "pioneer" of modern birth control, was arrested for her publication of *Woman Rebel*—a magazine publicizing contraceptive devices and their accessibility. Arguments on race-suicide theory or eugenics, birth control and feminism were intimately connected. For example, Linda Gordon observed that the most common eugenic position was "virulently anti-feminist" and that most, but all not, eugenists were opposed to birth control.[43] In contrast, however, feminists and birth control campaigners such as Goldman and Sanger were not against eugenic principles and, in fact, incorporated many of them into their respective campaigns. Jeffrey Weeks has pointed out that sex reform is "constructed across the dialectic of social control on the one hand and individual freedom on the other, and this, as eugenics had pinpointed, was particularly the case with the issue of contraception."[44] Central to race-suicide and eugenic arguments were class and race implications.[45] Policies and campaigns for a "healthier" more "fit" society implied the breeding of the right kind of stock—those of middle- and upper-class status and Anglo-Saxon extraction. Eugenicists were concerned with the declining birth rate in general and, in particular, with the inadequate reproduction of "superior" stock and the excessive reproduction of "inferior" stock.[46]

Eugenics gained a secure foothold in policies relating to immigration, education, health, economics and foreign affairs. As Jeffrey Weeks explains:

...The task of state policy was to encourage methods to induce a sense of sexual responsibility in the population at large. Theoretically, there were two ways to do this: by encouraging the best to breed, or by discouraging the worst. But in practice, social policy had to be directed at the latter—who...were inevitably seen in class terms.[47]

Goldman's passion to enable women to control their reproductive faculties, and thus their destiny, grounded in eugenic principles, was a passion which met with great opposition from others representing different factions within the eugenics movement. Theodore Roosevelt,[48] for example, denounced family limitation as being a submission to "coldness, to selfishness, to love of ease, to shrinking from risk, to an utter and pitiful failure in sense of perspective."[49] Roosevelt saw family planning as a sign of decadence and moral disease—a sign of the deterioration of the human race.[50] The race-suicide debate did not emerge solely out of Theodore Roosevelt's protestations that small families were a sign of decadence and moral disease, but was fuelled by upper- and middle-class fears of actual social changes—a decreasing birth rate, a more compact family structure and birth-control use.[51]

Subsumed under the slogan "race suicide" were a number of objections to birth control which, although distinct thematically, tended to reinforce one another.[52] Perhaps the strongest objection to birth control, presenting the most difficult and pervasive preconception to counter, was the simple view that birth control was sinful. This view was articulated by members of religious organizations, the medical establishment, and the social purity movement.[53] This uncomplicated, yet powerful objection fed into Goldman's philosophy in a number of ways. Goldman's world view ran directly counter to the world view which she referred to metaphorically as "puritanism":

Puritanism.... rests on a fixed and immoveable conception of life; it is based on the Calvinistic idea that life is a curse, imposed upon man by the wrath of God. In order to redeem himself man must do constant penance, must repudiate every natural and healthy impulse, and turn his back on joy and beauty.[54]

For Goldman, "puritanism" was the body of thought which legitimized and perpetuated sexual repression. Both church and State proselytized the virtues of "puritanism," either, explicitly, through religious dogma or, implicitly, through legislation. "Puritanism," to the anarchists, was the force which perverted the inherent goodness of humankind by convincing its followers of their innate impurities and imperfections.

Being critical of the hypocrisy that was inherent in "puritanism," Goldman slammed arguments which were based on moral or religious practice. "Puritanism," for Goldman, was a prison of hypocrisy which entrapped those who gave in to its moralistic demands. "Puritanism's" consequences for women were great, as its values— permeating family, religion and State—confined women to three choices: that of celibate, prostitute, or "reckless, incessant breeder of hapless children."[55]

The opposition to birth control on the grounds of its "sinfulness," according to Goldman, contributed not only to woman's sexual and reproductive powerlessness, but also to her economic and political powerlessness. Having frequent pregnancies and births simply incapacitated women for long periods of time, allowing only limited amounts of energy to be spent in non-domestic activity (e.g., her own self-expansion). To remove birth control from the encompassing category of "sinful" would be to admit a separation between reproduction and sexuality and a different destiny for women, other than that of biology. While Theodore Roosevelt considered the behaviour of those who avoided having children as "criminal against the race,"[56] Goldman emphasized that the very mention of safe methods of birth control was considered criminal.[57]

In "The Hypocrisy of Puritanism," a popular Goldman lecture first published in *Anarchism and Other Essays* (1911), Goldman states that "puritanism continuously exacts thousands of victims to its stupidity and hypocrisy."[58] Women were forced to bear children irrespective of their economic and physical resources to provide for their offspring. The result was that many women were forced to "risk utmost danger rather than continue to bring forth life."[59] Goldman cited statistics indicating that the number of abortions had reached a "fearful percentage," consistent with her own experience as a midwife in New York City's East Side, in 1896, where she came face to face with "the fierce, blind struggle of the women of the poor against frequent pregnancies."[60] Frequently, Goldman, the midwife, was called for the purpose of performing an abortion. In *Living My Life*, Goldman reconstructed her reason for not performing abortions as one based on considerations of safety:

> Many women called for that purpose [requests for abortion] even going down on their knees and begging me to help them, "for the sake of the poor little ones already here."...I tried to explain to them that it was not the monetary considerations that held me back; it was the concern for their life and health.[61]

Women *were* forced to take their reproductivity into their own hands, inventing abortion procedures or duplicating concoctions that had been used in ancient times. Jewish women on the Lower East Side of New York City, in 1896 when Goldman acted as midwife, attempted to abort themselves by sitting over a pot of steam or hot stewed onions.[62] This procedure was one of the more benign methods of abortion used at the time, unequalled in its effectiveness and harmfulness to the more common method of inserting sharp objects into the uterus. The choice of objects, limited only by the confines of one's imagination and the availability of materials, included "knitting needles, crochet hooks, nail files, nutcrackers, knives, hatpins, umbrella ribs and pieces of wire."[63] Although abortion increased steadily throughout the nineteenth century, so did other forms of contraception.[64] By the early 1900s, male withdrawal and the condom (combined with other methods) had greatly increased in popularity; however, homemade suppositories, pessaries and spermicidal jellies retained their prominence in the earlier decades of the twentieth century.[65]

Another theme, although not entirely separable from others in the "race suicide" debate against birth control, was the argument for large families as the basis for American economic and social life.[66] The birth control movement was perceived as a threat to the traditional American institution of the family—seen as the moral and social foundation of the society. Roosevelt echoed this theme when he announced: "The whole fabric of society rests upon the home."[67] Linda Gordon reported that Roosevelt associated the ideal home with the large family. Six children were considered to be the minimum for those of "normal stock; more for those of better stock."[68] Fighting on a eugenic battleground, Goldman used her own eugenic arguments in *defense* of birth control:

Woman no longer wants to be party to the production of a race of sickly, feeble, decrepit, wretched human beings. Instead she desires fewer and better children.[69]

Her opponents, arguing *against* birth control and *for* a brand of eugenics (i.e., race suicide), proposed that women "save the race" through their reproductivity. Race-suicide "spokesmen" wanted to encourage "better stock" (i.e., white, middle-class families) to refrain from using birth control and to have larger families.[70] Anarchists and socialists charged that "the call for large families was the capitalists' desire to fill their factories and armies."[71] Feminists argued for the need to view reproduction from the perspective of "quality," not "quantity," accusing the race suicide proponents of ignoring the sick and impoverished children that had already been born. Because of her commitment to anarchism, Goldman's views and tactics on birth control differed sharply from those of Margaret Sanger. Goldman saw birth control as one issue subsumed in a larger framework of freedom and was tactically unwilling to use what she considered undesirable means to achieve a desirable end. Sanger, who viewed birth control as the key issue of women's freedom, gradually moved into middle-class circles and collaborated with various arms of the State in order to gain greater support for the birth control movement. Candace Falk explains the difference in approach between Sanger and Goldman:

Sanger, a woman with a single purpose, was pragmatic in her approach to the birth-control issue. She was willing to compromise to reach her desired end. Emma.... saw birth control as only one facet of the larger issue of freedom and love.[72]

To reiterate, Goldman's attempts to present birth control as a key element of women's emancipation were made in the midst of the raging "race-suicide" debate. Intermingled with arguments about the sinfulness of birth control and the need for a steadily growing population of the "right stock" was the position that birth control contributed to woman's growing egoism and thus detracted from her primary social duty—motherhood. Goldman's critiques of the motherhood campaign contained its own eugenic arguments marshalled to expose the hypocrisy of the sanctimonious invocation of "motherhood":

The woman, physically and mentally unfit to be a mother, yet condemned to breed; the woman economically taxed to the very last spark of energy, yet forced to breed; the woman, tied to the man she loathes, whose very sight fills her with horror, yet made to breed; the woman, worn and used-up from the process of procreation, yet coerced to breed more, even more. What a hideous thing this much-lauded motherhood![73]

Theories on the Individual: Individualism as a Societal Ideology

Patricia Marchak defines a societal ideology as a "screen" through which the social world is perceived.[74] During the "Progressive Era," liberalism, with its central tenet of individualism, comprised the dominant ideological "screen" through which life in America was viewed.

Goldman, therefore, was in the midst of a growing national cult of individualism, which might have been expected to produce "individualistic" gains for women. Goldman herself had a great deal to say about the societal ideology of individualism as "the individual" was the basic unit upon which her theory of anarchism was constructed. Claiming that "the individual is the true reality in life," Goldman argued that the "very essence of individuality is expression."[75]

Since liberalism as a societal ideology in American life advocated individualism as a means for social and economic progress, Goldman went to great lengths to make the distinction between her theory of the individual and that of the liberal societal ideology. While Goldman's theory of the individual, or what she calls "individuality," rests upon the "consciousness of the individual as to what he is and how he lives,"[76] the individualism of laissez-faire liberalism, in Goldman's view, was built upon an economic or social agenda in the name of State democracy. Goldman elaborates:

> Individuality is not to be confused with the various ideas and concepts of individualism; much less with that "rugged individualism" which is only a masked attempt to repress and defeat the individual and his individuality. So-called individualism is the social and economic laissez-faire.... that corrupt and perverse "individualism" is the straight jacket of individuality.[77]

Goldman viewed the social philosophy of individualism as a form of indoctrination whereby individuals were encouraged to work hard and achieve in order to improve their own position, while, in fact, they would be improving the position of those possessing economic and political power:

> Rugged individualism has meant all the "individualism" for the masters, while the people are regimented into a slave caste to serve a handful of self-seeking "supermen."[78]

Goldman was writing in a time dominated by a world view of competitive individualism. Charles Darwin's *Origin of Species* was used by social theorist, Herbert Spencer, to develop a "Social Darwinism," which contained strong racist overtones and provided the basis for

eugenics arguments and "Superman" theories. The anarchist
philosopher, Peter Kropotkin, rejected Darwin's view of competition, arguing for the existence of a system of "mutual aid." As we
saw in chapter one, Kropotkin's *Mutual Aid* (1902) greatly influenced
Goldman's view of community or group life.

Naomi Scheman's "From Hamlet to Maggie Verver: The History
and Politics of the Knowing Subject" makes a similar distinction (to
that of Goldman) between the concepts "individuality" and "individualism."[79] Scheman suggests, not unlike Goldman, that "individuality" presents possibilities for a new epistemic or political
order. Individuality, Scheman argues, is grounded in diversity, while
individualism's power, as manifested through the liberal State, rests
on "the essential indistinguishability of atomic individuals."[80]
Scheman writes:

> Selves distinguished, as the privileged self of modernity
> is, by their mutual independence, need similarity to con-
> stitute epistemic, as well as political community. In-
> dividuality is an ironic threat to an individualistic
> epistemic or political order: it is the essential indistin-
> guishability of atomic individuals that makes the liberal
> State possible, and, analogously, it is the discovery or
> positing of similarity among knowers that makes pos-
> sible a workable constructivist epistemology. Difference
> is threatening to either enterprise, since only similarity
> can provide for widespread consent to the power of the
> State or for intersubjective agreement.[81]

While women did not reap the benefits of a philosophy which
espoused the belief in individual self-fulfilment, according to
Goldman, neither did the men of the working classes. As if making
direct reference to her own circumstances, Goldman drew attention
to the great contradiction of American individualism:

> America is perhaps the best representative of this kind of
> individualism, in whose name political tyranny, and so-

cial oppression are defended and held up as virtues; while every aspiration and attempt of man to gain freedom and social opportunity to live is denounced as "un-American" and evil in the name of that same individualism.[82]

While the societal ideology of liberalism did produce modest gains for the individuation of women, it also produced a reaction which led to the re-articulation of woman's "nature" and role. The liberal ethos of individualism was a culturally created social ideology resting on the premise that the individual is the primary unit of society. Yet when individual expression on the part of women was advocated, either through demands for higher education or greater access to birth control, arguments negating female individuality and supporting female responsibility to the group (i.e., the family and society) were presented.

The contradictory message of liberalism's ethos of individualism was that although liberalism was based on universality, men and women would be "differentially" governed by an ethos of individualism. In Goldman's proclamations of the value of individual instinct, nowhere did she argue that male "instinct" was more valuable than female "instinct" or that woman embodied "instinct" and men "intellect." Goldman, therefore, was fighting a battle of opposing world views over the placement of men and women. The world view that excluded women from the liberal, individualist domain which included men was one which equated women with "nature" and men with "culture."[83]

The dichotomy of women/nature and man/culture so influenced the view of the difference between the sexes and their appropriate location in private and public spheres, that even liberalism's pervasive appeal of shared material and social progress could not erode this distinction. Mary Poovey explains:

Locating the difference between men and women also helped set limits to the groups that actually had access to liberalism's promise of universal economic oppor-

tunities....If women were governed not by reason (like
men), but by something else, then they could hardly be
expected (or allowed to) participate in the economic and
political fray.[84]

Individualism was not compatible with woman's nature
which linked her, by nature and instinct, to the family. An organis-
tic conception of female life precluded detachment on the part of
women and implied a form of biological determinism;[85] for men,
who were equated with culture, the detachment that individualism implied was channelled into the performance of roles
in civil society. Woman's "natural" attachment to the group limited
the applicability to women of liberal individualistic conceptions of
life.

Individualism, although a societal ideology and norm, was apparently to be applied only to men—not women. The social duty of
motherhood precluded woman's entitlement to the enjoyment of
the national ethos. Values such as achievement, social ambition,
material prosperity, progress were ones which, although espoused
in terms of universality, when applied were limited by the specificity
of sex/gender. As Linda Gordon observes:

These views reflected a double standard. The very attitudes that were attacked in women—social ambition,
desire for wealth—were applauded in men. Individualist, self-aggrandizing, and materialist values were
the norm in the world of men—in politics and economics.
In the world of women they were unnatural and sinful.[86]

Birth control, without a doubt, would contribute to a woman's individualism, offering her the ability to make choices about how
many children she would have and when she would have them. The
cult of individualism, if enjoyed by women, would have ensured a
central location of birth control in their private lives allowing
women to pursue their own interests and not just "serve" those of
"the family." Birth control, as subsumed within the larger theme of

individualism, was perceived as a force which would separate woman from her natural and organic location—home. Women could not be allowed to be individuals for fear they would desert the family. As one physician during this period noted: "the family idea is, indeed, drifting into individualism.... Now [woman] has weaned herself from the hearthstone and her chief end is self. Pray!... By...the avoidance of offspring, our women are no longer compelled to stay at home—the home-tether is broken."[87]

The Role of the State/Legislative Realm

Another formidable historical force with which Goldman came face-to-face was one which appeared to be insurmountable, given its wide-ranging presence and momentum for further development. This force was the growth of the bureaucratic State in America. Defining the "State" as the "legislative and administrative machinery whereby certain business of the people is transacted," Goldman boldly asserted that the "State has no more conscience or moral mission than a commercial company for working a mine or running a railroad."[88]

The increasing rationalization and bureaucratization of American public life ran counter to the ideals of Emma Goldman. Following the model of Peter Kropotkin, Goldman argued for "external"[89] or economic arrangements consisting of "voluntary productive and distributive associations" in which individuals would work in "harmony with their tastes and desires,"[90] the internal factors. On an "internal" level, Goldman argued that the "progression" to State-run enterprises had the effect of automatizing individuals, leading them towards conformity and away from individual expression. Since sexuality and reproduction were at the core of Goldman's view of individual expression, the shift towards legislative and administrative control represented a concomitant shift away from sexual expression and toward inhibition. Goldman viewed the machinery of the State as omnipresent,[91] imposing itself on every facet of an individual's life—subordinating the individual to the demands of organized authority, leaving little energy or inclination for the expression of basic (i.e., sexual) desires. Goldman, who in Candace Falk's words "wanted to improve the fundamental fabric of human relationships,"[92] was uncompromising in her denunciation of the State, unwilling to admit that particular arms of State bureaucracy could perhaps assist her in meeting some of her goals. Goldman's goal of providing women greater access to birth control, for example, was one which might have been accomplished more fully through the use of State mechanisms (e.g., public health organizations). However, Goldman was not a pragmatist and "would not consciously compromise on anything, wanting all or nothing."[93]

For Goldman, freedom from the omnipotence and omnipresence of the State was seen as a primary principle, not to be deviated from for pragmatic purposes (e.g., the advancement of birth control). The antithesis of "State" life was, for Goldman, "associational" life through which "internal" dynamics, the most important being sexuality, find expression.

Referring to the State as the worst enemy men and women have, Goldman maintained that the State is a "machine that crushes you in order to sustain the ruling class, your masters."[94] She condemned government authority, calling it oppressive and tyrannical:

> ...The State is the altar of political freedom and, like the religious altar, it is maintained for the purpose of human sacrifice....government, organized authority, or the State, is necessary only to maintain or protect property and monopoly.[95]

Nineteen sixteen, the year Goldman was arrested for giving a public lecture on birth control, marked, in historian Robert Wiebe's assessment, "the completion of the federal scientific establishment" as government agencies "accumulated their files and procedures and precedents."[96] American organizations were permeated with the bureaucratic values of rationality, regularity, continuity, universality and functionality. According to Wiebe:

A bureaucratic orientation now defined a basic part of the nation's discourse. The values of continuity and regularity, functionality and rationality, administration and management set the form of problems and outlined their alternative solutions.[97]

While the State sought a greater role in the organization of American life, Goldman fought against what she perceived to be the oppressors of the human spirit—the church and State being identified by her as the arch villains.

In the 1880s, Max Weber had sensed the shift in patterns of authority away from such traditional sources as patriarchy (in an androcentrically-defined and historically-specific sense) and monarchy, toward what he called "legal-rational" forms of authority.[98] Legal-rational authority was legitimized and operationalized through the creation of bureaucracy, a form of social organization based, in theory, on universalism rather than particularism. A hierarchy of offices and positions, centralization of power and control, specifically designated channels of communication, jurisdictional territories setting out areas of responsibility, record-keeping and paper work, a reward system based on qualifications and achievements, formal rules and regulations, and positions as "careers" were identified by Weber as characteristics of the bureaucratic model.

While Weber expressed concern over the process of bureaucratization leading to depersonalization, the American industrial engineer, Frederick W. Taylor, author of *The Principles of Scientific Management* (1911), saw bureaucracy, and more specifically, scientific management, as an economic and social panacea to promote greater efficiency, regulation, productivity and, ultimately, greater social control. Premised upon the theory of social Darwinism, Taylor's theory placed the industrial worker in a competitive context struggling to do better than his fellow workers in order to maintain his position of employment. The principle of competition was seen to operate in the relations between workers as well as in those between corporations. The primary features of scientific management include the following principles:

1. Workers were to contribute to the workplace according to their biological capacity;

2. A specialized division of labour involving the simplification and compartmentalization of tasks was viewed as desirable, eliminating variant non-repetitive tasks;

3. A central plan of action or "blueprint" was required by every organization in order that questions addressing the "how," "what," and "time taken" of the production process could be answered;

4. The worker was viewed as possessing an innate laziness and dislike for work;

5. The workplace was to possess, based on the requirements of hierarchy and specialization, a high degree of centralization of control.[99]

The scientific or "classical" school of management came into its fullest being in the factory or assembly line context. Henry Ford, best and/or perhaps infamously, known as the father of assembly line production in America, considered the principles of accuracy, economy, continuity, speed, repetition, subdivision of tasks, predetermination of work techniques, and centralization of intelligence in the design room, removed from the shop floor, to be instrumental in the success of his company in America during the early twentieth century. Scientific management dominated the organizational design of bureaucracies in the United States throughout the Progressive Era.

Goldman's obvious sense of dismay at witnessing the growth of the State and of scientific management was rooted in her philosophical conception of associational life and economic co-operation. Calling Darwinian theory "one-sided and entirely inadequate," and the results of Kropotkin's work on *Mutual Aid* (1902) as "profound" and "wonderful," Goldman denounced a model of social life based on "internecine strife and struggle." The basis of a free individual and associational life is not the "omnipotent, all devastating State" but "mutual aid" and voluntary co-operation. Viewing the growth of bureaucracy as a process which would divert individuals' attention and preoccupation from their inner emotional and sexual desires, Goldman perceived the State as destroying or deadening libidinal impulses and the emotional side of life.

Wiebe has argued that the "heart of progressivism was the ambition of the new middle class to fulfil its destiny through bureaucratic means."[100] In pursuit of this goal, sectors such as government, education and industry become central targets for bureaucratization, as the "reformers" attempted to exercise political control with the hope of altering the structure of authority and decision-making. This group realized that traditional forms of authority (i.e., based on ascription) and social organization were no longer appropriate in an urban, industrial society. The leaders of various professional groups as well as "experts in administration" sought regularity and continuity of rules as well as "proper procedures" as solutions to the cities' and country's problems.

The "progress" of bureaucratization was seen, by the reformers, as a way of equalizing opportunity by making universal the rules, regulations and procedures by which industry, education and government were run. For Goldman, the move away from particularism was a move towards conformity and uniformity. This movement toward standardization struck at the heart of the central anarchist ideal—individuality. The relationship between the individual and the State was, according to Goldman, characterized by conflict and domination. It was inconceivable to Goldman that the State, through greater influence in public life, would work *for*, and in the best interests *of*, the individual. Condemning the State's intentions, Goldman stated:

> The interests of the State and those of the individual differ fundamentally and are antagonistic. The State and the political and economic institutions it supports can exist only by fashioning the individual to their particular purpose; training him to respect "law and order"; teaching him obedience, submission and unquestioning faith in the wisdom and justice of government...[101]

The move to "standardize" and "rationalize" the key institutions of public life took on an element of contagious fervour as institutional leaders strove to become a part of this wave of "efficiency."

The educational system, for example, saw the need to establish an overall blue-print or central plan of action—a well-articulated *modus operandi*. In 1913, Paul Hanus, Professor of Education at Harvard University, developed a bureaucratic model adapted to the school system, based upon the principles of scientific management. Hanus stressed the importance of a clearly articulated purpose for the school system, the centralization of authority, a system for financial accounting, and a system of record-keeping which is "clear, adequate, incontestable and accessible."[102]

Goldman argued that schooling was a pivotal force in the development of oppression by the State, and, therefore, was not surprised to witness the growing allegiance of educational and industrial philosophies. For Goldman, economic liberalism and a complementary brand of public education went hand-in-hand. Stating that "individualism" in America is an individualism of social and economic laissez-faire, Goldman maintained that education is the process through which exploitation, spiritual debasement and systematic indoctrination of the masses takes place.[103] Education is the means through which the masses grant "consent" to State undertaking. In Goldman's words:

> Constitutionalism and democracy are the modern forms
> of that alleged consent; the consent being inoculated
> and indoctrinated by what is called "education"...[104]

Throughout the progressive period, the philosophy of utilitarianism in education was a popular one in trade schools and public schools alike; one which seemed appropriate in an age geared towards productivity, efficiency and scientific advancement. Schools were viewed as "training grounds" for the inculcation of corporate and industrial values such as regularity, persistency and punctuality, which would prepare students for the workplace.

Industry, or more specifically its way of viewing the world, was seen as "a controlling factor in social progress" as the American National Education Association's 1910 Report of the Committee on the Place of Industries in Public Education argued for a close alignment of the needs of industry and those of education. The committee's report included the following principles:

1. Industry, as a controlling factor in social progress, has a fundamental and permanent significance for education;

2. Educational standards, applicable in an age of handicraft, presumably need radical change in view of the complex and highly specialized industrial development;

3. The social aims of education and the psychological needs of childhood alike require that industrial (manual-constructive) activities form an important part of school occupations;

4. The differences among children as to aptitudes, interests, economic resources, and prospective careers furnish the basis for a rational as opposed to a merely formal distinction between elementary, secondary, and higher education.[105]

Goldman's perception of education's role in indoctrination and spiritual debasement on behalf of the State was consistent with the close partnership enjoyed by education and industry during this period. Her view that education was the process through which "consenting" citizens were produced, reinforced her perception of the alienation of the citizenry, as they occupied jobs dictated by a system of economic laissez-faire. Sounding strikingly similar to Marx and his theory of alienation, Goldman wrote:

The average worker has no inner point of contact with the industry he is employed in, and is a stranger to the process of production of which he is a mechanical part. Like any other cog of the machine, he is replaceable at any time by other similar depersonalized human beings.[106]

In conclusion, the sweeping expansion of the bureaucracy, to which Goldman was philosophically and practically opposed, created a growing gulf between her anarchist ideals and the realities of American life. While Goldman preached for the freedom of the individual spirit, a passion for efficiency, including principles such as regularity, consistency and conformity, was sweeping the nation. Bureaucratic ideals were infiltrating institutions in the private realm as well as the public sphere. For example, the State Supervisor of Home Economics for Arizona drew parallels between factory management (for men) and home management (for women), articulating the need for a "plan of home management" and for the frequent assessing of the plan to ensure that it is meeting the family's needs. Record-keeping and the development of a central plan of management did not pass by what is considered by many to be an expressive rather than instrumental activity—the running of a home and the "management" of a family. In this industrially designed model, home management included: a) studying the needs of the family, b) considering resources, c) making a plan, d) living by the plan, e) checking on results, f) perfecting the plan. Meal planning in the home and executive planning in the factory were paralleled, tenuously one might argue, in this way:

> Executives in well-managed factories are not content with dictating sets of instructions or handing out work sheets. Nor are they satisfied in knowing that plans have not been followed. Neither are homemakers satisfied in planning new combinations for meals or new methods of serving without seeing whether they will be satisfactory to family members and to other factors of time and effort.[107]

Like all social cults or ideologies, the "cult of efficiency,"[108] as manifested by the model of scientific management, permeated the entire social fabric, creating a high degree of attitudinal homogeneity among Americans. Wiebe refers to Frederick Taylor as a "folk hero," as the list of bureaucratic applications included the national

Republican party, universities such as Chicago and Columbia and prestigious law offices:

> Law offices that had once depended upon the magnetism of one or two prominent names were transforming themselves into sets of highly specialized subdivisions, each with its own hierarchical staff. "Law factories" they were called. Such universities as Chicago and Columbia which had once sought fame by pursuing a single educational ideal were now increasingly eclectic centres directed by professional administrators.[109]

Goldman lamented this growing uniformity:

> The wholesale mechanization of modern life has increased uniformity a thousandfold. It is everywhere present, in habits, tastes, dress, thoughts and ideas.[110]

The development of the American "State" was viewed by Goldman as more than a simple intrusion into people's work lives. Its creeping presence represented, to Goldman, the need for her theory of anarchism which uncompromisingly rejected the control of organized authority. Goldman's placement of the issues of sexuality and reproduction, within the framework of her discussion of the State, represents Goldman's view that sexual freedom is to be treated on a par with all other forms of freedom.[111] In typical Goldman fashion, there are no compromises to this position; according to Goldman, the presence and power of the State dull the spirit and diminish the senses. As a result, sexual and reproductive energy is repressed if not depleted; "instinct" remains unexplored and unexpressed.

Goldman's perception of "power" is grounded in the presence of the "State"; it is a unitary vision rather than a diffuse one in which power could rest in a multitude of relations, including those of sex.[112] Instead, Goldman views "sex" and the "State" or society as dichotomous realms positioned in opposition to one another. Following Goldman's logic, if "power" rests in the exclusive domain of the State, power relations would not reside in sexual relations. As will be later discussed, Goldman may have been rather shortsighted in suggesting that the power of the State represented a unitary threat to sexual freedom, while overlooking relations of power which might reside in customs, habits, and informal patterns of behaviour, including sexuality itself.

NOTES

1. Alix Kates Shulman, *To the Barricades: The Anarchist Life of Emma Goldman* (New York: Thomas Y. Crowell, 1971), p. 130.
2. Ibid., p. 131.
3. Ibid., pp. 131-132.
4. Ibid.
5. Ibid., p. 130.
6. Ibid., p. 132.
7. Mary Poovey, *Uneven Developments: The Ideological Work of Gender in Mid-Victorian England* (Chicago: University of Chicago Press, 1988), p. 35.
8. Linda Gordon, *Woman's Body, Woman's Right: A Social History of Birth Control in America* (New York: Grossman Publishers, 1976), p. 261.
9. Ludmilla Jordanova, "Natural Facts: a historical perspective on science and reality," in *Nature, Culture and Gender,* edited by Carol MacCormack and Marilyn Strathern (Cambridge University Press, 1980), p. 64; Poovey, *Uneven Developments: The Ideological Work of Gender in Mid-Victorian England,* p. 35.
10. Poovey, *Uneven Developments: The Ideological Work of Gender in Mid-Victorian England,* p. 36.
11. Carroll Smith-Rosenberg, *Disorderly Conduct: Visions of Gender in America* (Oxford University Press, 1986), pp. 262-63.
12. Carroll Smith-Rosenberg and Charles Rosenberg, "The Female Animal: Medical and Biological Views of Woman and Her Role in Nineteenth Century America," *The Journal of American History,* 60 (March 1974), p. 340.
13. Ibid., p. 348.
14. Gordon, *Woman's Body, Woman's Right,* p. 260.
15. Alice Wexler, *Emma Goldman: An Intimate Life* (New York: Pantheon Books, 1984), p. 215.
16. Gordon, *Woman's Body, Woman's Right,* p. 220.
17. Quoted in Ibid., p. 261.
18. Ibid., p. 260.
19. Ibid., p. 167.
20. Ibid., p. 261.
21. Quoted in Ibid., p. 170.
22. Ibid., p. 64.
23. Ibid., p. 170.
24. Ibid.
25. Emma Goldman, *Living My Life* (New York: Alfred A. Knopf, 1931. Reprint, New York: Dover Publications, 1970), p. 186.
26. Ibid., p. 187.
27. Ibid.
28. Ibid.
29. Ibid.
30. Gordon, *Woman's Body, Woman's Right,* p. 171.

31. Ibid., p. 261.
32. David Kennedy, *Birth Control in America: The Career of Margaret Sanger* (New Haven: Yale University Press, 1970), p. 140.
33. Ibid.
34. Gordon, *Woman's Body, Woman's Right*, p. 171.
35. Ibid.
36. Kennedy, *Birth Control in America*, p. 144.
37. Ibid., p. 141.
38. Jeffrey Weeks, *Sex, Politics and Society*, 2nd ed. (New York: Longman, 1989),   p. 23.
39. Gordon, *Woman's Body, Woman's Right*, p. 278. Linda Gordon argues that "race-suicide" theory was a response to demographic change and birth control use in the early twentieth century (p. 137).
40. Weeks, *Sex, Politics and Society*, p. 128.
41. Gordon, *Woman's Body, Woman's Right*, p. 137.
42. Ibid., p. 289.
43. Ibid., p. 279.
44. Weeks, *Sex, Politics and Society*, p. 187.
45. Weeks, Sex, Politics and Society, p. 128; Gordon, *Woman's Body, Woman's Right*, pp. 278-279.
46. Gordon, *Woman's Body, Woman's Right*, p. 279.
47. Weeks, *Sex, Politics and Society*, p. 133.
48. Linda Gordon explains that the term "race-suicide" became the popular label for Roosevelt's ideas. Roosevelt became one of the chief spokesmen for the race-suicide theory. See Gordon's *Woman's Body, Woman's Right*, p. 137.
49. Kennedy, *Birth Control in America*, p. 47.
50. Ibid.
51. Gordon, *Woman's Body, Woman's Right*, p. 137.
52. Ibid.
53 Weeks, *Sex, Politics and Society*, p. 41-45.
54. Emma Goldman, *Anarchism and Other Essays* (New York: Mother Earth Publishing Association, 1910), p. 173.
55. Martha Solomon, *Emma Goldman* (Boston: G. K. Hall, 1987).
56. Gordon, *Woman's Body, Woman's Right*, p. 136.
57. Goldman, *Anarchism and Other Essays*, pp. 171-172.
58. Ibid.
59 Ibid.
60. Emma Goldman, *Living My Life*, Vol. I: (New York: Alfred A. Knopf, 1931; Reprint. New York: Dover Publications, 1970), p. 186.
61. Ibid.
62 Gordon, *Woman's Body, Woman's Right*, p. 38.
63. Ibid.
64. Ibid., p. 62.
65. Norman Himes, *Medical History of Contraception* (New York: Gamot Press, 1963), pp. 335-337.
66. Gordon, *Woman's Body, Woman's Right*, p. 137.
67. Ibid., p. 140.
68. Ibid.
69. Ibid., p. 219.
70. Ibid., p. 278.
71 Ibid., p. 145.
72. Candace Falk, *Love, Anarchy and Emma Goldman* (New York: Holt, Rinehart and Winston, 1984), p. 238.
73. Emma Goldman, in *Red Emma Speaks: Selected Writings and Speeches by Emma Goldman*, compiled and edited by Alix Kates Shulman (New York: Random House, 1972), p. 131.
74. M. Patricia Marchak, *Ideological Perspectives on Canada*, 3rd edition (Toronto: McGraw-Hill Ryerson), 1988.

75. Goldman, *Red Emma Speaks: Selected Writings and Speeches by Emma Goldman*, p. 88.
76. Ibid.
77. Ibid., p. 89.
78. Ibid.
79. Naomi Scheman, "From Hamlet to Maggie-Verver: The History and Politics of the Knowing Subject," *Poetics*, 18, 4-5 (1989), p. 450.
80. Ibid.
81. Ibid.
82. Ibid.
83. Jordanova, "Natural Facts: A Historical Perspective on Science and Reality."
84. Poovey, *Uneven Developments: The Ideological Work of Gender in Mid-Victorian England*, pp. 10-11.
85. Jordanova, "Natural Facts: A Historical Perspective on Science and Reality," p. 64.
86. Gordon, *Woman's Body, Woman's Right: A Social History of Birth Control in America*, p. 140.
87. Ibid., p. 157.
88. "External" and "internal" are used by Goldman to mean roughly economic/structural and psychosexual factors respectively.
89. Goldman, *Anarchism and Other Essays*, p. 62.
90. Goldman, *Red Emma Speaks: Selected Writings and Speeches by Emma Goldman*, p. 95.
91. Falk, *Love, Anarchy and Emma Goldman*, p. 238.
92. Ibid.
93. Ibid.
94. Goldman, *Living My Life*, p. 122.
95. Ibid., p. 64.
96. Robert Wiebe, *The Search for Order* (New York: Hill and Wang, 1967), p. 295.
97. Ibid.
98. Max Weber, *Economy and Society* (New York: Bedminster Press, 1968), pp. 217-226.
99. Charles Perrow, *Complex Organizations* (New York: Random House, 1979), pp. 63-65.
100. Weibe, *The Search for Order*, p. 166.
101. Goldman, *Red Emma Speaks: Selected Writings and Speeches by Emma Goldman*, p. 96.
102. Paul Hanus, *Proceedings of the National Education Association of America*, 1913, p. 259.
103. Goldman, *Red Emma Speaks: Selected Writings and Speeches by Emma Goldman*, p. 89.
104. Ibid., p. 90.
105. "Report of Committee on the Place of Industries in Public Education," *Proceedings of the National Education Association of America*, 1910.
106. Goldman, *Red Emma Speaks: Selected Writings and Speeches by Emma Goldman*, p. 96.
107. Mildred Wood, *Proceedings of the National Education Association of America*, 1928, p. 99.
108. Robert Callahan, *Education and the Cult of Efficiency* (Chicago: University of Chicago Press, 1962).
109. Wiebe, *The Search for Order*, p. 295.
110. Goldman, *Red Emma Speaks: Selected Writings and Speeches by Emma Goldman*, p. 93.
111. Alix Kates Shulman, "Emma Goldman: A Life of Anarchy," CBC *Ideas* transcripts, 1983, p. 11.
112. Weeks, *Sex, Politics and Society*, p. 7.

CHAPTER 4

Theoretical Perspectives on Sexuality and Reproduction

Emma Goldman's articulations on sexuality and reproduction can be more fully understood through a broader discussion of the contemporary theoretical positions on sexuality. In this chapter, I will draw on the taxonomy of sexual theories developed by the British social construction theorist, Jeffrey Weeks, in an attempt to "fit" Goldman's views on sexuality into Weeks' scheme of categories. Weeks' taxonomy will be employed in order to enhance our understanding of Goldman's views on sexuality and reproduction, as well as to illuminate Goldman's thought relative to competing theoretical positions, including those of the contemporary "sex debates."

Essentialist and Non-Essentialist Approaches to the Study of Sexuality

According to Jeffrey Weeks, theoretical approaches to the study of sexuality can be categorized as either "essentialist" or "non-essentialist."[1] The essentialist approach is the most common. It is described by Weeks as a view of sexuality in which "sex is conceptualized as an overpowering force in the individual that shapes not only the personal but the social life as well. It is seen as a driving, instinctual force, whose characteristics are built into the biology of the human animal, which shapes human institutions..."[2] Weeks characterizes essentialist approaches to the study of sexuality by their reductionist and deterministic methods.[3] In the study of sexuality, essentialism reduces sexuality to a biological drive through which complex patterns of social organization are to be understood. The "social" is reduced to the "biological/nature" which determines both individual personality and social structures and interaction.

Essentialist approaches, according to Weeks, can be divided into two categories—"naturalist" theories and what sociologist Kenneth Plummer (1975) calls "meta-theoretical" perspectives. "Naturalist" theories include those of early twentieth-century sexologist and Goldman contemporary, Havelock Ellis, who considered such social phenomena as male sexual dominance, female sexual submissiveness, maternalism and male homosexuality to be biologically determined. Weeks describes Ellis's "naturalist essentialism" in the following manner:

> Ellis believed in the existence of an essential and basically healthy nature which was distorted by modern ways. His aim was to find ways of chipping away at the residues of the old, to allow the healthy organism to develop, and so to build on the solid groundwork of natural laws.[4]

Anthropologist, Bronislaw Malinowski, who wrote *The Sexual Life of Savages* in 1929, also viewed sexuality from a "naturalist" perspective. However, in contrast to Ellis, he argued that this "instinct" must be regulated, suppressed, and directed by social regulation:

> Sex is a most powerful instinct...there is no doubt that masculine jealousy, sexual modesty, female coyness, the mechanisms of sexual attraction and of courtship—all these forces and conditions made it necessary that even in the most primitive human aggregates there should exist powerful means of regulating, suppressing and directing this instinct.[5]

"Meta-theoretical" approaches are based on psychodynamic/ Freudian premises. Instead of reducing individuals or social patterns to broad biological imperatives, meta-theoretical reductionism operates on the basis of more specific psychodynamic imperatives— reducing sexuality to the "natural" expressions of the id and its relationship with the superego.

Essentialism, as a methodological/theoretical framework, encompasses not only the sub-groups which Weeks refers to as naturalist and meta-theoretical, but, in addition, can accommodate seemingly antithetical ideologies, of opposing political agendas. Ideologies of "the right" and "the left" can both find a home, ironically, under the umbrella of essentialism. This co-existence of opposing political ideologies within the confines of essentialism creates an unthinkable commonality among and between ideologies such as sociobiology, libertarianism, and functionalism. Functionalists such as Malinowski and Emile Durkheim argue sexual instincts must be controlled and regulated as they represent potentially disruptive forces for both the individual and the social group. The "means of regulating, suppressing and directing" the sexual instinct, in Malinowski's words, have been historically plentiful, taking the form of customs, taboos and mores and, in industrialized societies, marriage patterns, laws and institutionalized religion. The view that sex "really is dangerous"[6] was behind the need for close social control of sexual impulses. Durkheim, writing in France in the late 1800s, expressed a similar belief when he argued "to be free is not to do what one pleases; it is to be the master of oneself…"[7] Through the *control* of one's "unthinking physical forces," and not through the unrestricted expression of such forces, freedom is gained. Durkheim wrote:

> …Rights and liberties are not things inherent in man as such….Society has consecrated the individual and made him pre-eminently worthy of respect. His progressive emancipation does not imply a weakening but a transformation of the social bonds….The individual submits to society and this submission is the condition of his liberation. For man freedom consists in the deliverance from blind, unthinking physical forces; this he achieves by opposing against them the great and intelligent force which is society, under whose protection he shelters. By putting himself under the wing of society, he makes himself also, to a certain extent, dependent upon it. But this is a liberating dependence.[8]

The functionalist perspectives of Durkheim, and later Malinowski, represent a "right-wing," conservative perspective within
essentialism, in which individuals must sexually submit to the
control of the social structure. In contrast to this conservative position, "radical" sexual ideologies also take their place within essentialism as they, too, assume a basic "biological mandate."[9] Weeks
states:

> ...The instinctual (or 'drive reduction') model has been
> embraced by all shades of opinion, from the conservative
> moralist anxious to control this unruly force to the
> Freudian left (Wilhelm Reich, Herbert Marcuse, Erich
> Fromm) wanting to "liberate" sexuality from its capitalist
> and patriarchal constraints.[10]

However, as Weeks suggests, sexual ideologies of conservative
and "radical" persuasions do *not* share a common view of the morality
of sexual expression nor do they share a common view of the individual sexual being vis-à-vis her/his social world. While
functionalists such as Durkheim and Malinowski believed that
society must take precedence over the individual, the so-called "sex
radicals," like Emma Goldman writing in the early twentieth-century,
argued that society exists to meet the needs of individuals. Libertarian
theorists sought to overcome the oppressive constraints of social institutions and tended "to see sex as a beneficent force which is
repressed by a corrupt civilization."[11] According to Weeks, the sexual
liberationist Wilhelm Reich (1897-1957), for example, saw the libido as
a biological force that had the potential, depending on its expression,
to cause both illness and well-being. Weeks observes that "at the heart
of Reich's theory was a natural man and a natural woman whose
sexual urges were basically heterosexual and genital..."[12] In *The Function of the Orgasm: Sex-Economic Problems of Biological Energy*, first published in 1942, Reich argued that neurosis impedes the expression of
"natural" sexual impulses:

Beneath these neurotic mechanisms, behind all these
dangerous, grotesque unnatural fantasies and impulses I
found a bit of simple, matter-of-fact, decent nature.[13]

Reich's criticism of society stemmed from his view that sexual repression was rooted in economic and social conditions. Forces such as
authoritarianism and class oppression inhibited the full release of the
libido.[14] Thus, it was society which caused neurosis which in turn
stood in the way of full sexual release or what Reich called "orgastic
potency" and individual well-being; Reich maintained that "not a
single neurotic individual possesses orgastic potency."[15]

Non-Essentialist Perspectives

Non-essentialist perspectives on the study of sexuality do not assume, as was the case in essentialism, that sex is an unshakeable
driving force, biologically mandated and "free-floating."[16] Instead,
non-essentialist theories are based on the premise that sexuality is
socially constructed and organized; its meanings and definitions are
embedded in the social structures of the community or society. In
Weeks' formulation, non-essentialism regards "biology as a set of
potentialities which are transformed and given meaning only in social relationships."[17] This will be the formulation used in this thesis
in the analysis of Goldman's construction of sexuality. Contemporary non-essentialist anthropologists, Ellen Ross and Rayna Rapp,
elaborate upon non-essentialism's view of the social essence of
sexuality stating that "sexuality…is not simply released or free-floating. It continues to be socially structured."[18] The social structuring of
sexuality implies cultural, racial, gender, and class diversity in the expression of sexual behaviour. Ross and Rapp argue, as Margaret
Mead did in *Sex and Temperament in Three Primitive Societies* (1935),
that "sexual socialization is no less specific to each culture than is
socialization to ritual, dress, or cuisine."[19]

The origin of non-essentialism has its roots in the anthropology and sociology of sex, the new social history, and in the
"revolution" in psychoanalysis.[20] Weeks explains the common as-

sumptions of the approach. First, the non-essentialist approach rejects the view that sex exists as an autonomous realm, a "natural" domain in which biological instincts wage war against the social control of the culture. Non-essentialist theorists argue that sex is inextricably interconnected to and dependent upon the society in which it is located. Non-essentialism posits that sexual forms, behaviours, and ideologies vary greatly in relation to social and cultural differences, and they reject the essentialist conception of a standard, undemarcated, pansexual impulse. As Ross and Rapp suggest:

> Sexuality both generates wider social relations and is refracted through the prism of society. As such, sexual feelings and activities express all the contradictions of power relations—of gender, class, and race.[21]

As Carole Vance, another non-essentialist, argues, "sexuality may be thought about, experienced, and acted on differently according to age, class, ethnicity, physical ability, sexual orientation and preference, religion and region."[22] Non-essentialism, attempts to "deconstruct" what Weeks calls "the apparent unity of this world of sexuality."[23]

Non-essentialist theoretical approaches also reject the notion that sexuality can be understood in terms of such dichotomies as repression and liberation, pressure and release. This dichotomous thinking is replaced by a view that society creates sexuality in complex ways. Weeks elaborates:

> Existing languages of sex, embedded in moral treatises, laws, educational practices, psychological theories, medical definitions, social rituals, pornographic or romantic fictions, popular music and commonsense assumptions (most of which disagree) set the horizon of the possible. They all present themselves as true representations of our intimate needs and desires.[24]

Weeks classifies the various theorists writing from a non-essentialist position into three methodologically distinct perspectives—the discursive, the neo-interactionist, and the psychoanalytic.[25]

Theories of the social construction of sexuality are perhaps most eminently and prominently represented by the work of the contemporary French philosopher and historian, Michel Foucault. Foucault's *The History of Sexuality* (1979), a significant contribution to the theory of non-essentialism, introduces the notion of sexuality as a "historical construct":

> Sexuality must not be thought of as a kind of natural given which power tries to hold in check, or as an obscure domain which knowledge tries gradually to uncover. It is the name that can be given to a historical construct.[26]

Foucault's "discursive" approach to sexuality involves a "deconstruction" of what has been considered to be a unitary theory containing "laws" of its own. "Sexuality," according to Foucault, has ideologically constructed and brought together elements such as "bodies, organs, somatic localisations, functions, anatomophysiological systems, sensations and pleasure..."[27] These elements, Foucault suggests, are greatly dissimilar and possess little or no basis for unification.

The interactionist perspective (or symbolic interactionist perspective) is best represented by the work of J. H. Gagnon and William Simon as well as that of Kenneth Plummer. Gagnon and Simon, in *Sexual Conduct: The Social Sources of Sexuality* (1973), argue that sexuality takes the form of "scripts" which mediate between bodily function and pleasures and the social world. Challenging the long-standing notion of a "biological mandate," Gagnon and Simon suggest that sexuality is subject to "socio-cultural moulding to a degree surpassed by few other forms of human behaviour."[28] The social construction of "scripts" of masculinity and femininity engender the emergence of particular definitions of sexuality. As Gagnon and Simon argue, sexual impulse or "nature" does not create a version of masculine or feminine sexuality. Instead, the authors suggest:

Social roles are not vehicles for the expression of sexual impulse.... Sexuality becomes a vehicle for expressing the needs of social roles.[29]

A non-essentialist "neo-psychoanalytic" approach can be found in the work of contemporary theorists such as Juliet Mitchell (*Psychoanalysis and Feminism,* 1974). According to Weeks, feminist re-interpretation of psychoanalytic theories regarding sexuality by Mitchell and, before her, Karen Horney, (*New Ways in Psychoanalysis,* 1939), "has offered a most important emphasis on psychological structuring in the creation of historically specific forms of 'masculinity' and 'femininity' and has encouraged a break away from discussion in terms of social roles', with all that concept's inherent functionalism."[30] Mitchell argued that the historically specific notions of sexuality, "masculinity" and "femininity" are grounded in the patriarchal culture and pointed to confusion and ambiguity in Freud's own writing in his theorization of the relationship between the concepts "feminine" and "masculine."[31] Weeks has suggested that Juliet Mitchell persuasively argued that Freud was a "patriarchal exponent of female inferiority ('anatomy is destiny' is a description not a prescription) ..."[32]

Theoretical Approaches to the Regulation of Sexuality

Weeks explains that it is difficult to differentiate the meaning we give to sexuality from the forms of social control we advocate for its regulation. Weeks states:

What we believe sex is, or ought to be, structures our response to it. So it is difficult to separate the particular meanings we give to sex from the forms of control we advocate.[33]

According to Weeks' categorizations, the various theoretical perspectives on the regulation or non-regulation of sex encompass the absolutist position, the libertarian position, the liberal-pluralist position and the radical pluralist position.[34] These perspectives provide a screen, subliminal or conscious, through which we view the subject of sexual politics.[35] The degree to which we advocate social control or regulation of sexuality and by what social institutions or agencies, or whether we advocate control or regulation at all, depends on our ideological screen. Our respective screens may be tightly meshed, allowing only a select number of sexual behaviours to fall within the "acceptable zone." On the other hand, our ideological screen may be broadly meshed enabling a rich diversity of sexual behaviour to be expressed without the perceived necessity for "regulation" on the part of society or the social group.

"Historically," Weeks argues, "we are the heirs of the absolutist tradition."[36] Absolutist perspectives on sexuality are based upon a belief in the inherent malevolence of sexual expression. The absolutist morality of this perspective directs and divides sexual behaviours into acceptable and unacceptable zones, funnelling what potentially could be destructive and unacceptable behaviour into "acceptable" outlets of sexual expression—monogamy, marriage, biological reproduction, and heterosexuality. The absolutist position views sexuality as the uncivilized or unsocialized component of human behaviour. Society with its various institutional arms— religion, the family and legal system are its civilized and civilizing counterpart. From an absolutist perspective, human desire is bad and social control is good. If sexuality is to be expressed at all, it must be expressed through socially sanctioned institutions in a socially sanctioned manner. To be fully human is to be in *control* of one's sexual impulses and not to permit them to control one's life.

Weeks asserts that moral absolutism is deeply embedded in the Christian culture's perception of sexuality and the appropriate means for its regulation. He states:

> Moral absolutism has deeply influenced our general culture, and, in particular, the forms of legal regulation, many of which still survive. The major set of legal changes in Britain in the last decades of the nineteenth century and the early part of this century...were pushed for

by absolutist social moral movements, propelled in many cases by a religious fervour, and frequently in alliance with moral feminism. Though tempered by selective enforcement and pragmatic adjustments...these laws continued to define sexual offenses until the 1960s and sometimes beyond.[37]

The libertarian position on the regulation of sexuality is also embedded in a set of values about the desirability of sexual expression and the evils of regulation.[38] Like moral absolutism, libertarianism assumes an essentialist perspective on sexuality, considering it to be a natural "given." Like moral absolutists, sexual libertarians have considered sexuality to be outside of and opposed to society, thus perpetuating the schism between sex and society.[39] Unlike moral absolutist positions, however, libertarianism does *not* view sexuality as a dangerous, regressive, antisocial force; instead, sexuality is imbued with a sense of personal and social significance. Sex, according to libertarian perspectives, is a healthy, positive, "natural" phenomenon which has been repressed and diverted by the so-called development or "civilization" of the social world. Assuming the inherent goodness of the sexual impulse, libertarians argue for complete freedom of sexual expression. Libertarians call for an end to sexual repression as it manifests itself through the socializing agents of the church, the family, and the State.

Sexual libertarians have included such writers and thinkers as Charles Fournier, Edward Carpenter, Emma Goldman, A. S. Neill, Wilhelm Reich, and Herbert Marcuse who have believed that sexual liberation "is a (perhaps *the*) key to social freedom, a disruptive energy that can help break the existing order."[40] What is required, according to the libertarian theorists, is not regulation, control, and discipline of sexual activity, but, rather, release, openness, and freedom. Through the unfettered expression of presumably "basic" and "natural" impulses, the individual may gain her/his physical and emotional well-being, while the society may gain integrity and honesty, throwing off the shackles of moralist hypocrisy and the double standard which separates and governs behaviours in private and public realms.

While the libertarian framework offers a liberatory and optimistic message to those who have suffered from the "puritanism" and sexual repression of moral absolutist influences, libertarianism does not come without its attendant problems. In stressing what can be gained by "releasing" sexuality from the confines of social institutions such as the family and the State, libertarians create, according to Weeks, the erroneous impression that sexual freedom is an unqualified "good" and that sexuality unproblematically speaks "its own truth."[41] Consequently, libertarian approaches may be perceived to be uncritical sources of male sexual "glorification,"[42] lacking in a counterbalance wherein the attendant problems or "dangers" of sexual liberation are addressed. Weeks notes that feminists (moral feminists and others) have pointed out the deleterious effect of libertarian theory:

> As a result its [the libertarian approach] celebration of sex can easily become a glorification of all manifestations of desire. The effect of this, as feminists have pointed out, can be to impose a view that sexual expression is not only pleasurable, but necessary—often at the expense of women. The real problems, of defining alternatives and constructing new forms of relating, are ignored.[43]

In other words, libertarian theories of sexuality embody a fundamental flaw stemming from their essentialism. By assuming that sexuality is "free-floating"[44] and a product of "nature" and not society, the possibility that there may exist "alternate" (i.e., female same-sex relationships) forms of "sexual" activity has been ignored. Paradoxically, there is an inherent conservatism in libertarianism, as it attempts to liberate the sexual practices of the status quo while ignoring, as Weeks suggests, the "problems of defining alternatives and constructing new forms of relating."[45]

A third position on the regulation of sexuality is the liberal-pluralist perspective.[46] Rooted in the nineteenth-century liberalism of J. S. Mill, liberal perspectives on sexuality attempt to bring about greater sexual "rights" for the individual, while leaving unchallenged the basic underpinnings of the social structure. Essentialist in their theoretical orientation, liberal-pluralist perspectives assume the characteristic "biological mandate" of sexuality, at the same time attempting, however, to mediate between "the individual" and the society to achieve greater "rights" for the individual. Endorsing sexual pluralism, although in a narrow and hesitant fashion,[47] liberal-pluralist models reject the moral claims of absolutism which suggest that some sexual behaviours are inherently good, while others are inherently evil. For the liberal-pluralist regulation of sexuality is based on whether or not a particular sexual act is seen to be injurious to another—whether the act violates another's "individual rights." Or as Havelock Ellis stated in *The Psychology of Sex:*

> The question is no longer:
> Is the act abnormal?
> It becomes: Is the act injurious?[48]

While liberal-pluralist perspectives reject moral absolutism, attempting to broaden the scope of what is perceived to be acceptable sexual behaviour, liberalism falls short in its liberatory capacity. Unlike the libertarians the liberal-pluralists do not advocate the full release of sexuality from the control of so-called "repressive" social institutions. Instead, a framework based on the artificial distinction between private morality and public law is offered as a means to "regulate" sexuality publicly and to "liberate" sexuality privately.[49] According to Weeks, the liberal-pluralist perspective, promoting individual "rights," creates a sense of "false consciousness" through its explicit separation of "private" and "public." "Private rights" and "public morality" as theoretically constructed concepts imply the experiential separation of private and public/social life.[50] Weeks and others would contend, on the contrary, that in one's private life and seemingly intimate sexual practices, the social world invades one's unconsciousness as well as consciousness, leaving perceived "unique" or uninhibited sexual practices very much conditioned by social influences. Contemporary feminist, Angela Carter, explains:

...In bed, we even feel we touch the bedrock of human nature itself. But we are deceived, flesh is not an irreducible human universal. Although the erotic relationship may seem to exist freely, on its own terms, among the distorted relationships of the bourgeois society, it is, in fact, the most self-conscious of all human relationships, a direct confrontation of two beings whose actions in the bed are wholly determined by their acts when they are out of it .... Flesh comes to us out of history; so does the repression and taboo that governs our experience of flesh.[51]

Sex may *feel* "private" or "individual," but as Ross and Rapp argue, those feelings incorporate "roles, definitions, symbols, and meanings of the world in which they are constructed."[52] The ideological separation between private and public creates a "space" which Ross and Rapp refer to as "personal life" in which sexual identity is located:

The separation, with industrial capitalism, of family life from work, of consumption from production, of leisure from labour, of personal life from political life, has completely reorganized the context in which we experience sexuality. These polarities are grossly distorted and precast as antinomies in modern ideological formulations, but their seeming separation creates an ideological space called "personal life," one defining characteristic of which is sexual identity.[53]

Against the "certainties" of the three positions outlined thus far, Weeks proposes a fourth perspective—radical pluralism.[54] Weeks calls the radical pluralist position one "in the making rather than a fixed set of ethical or political practices," explaining it bears some similarity to other positions.[55] For example, radical pluralism recognizes the needs of the individual, as does the liberal-pluralist position, and, like libertarians, it recognizes the legitimacy of "denied" sexual practices. However, radical pluralism is at odds with moral absolutism in its rejection of the dogmatism and certainties of absolutist perspectives.

Weeks argues that two aims must be pursued in relation to the full development of the radical-pluralist perspective. The first is a "challenge...to the idea that sexuality embodies the working out of an immanent truth."[5] We must, according to Weeks, begin to explore the complexity of sexuality as a biological, psychic, and social force, and discard the assumptions of sex as good or bad, natural or unnatural and so on. The second and related aim of a radical-pluralist perspective would be to create a sensitivity to the issues of "the social nature of identity, the criteria for sexual choice, the meaning of pleasure and consent, and the relations between sexuality and power."[57] Weeks argues that radical pluralism does not attempt to create a "utopian" view of sexuality, set outside of and apart from history; rather it is in and through history that sexuality gains its meaning.[58] As contemporary historian, Michael Ignatieff, writes: "If human nature is historical, individuals have different histories and therefore different needs." Radical-pluralism is, as an emerging model for the "regulation" of sexual practice, grounded in history rather than utopian ideals, committed to diversity of practice rather than uniformity, and sensitive to the reality that "individuals have different histories and therefore different needs."[60]

The Social Organization of Sexuality: The Link Between Gender and Sexuality

Theorists working within non-essentialist frameworks argue that just as sexuality is socially constructed, is it socially organized. Far beyond the boundaries of "natural impulse" or "private" experience, "sexuality" is constructed and organized by forces such as kinship and family systems (e.g., patriarchy), communities as "loci of social relations" (e.g., traditions of courting behaviour), economic and social organization (e.g., capitalism, industrialization, urbanization), social regulation (e.g., religion, education), political interventions (e.g., movements such as the contemporary New Right), and the development of "cultures of resistance" (e.g., pro-choice movements lobbying against abortion legislation).[61]

The social organization of sexuality by systems of kinship and family, local community structures and social/economic development has historically been predicated upon an assumption of a previously existing link between "gender" and "sexuality," as inextricably interconnected concepts. According to Weeks, "gender," the social condition of being female or male, and "sexuality," the cultural manner of "living out bodily pleasures,"[62] are seen to be "naturally" connected and mutually complementary. As Weeks argues, "we still cannot think about sexuality without taking into account gender; or, to put it more generally, the elaborate facade of sexuality has in large part been built upon the assumption of fundamental differences between men and women, and of male dominance over women."[63]

Gayle Rubin's "The Traffic in Women: Notes on the 'Political Economy' of Sex" (1975) provides a foundation for discussion of the socially-constructed and imposed link between the concepts of gender and sexuality. Rubin writes:

> Gender is a socially imposed division of the sexes. It is a product of the social relations of sexuality. Kinship systems rest upon marriages. They therefore transform males and females into "men" and "women," each an incomplete half which can only find wholeness when united with the other.... The idea that men and women are more different from one another than either is from anything else must come from somewhere other than nature.... But the idea that men and women are two mutually exclusive categories must arise out of something other than a nonexistent "natural" opposition. Far from being an expression of natural differences, exclusive gender identity is the suppression of natural similarities.[64]

Rubin's concept of the "sex-gender system" aids our understanding of how sexual or biological characteristics become socially transformed into characteristics possessing social and symbolic meaning (e.g., the penis becoming "the phallus"—a symbol of domi-nance or control). Rubin's "sex-gender system," defined as "the set of arrangements by which society transforms biological sexuality into products of human activity,"[65] encapsulates relations of reproduction, production, and family life. It is, in Rubin's words, "the part of social life which is the locus of the oppression of women, of sexual minorities, and of certain aspects of human personality within individuals."[66]

Carol Vance's "Gender Systems, Ideology and Sex Research" adds to Rubin's conceptualization of the sex-gender system. Vance argues that every gender system, regardless of its "unique" content, possesses its own ideology in which gender is viewed as "natural," thereby providing a sense of order and structure.[67] Sexuality, therefore, is inextricably linked to and embedded in relations of power—relations which attempt to maintain the conditions of the present order, whether they relate to gender, race, class, or sexual preference.

Foucault's *History of Sexuality* points to the ways in which power is created and maintained, not in a unitary superstructural manner, but through "concrete mechanisms and practices" among and between individual participants. Weeks adds, that power "is not a single thing: it is relational, it is created in the relationships which sustain it."[68] As an agency through which power is exercised, discourses on sexuality serve not only to reflect the power imbalances of the social world, but to further perpetuate relations of power and inequality. In this way, sexuality, its meaning, and attendant consequences are unequally experienced, according to one's relative position of power outside of the bedroom. As contemporary feminists, Ellen Carol DuBois and Linda Gordon state:

> It is often alleged that female sexuality is a more complex matter than men's, and, if so, a major reason is that sex spells potential danger as well as pleasure for women. A feminist politics about sex, therefore, if it is to be credible as well as hopeful, must seek both to protect women from

sexual danger and to encourage their pursuit of sexual pleasure.[69]

Biological Reproduction: Theoretical Perspectives

Biologically men have only one innate orientation—a sexual one that draws them to women—while women have two innate orientations, sexual towards men and reproductive toward their young (Alice Rossi, 1976).

Biological sexuality is the necessary precondition for human sexuality. But biological sexuality is only a precondition, a set of potentialities, which is never unmediated by human reality (Robert Padgug, 1979).

The above articulations by Alice Rossi and Robert Padgug illustrate the divergence of theory on the "essential" nature of biological reproduction. Just as theories of sexuality are based upon either essentialist or non-essentialist assumptions, theories of reproduction tend to fall into opposing positions according to assumptions about "what reproduction is."

Prior to recent advances in reproductive technology, sexual intercourse was the primary precondition to biological reproduction. Sexuality and biological reproduction, although commonly coupled as closely-associated practices, are greatly dissimilar in their meaning, scope, and intention. While heterosexual intercourse is, in most cases, a necessary precondition to biological reproduction, biological reproduction comprises only a sub-set of practices covered by the umbrella "sexuality." While it cannot be denied that reproduction involves a biological component, essentialist and non-essentialist frameworks differ over its importance. From an essentialist perspective, the act of reproduction is viewed in a deterministic fashion whereby women's existence is defined and determined by her reproductive capacity. Women's reproductivity, in this light, is thought of as an innate orientation, an orientation governed by natural laws and biological predispositions. Essentialists reduce the essence of women's existence to her biological reproductivity (or their *capacity* to be biologically reproductive) and reduce biological reproduction to an innate impulse or natural instinct. Motherhood is viewed as a "natural" consequence of an innate "need" for its expression. Proponents of this view represent a wide variety of political opinion, both radical and conservative: sexologists such as, Havelock Ellis, and Edward Carpenter, "sex radicals" such as Emma Goldman and Margaret Sanger, sexual liberation theorists such as Wilhelm Reich, sociobiologists, and moral absolutists all appear to make similar assumptions about the "nature" of reproduction even though they disagree over issues of regulation of sexuality and reproduction.

Non-essentialists argue that although most women share a biological capability to produce a child, social and cultural practices "construct" what essentialism perceives to be a natural given. The social construction of reproduction involves the transformation of a biological potentiality into a set of social and cultural practices governing notions about how reproduction is to take place, how often (if at all), with whom, and under what conditions or circumstances. In this way, non-essentialism rejects the assumption that reproduction is "private" or "personal"; instead "reproduction" and "society" are considered to be coterminous and interdependent variables rather than dichotomous antinomies.

The unitary view of reproduction in which female reproduction is reduced to a single reproductive drive or instinct is "deconstructed" by non-essentialist frameworks. This process of "deconstruction" exposes the variability of the ideological, behaviourial, and cultural contexts of reproduction. Non-essentialism recognizes that there may be as many versions of what reproduction is as there are social and cultural contexts in which the "practice of reproduction" takes place.

Thus, in Weeks' formulation, "the practice of reproduction" central to non-essentialism replaces the "instinct of reproduction" assumed in essentialist frameworks. Reproduction, like sexuality, is constructed, organized, and mediated by the reality of power relations. These relations of power, as Foucault has suggested, are created and maintained through mechanisms and practices related to biological reproduction governed by what Rubin calls the "sex-gender system." Marilyn French, discussing theories of the origin of patriarchy, explains:

> ...the discovery of the male role in procreation must have been of extreme importance to attitudes of matricentric groups. The male role can be interpreted as a controlling one: a "shudder in the loins" that brought ecstasy to a man was all that was required of him to procreate: the woman bore the entire burden after that. Possibly men began to see women not as miraculous bearers of babies but as the soil, as a mere receptacle.... for male seed which by itself engendered the new growth.
>
> Over centuries, perhaps, these ideas led to the emergence of a new value: *the idea of control*.... It [the idea of control] is valued simply because it exists more than for what it accomplishes or creates.[70]

Applying Weeks' Classification of Theoretical Perspectives on Sexuality to Goldman's Views

Drawing on Weeks' taxonomy of sexual theories, Goldman's views on sexuality "fit" Weeks' scheme of categories in the following manner. First, according to Weeks' classification, Goldman is an essentialist. Goldman believed that sexuality possesses an essential essence (specific to each gender) which remained stable and constant regardless of culture, history, class, or race. Assuming that sexuality was a driving instinctual force, rooted in the biology of women and men, Goldman placed sexual expression on a par with other biological "needs" such as those for air, food and water. Her views on sexuality, therefore, fit into Weeks' more specific classification of "naturalist essentialism." That is, sexuality is both an essential and "natural" phenomenon. Goldman's views were predicated on a biological determinism, typical of naturalist essentialist perspectives, as she argued that, in relation to sexuality, the natures of men and women were due to distinct biological predispositions. Goldman's "naturalist" perspective was greatly influenced by the British sexologist, Havelock Ellis, who championed the view that sex was healthy and needed to be more freely expressed.

Goldman's label of naturalist essentialist can be even more fully elucidated using Weeks' taxonomy of theoretical approaches to the *regulation* of sexuality. The naturalist essentialism of Goldman is coupled with a theory of libertarianism, making her, according to Weeks' taxonomy, a libertarian naturalist essentialist. Goldman's libertarian view of the church and the State as oppressive forces in society is joined by a view that sexuality is a healthy and positive force which is distorted by these institutions. While positions of naturalist essentialism expressed by theorists such as Malinowski advocated greater control of the "natural" sex impulse, Goldman's libertarian naturalist essentialism was one based on a belief in the need to "liberate" sexuality from the confines of social institutions and attitudes which inhibited sexual freedom. Goldman, the so-called "sex radical," championed the cause of sexual freedom while ignoring the ways in which sexuality might negatively affect women's lives. In this way, Goldman's uncritical view of sexuality could be perceived as a glorification of "desire," stemming from her essentialist view that sexuality is a product of "nature" and not society.

Summary

Weeks argues that "values and theoretical assumptions about the nature of sex [and reproduction as a sub-set of sexuality] are closely related."[71] Values and theoretical assumptions about sexuality and reproduction, essentialist or non-essentialist, are often outgrowths of more general intellectual or political positions.[72]

Feminist positions on sexuality include those which embrace the moral absolutist position that sex is essentially dangerous and disruptive, those which accept the libertarian position that sex is essentially liberatory and pleasurable, and those which reject the view that sex must be *either* dangerous and disruptive *or* liberatory and pleasurable. This last position, that entails a rejection of both moral absolutism and libertarianism, involves the development of a feminist politics on sex that encourages women to seek sexual pleasure while, at the same time, protecting themselves from sexual danger.[73] The social purity movement of the late nineteenth century, to which Goldman was strongly opposed, represented the view that sex offered danger with little pleasure, thereby limiting women's opportunity and encouragement to explore and expand their sexuality. In contrast, what DuBois and Gordon call the "pro-sex" feminists (e.g., Goldman) of the early twentieth century, "encouraged women to leap, adventurous and carefree, into sexual liaisons, but...failed to offer a critique of the male construction of the sexual experience available to most women."[74] DuBois and Gordon argue that the theory and politics of women's sexuality must be grounded in the real world, recognizing the potential danger sex presents for women while, at the same time, encouraging women to experiment with and explore the limits of their sexuality. Highlighting the dangers for women, contemporary feminist, Lynne Segal, suggests sexual excitement "is generated by, and in the service of, a multitude of needs, not all of them 'nice.'"[75] However, libertarianism is still a strong force. Contemporary feminist, Alice Echols, defends the "radical" traditions of libertarianism, suggesting that the link between "sexual liberation" and "women's liberation" be maintained.[76] Echols argues that the "struggle for sexual pleasure is legitimate and need not imply a callous disregard of sexual danger."[77]

From the point of view of some present-day feminists, a tenable feminist theory of sexuality, then, must recognize both the dangers and the pleasures[78] without, in Echols' words, "foreclosing" on sexuality.[79] A tenable feminist theory, these writers maintain, must also reject the temptation to construct sexuality in a manner which neatly categorizes right and wrong, good and bad, acceptable and unacceptable, liberated and repressed, moral and immoral. In their view, a tenable theory must learn from the moralistic perspectives of both the social purity and libertarian movements, which "condemned those who see sexual behaviour deviated from the standard..."[80] and take a more complex approach to sexuality. The social construction theory of sexuality must acknowledge, as Alice Echols suggests, "the complexities and ambiguities of sexuality."[81] As Jeffrey Weeks argues, sexuality is too difficult and elusive a concept to be compartmentalized neatly in the categories of right or wrong. Instead, Weeks contends, "we need to be alive to its ambivalent and ambiguous qualities, and act accordingly.... Sexual 'choice,' then suggests a recognition of limits as well as possibilities, hazardous paths as much as positive goals."[82]

Goldman's essentialist and libertarian perspective on sexuality and reproduction was one which did not recognize the complexities and ambiguities of sexuality. Instead, Goldman neatly categorized sexuality as positive and liberatory for both men and women, without attending to the ways in which so-called "sexual liberation" could be unequally experienced according to one's gender.

NOTES

1. See Jeffrey Weeks' work, *Sex, Politics and Society*, 2nd ed. (New York: Longman, 1989); *Sexuality* (London and New York: Tavistock Publications, 1986); and *Sexuality and Its Discontents* (London: Routledge and Kegan Paul, 1985).
2. Weeks, *Sex, Politics and Society*, p. 2.
3. Ibid., pp. 1-3.
4. Ibid., p. 198.
5. Malinowski in Weeks, *Sexuality*, p. 24.
6. Bronislaw Malinowski, *Sex, Culture and Myth* (London: Rupert-Hart-Davis, 1956), p. 127.
7. Emile Durkheim, *Education and Sociology* (London: Glencoe, 1956), p. 90.
8. Emile Durkheim, *The Division of Labour in Society*, translated by George Simpson (Glencoe, Ill.: Free Press, 1964), p. 72.
9. Weeks, *Sexuality*, p. 72.
10. Weeks, *Sex, Politics and Society*, p. 3.
11. Weeks, *Sexuality*, p. 24.
12. Weeks, *Sexuality and Its Discontents*, p. 162.
13. Wilhelm Reich, *The Function of the Orgasm: Sex-Economic Problems of Biological Energy* (London: Panther Books, 1972), p. 179.
14. Ibid., p. 231.
15. Ibid., p. 114.
16. Ellen Ross and Rayna Rapp, "Sex and Society: A Research Note from Social History and Anthropology," in Christine Stansell, Ann Snitow and Sharon Thompson, eds., *Powers of Desire: The Politics of Sexuality* (New York: Monthly Review Press, 1983), p. 68.
17. Weeks, *Sexuality*, p. 25.
18. Ross and Rapp, in *Powers of Desire: The Politics of Sexuality*, p. 68.
19. Ibid., p. 109.
20. Weeks, *Sexuality*, p. 25.
21. Ibid., p. 53.

22. Carol S. Vance, "Pleasure and Danger: Toward a Politics of Sexuality," in *Pleasure and Danger: Exploring Female Sexuality*, edited by Carole S. Vance (Boston and London: Routledge and Kegan Paul, 1984), p. 17.
23. Weeks, *Sexuality*, p. 16.
24. Ibid., p. 16.
25. Weeks, *Sex, Politics and Society*, p. 3.
26. Michel Foucault, *The History of Sexuality*, Vol. I, translated by Robert Hurley (London: Allen Lane, 1979), p. 105.
27. Ibid., p. 153.
28. J.H. Gagnon and William Simon, *Sexual Conduct: The Sources of Sexuality* (London: Hutchinson, 1973), p. 26.
29. Ibid., p. 45.
30. Weeks, *Sex, Politics and Society*, p. 6.
31. Ibid., p. 154.
32. Ibid.
33. Weeks, *Sexuality*, p. 100.
34. Ibid., pp. 100-105; Weeks, *Sexuality and Its Discontents*, pp. 55-56.
35. Weeks, *Sexuality*, p. 100.
36. Ibid.
37. Ibid.
38. Ibid., pp. 100-101.
39. Ibid., p. 101.
40. Ibid.
41. Weeks, *Sexuality and Its Discontents*, p. 56.
42. Ibid.
43. Ibid.
44. Ross and Rapp, "Sex and Society: A Research Note from Social History and Anthropology," p. 68.
45. Weeks, *Sexuality and Its Discontents*, p. 56.
46. Weeks, *Sexuality*, p. 101; Weeks, *Sexuality and Its Discontents*, p. 55.
47. Weeks, *Sexuality*, p. 104.
48. Havelock Ellis, *Sex in Relation to Society: Studies in the Psychology of Sex*, Vol. VI (London: Heinemann, 1946), p. 183.
49. Weeks, *Sexuality*, p. 104.
50. Ibid.
51. Angela Carter, quoted in Rosalind Coward, *Female Desire: Women's Sexuality Today* (London: Paladin, 1984), pp. 247-248.
52. Ross and Rapp, "Sex and Society: A Research Note from Social History and Anthropology," p. 53.
53. Ibid., p. 68.
54. Weeks, *Sexuality and Its Discontents*, p. 56.
55. Ibid.
56. Ibid.
57. Ibid.
58. Ibid., p. 57.
59. Michael Ignatieff, *The Needs of Strangers* (London: Chatto and Windus, 1984), p. 135.
60. Ibid.
61. Weeks, *Sexuality*, pp. 27-31; Ross and Rapp, "Sex and Society: A Research Note from Social History and Anthropology," pp. 54-67.
62. Weeks, *Sexuality*, p. 45.
63. Ibid.
64. Gayle Rubin, "The Traffic in Women: Notes on the 'Political Economy' of Sex," in Rayna R. Reiter, ed., *Toward an Anthropology of Women* (New York: Monthly Review Press, 1975), pp. 175-180.
65. Ibid.
66. Ibid.

67. Carole S. Vance, "Gender Systems, Ideology, and Sex Research," in *Pleasure and Danger*, edited by Carole S. Vance (Boston and London: Routledge and Kegan Paul, 1984), p. 372.
68. Weeks, *Sex, Politics and Society*, p. 7.
69. Ellen Carol Du Bois and Linda Gordon, "Seeking Ecstasy on the Battlefield: Danger and Pleasure in Nineteenth Century Feminist Thought," *Feminist Studies*, 9 (Spring 1983), p. 71.
70. Marilyn French, *Beyond Power: On Women, Men and Morals* (London: Abacus, 1986), p. 50.
71. Weeks, *Sexuality*, p. 101.
72. Bernard Berelson, "Population Policy: Personal Notes," *Population Studies*, 24 (1971), p. 175.
73. DuBois and Gordon, "Seeking Ecstasy on the Battlefield: Danger and Pleasure in Nineteenth Century Feminist Thought," p. 31.
74. Ibid.
75. Lynne Segal, "Sensual Uncertainty, Or Why the Clitoris is Not Enough," in Sue Cartledge and Joanna Ryan, eds., *Sex and Love: New Thoughts on Old Contradictions* (London: The Women's Press, 1983), p. 45.
76. Alice Echols, "The Taming of the Id: Feminist Sexual Politics, 1968-83," in Carole S. Vance, ed., *Pleasure and Danger* (Boston and London: Routledge and Kegan Paul, 1984), p. 66.
77. Ibid.
78. DuBois and Gordon, "Seeking Ecstasy on the Battlefield: Danger and Pleasure in Nineteenth Century Feminist Thought."
79. Echols, "The Taming of the Id: Feminist Sexual Politics, 1968-83."
80. DuBois and Gordon, "Seeking Ecstasy on the Battlefield: Danger and Pleasure in Nineteenth Century Feminist Thought," p. 32.
81. Echols, "The Taming of the Id: Feminist Sexual Politics, 1968-83," p. 66.
82. Weeks, *Sexuality*, p. 118.

CHAPTER 5

Goldman and the Sexologists

The deference and reverence with which Goldman viewed the sexologists—Freud and Havelock Ellis in particular— reflected her unconditional and uncritical acceptance of their theories. It would not be unfair to suggest that Goldman perceived the sexologists to be virtual icons, beyond and above criticism. Because sexology, in Goldman's view, had taken sex out of the closet and into the domain of open conversation, the messengers and their theories were to be treated with the utmost deference and respect. Emma Goldman's construction of sexuality and reproduction was shaped, in a fundamental way, by the discourse of sexology. This chapter will discuss the discursive shaping of Goldman's ideas which lead to her construction of a gender-bound and essentialist view of sexuality.

Goldman's frequent and generic use of the concept "instinct" was shaped by the sexologists' general usage of the term. Although Ellis most frequently employed the concept "impulse" and Freud "the drive," the concept of "instinct" filled the gap caused by inadequate explanations of the ultimate nature of impulses and drives.[1] Jeffrey Weeks has described the dominant view of instincts up to the 1920s as one which suggested instincts "laid down the basic and permanent ends of human activity, providing the fundamental 'cravings,' the persistently recurring impulses, common to all members of the species, which were heritable and to which the different behaviour patterns were a response."[2] Weeks notes that Darwin's *The Descent of Man* (1871), in which aesthetic and erotic responses are said to ensure selection, led sexologists such as Havelock Ellis to theorize on the complexity of the sexual instinct and its inclusion of both biological and psychological factors. This gave rise on the part of some sexologists "to a pansexualist vision where sex became the sole explanatory force for social phenomena."[3]

Havelock Ellis

In reviewing the history of the writings of sexuality in America and the influence of various sexologists, historians John D'Emilio and Estelle Freedman observe that although Freud had a more enduring influence, "in the short run the writings of the English sexologist Havelock Ellis had a greater impact."[4] Phyllis Grosskurth, Ellis's biographer, has described him as "one of the seminal figures responsible for the creation of modern sensibility,"[5] while Weeks considers Ellis's work to be "one of the springs from which the broad stream of sexual liberalism has flowed with apparent ease."[6] Sheila Jeffreys, in contrast, refers to what she considers the "mythology" surrounding Ellis's reputation:

> As the mythology of the sexual revolution was created, Ellis was given the reputation of having attacked and made inroads into puritan sexual morality of the nineteenth century, for having proclaimed that sex was good and enjoyable, for having destroyed the myth of woman's sexual anaesthesia and for having established her right to pleasure.[7]

According to D'Emilio and Freedman, Ellis believed sex to be the driving force behind all civilization and central to individual expression and satisfaction.[8] Consequently, Ellis defended (some, but not all) sexual variations or patterns of sexual expression which had previously been condemned. In the preface to the sixth volume of *Studies in the Psychology of Sex*, Ellis makes his primary argument that "sex lies at the root of life, and we can never learn to reverence life until we know how to understand sex."[9] Operating on the premise that society did not need "more restraint, but more passion," Ellis advocated pre-marital sexual experimentation and masturbation as a form of relaxation; as well, he fervently defended male homosexual rights.[10] Masturbation was viewed by Ellis as a prelude or experimental preparation for sexual relationships. Male homosexuality was a congenital condition "as natural for its practitioners as heterosexual relations were for the majority."[11]

Marriage, according to Ellis, was one of the great crimes perpetrated by religion against humanity, locking men and women into frequently passionless unions with little or no opportunity for escape. Ellis favoured a "companionate" union or ethical union between partners and advocated legal marriage only when children were involved.[12] Ellis's proposals on marriage advocated unions which are flexible enough to accommodate outside emotional and sexual interests. Ellis argued that the flexibility of marriage, and, at the same time, the stability of marriage were necessary as men and women were both "monogamic" and "polysexual,"[13] requiring sexual variety as well as familiarity.

Ellis claimed to have realized the significance of sexual matters early in his life. In the preface to the sixth volume of *Studies in the Psychology of Sex* he states:

> The origin of these *Studies* dates from many years back. As a youth I was faced, as others are, by the problem of sex. Living partly in an Australian city where the ways of life were plainly seen, partly in the solitude of the bush, I was free both to contemplate and to meditate on many things. A resolve slowly grew up within me: one main part of my life-work should be to make clear the problems of sex.[14]

A few sentences later, Ellis writes:

> In this particular field the evil of ignorance is magnified by our efforts to suppress that which never can be suppressed, though in the effort of suppression it may become perverted.[15]

In the first essay of the sixth volume of *Studies*, Ellis addresses the topic of human modesty in such a way as to "naturalize" the relations between the sexes as those between the pursuer (male) and the pursued (female). Ellis believed that modesty was rooted in the sexual periodicity of the female and was an inevitable by product of the "natural aggressiveness" of men in sexual relationships. Ellis argued that female modesty or innocence was an "instinctive demand" made by the male on the female; however, Ellis added, there was no such instinctive demand by women for the innocence of men.[16] "In the nature of things," Ellis exhorts, "this could not be" as "such emotion is required for properly playing the part of the pursued; it is by no means an added attraction on the part of the pursuer."[17]

Ellis's construction of male as pursuer and female as the pursued is grounded in a sexual paradigm in which sex-linked behaviour is biologically or evolutionally mandated. Attributing female modesty to an unconscious desire to engage in sexual relations, Ellis suggests that seeming female reluctance is really not reluctance at all. Rather, female modesty or reluctance is a sign to the male that she is interested in his advances. Ellis noted that his observation of female timidity and modesty had previously been popularized in the form of proverbs, such as "The girl who blushes most, is most disposed to the pleasures of love"; "Do as the lasses do—say no, but take it"; and the Welsh saying "The more prudish the more unchaste."[18]

As the above assertions reveal, Ellis was in many respects a man of his time, and not capable of fully casting off or rising above contemporary assumptions and prejudices; for his views on woman's "modesty" reinforced the right of men to, at best, "seduce" her and, at worst, overtake her against her will. In essence, Ellis's analysis validated the belief that a woman's "no" actually meant "yes."

Although Ellis rejected the view of female passionlessness, he maintained that woman's passivity and lack of initiative in sexual matters required an aggressive and insistent stance on the part of the male.

This "violent misogyny,"[19] which Weeks notes was inherent in the sexologists' message, is displayed unabashedly in Ellis's work on female arousal and, correspondingly, in his work on the male role in ensuring her arousal. For example, in the third volume of *Studies in the Psychology of Sex,* the sexual impulse is discussed in relation to pain. Here Ellis advocates female bondage as a way to heighten sexual excitement, claiming that any restriction on muscular activity heightens the woman's state of excitement. A dichotomous view of sexual need, pleasure, and response based on gender is exemplified in Ellis's discussion of the infliction of pain during sexual activity. Predictably, one might argue, Ellis suggests it is "normal" for men to enjoy inflicting pain upon their sexual partners, just as it is "certainly normal" for women to enjoy having the pain inflicted upon them:

> While in men it is possible to trace a tendency to inflict pain, or the simulation of pain, on the women they love, it is still easier to trace in women a delight in experiencing physical pain when inflicted by a lover, and an eagerness to accept submission to his will. Such a tendency is certainly normal.[20]

Ellis "normalized" male dominance and female subjugation in heterosexual relations claiming that women enjoy having pain inflicted upon them, citing cases of wife battering in Russia, Hungary, South America and England as well as cases of French prostitutes who were abused by their pimps.

The implications of Ellis's position of female pleasure and its conduit pain, are clearly anti-woman, despite Ellis's insistence that he was a "feminist." Contemporary feminist, Sheila Jeffreys, has argued that Ellis's position on female sexuality served to undermine feminist campaigns against male sexual abuse of women and children. Social purity campaigners challenged Ellis's conception of sexuality as they lobbied for greater protection of women and children at the hands of men. Ellis's biological and evolutionary model, which placed sexual behaviour and gender differences in the realm of "nature," was not unlike medical models of his day. However, Ellis claimed that his view that women enjoyed receiving pain while men enjoyed inflicting pain was *not* incompatible with his advocacy of women's emancipation. Appearing sensitive to the charges of female subjection, Ellis wrote:

I am well aware that in thus asserting a certain tendency in women to delight in suffering pain—however careful and qualified in the position I have taken—many estimable people will cry out that I am degrading a whole sex and generally supporting the subjection of women... I would point out to those who would deprecate the influence of such facts in relation to social progress that nothing is gained by regarding women as simply men of smaller growth. They are not so; they have the laws of their own nature; their development must be along their own lines and not along masculine lines.[21]

According to the logic of Ellis's argument, woman's behaviour is determined by the "laws of her nature" and, rape and sexual abuse by male partners are the consequences of that "nature." If women are victims, their victimization is due to their nature as well as to that of those who engage in their victimization. Ellis used this logic to explain how the cry of rape was employed as a cover to conceal women's voluntary sexual activity:

There can be little doubt that the plea of force is very frequently seized upon by women as the easiest available weapon or defence when her connection had been revealed. She has been so permeated by the current notion that no "respectable" woman can possibly have any sexual impulses of her own to gratify that, in order to screen what she feels to be regarded as an utterly shameful and wicked, as well as foolish, act, she declares it never took place by her own will at all.[22]

Although Ellis considered himself a champion of woman's expression and freedom as he strived to alter the vision of female "respectability" by suggesting that women, as well as men, were passionate, he did nothing to address the abuses that women would encounter at the hands of men. For Ellis, covert female passion and overt male aggression went hand-in-hand.

Like Emma Goldman, Havelock Ellis was influenced by the eugenic movements during this time. In *The Task of Social Hygiene* (1913) Ellis pointed to the ways in which "the race" would become regenerated and details the concomitant responsibilities of each gender. While Ellis advocated women's emancipation, the form that this emancipation would take was grounded in biological, evolutionary and eugenic imperatives. As a result, Ellis's platform has been interpreted as anti-feminist because of its glorification of motherhood and the accomplishment of inherent biological determinism.[23] While Goldman's view of the sexes, and their placement in the social world, rejected the philosophy of separate spheres, Ellis's view of sexual innatism necessitated separate placement of women and men, according to their biological differences. In *Studies in the Psychology of Sex,* Ellis concludes:

> Woman's special sphere is the bearing and the rearing of children, with the case of human life in the home. Man's primary sphere remains the exploration of life outside the home, in industry and inventions and the cultivation of the arts.[24]

Despite the difference of opinion over the notion of separate spheres, Goldman did view Ellis's ideas as emancipatory as she too believed that women's freedom occurred through the fulfilment of their biological "instincts."

The "woman movement," according to Ellis, had the potential of contributing to the "evolution of a super-mankind" since women had ultimate control over the regeneration of the race. Ellis placed woman's contribution to society firmly in the realm of her biological, reproductive and care-giving powers, acknowledging that it was she who was responsible for "breeding":

> The breeding of men lies largely in the hands of women. That is why the question of Eugenics is to a great extent one with the woman question. The realisation of eugenics in our social life can be attained with the realisa-

tion of the woman movement in its latest and completest phase as an enlightened culture of motherhood, in all that motherhood involves alike on the physical and psychic sides.[25]

The natural progression of the "woman movement," Ellis argued, leads women toward child-bearing and child-rearing within an "enlightened culture of motherhood." The enlightened culture of motherhood would make women *more* conscious of her reproductive role and more discerning and selective in her reproductive and child-rearing functions. Helping to create a "selectively bred race," women's reproductive power would no longer be considered a haphazard or uncalculated activity, but rather a consciously mediated act with social consequences.

Because of woman's biological nature, Ellis believed that her "equality" must take a particular form; a form which Sheila Jeffreys argues could be called "complementarity, but hardly equality."[26] Pregnancy, child-bearing, lactation and care-giving, argued Ellis, rendered women economically dependent for a considerable period of their lives.[27] In addition, Ellis asserted that men and women are not intellectual equals. To support these claims, Ellis referenced the animal kingdom, stating that among "animals which live in herds under the guidance of a leader, this leader is nearly always a male; there are few exceptions."[28]

If men and women were not to be economic or intellectual equals, what form did Ellis's notion of equality take? To this question Ellis would respond: "It is necessary to remember that the kind of equality of the sexes towards which this change of status is leading, is social equality—that is, equality of freedom."[29] Because women were, in Ellis's view, "the mothers of the race" and were not like men and would *never* be like men, Ellis created, in Sheila Jeffrey's opinion, a "strange sort of equality...in which women were always to be followers and men leaders."[30] Jeffreys concludes that what Ellis wanted for women was "equivalence," not equality.[31]

Similar to Swedish feminist, Ellen Key, in his perspective on motherhood and separate spheres,[32] Ellis found it absurd that women should engage in the same education, same occupations and same sports as men. Since men and women were biologically different their social roles should be different and the spheres in which each performed these roles should be separate.[33] In his introduction to Key's *The Woman Movement*, Ellis supported Key's form of feminism which held that men and women's work should not be identical, but rather complementary.

For Ellis the concept of "separate spheres" was deeply rooted in biology and he opposed forms of feminism which failed to recognize the biological foundation of separate roles and spheres for men and women. While denouncing the myth of women's inferiority and female subjection to male interests, Ellis's brand of "feminism" granted women "equality" provided she remained in her own sphere, performing her biologically-mandated role.

Ellis argued that woman's most significant contribution would be to "breed a firmly-fibred, clean-minded, and self-reliant race of manly men and womanly women."[34] Advances in the status for women should be based not on what would be good for women as *human beings,* but rather what would be good for them as *women.* He criticized the women's rights reformers who blurred the social distinctions between men and women and emphasized their common human rights:

> Those who propagandised this now rather antiquated notion of the "equality" of the sexes, in the sense of resemblance if not identity, were justified in so far as they were protesting against that superstition of the inferiority of women which had proved so influential, and, as many of us think, so mischievous in its applications within the social sphere. But the banner of Equality under which they fought, while a wholesome and necessary assertion in the social and political realms, had no biological foundation.[35]

Ellis clearly fits Week's description as one who attempted to uncover "animal nature"[36] in human activity. Despite Ellis's reputation as a "seminal figure" in the movement towards sexual liberalism,[37] in actuality, his ideas reinforced and entrenched the placement of female sexuality in a biologically-determined framework. What is more, although he provided cross-cultural examples of sexual variation, he failed to regard "culture" as being, at least, partially responsible for the sexual "nature" of women. Although Ellis spoke about previously unmentionable and/or inconceivable topics such as female passion, autoeroticism, and "polysexual" activity, he did nothing to dismantle the paradigm of "biology as destiny" for women. If anything, as Sheila Jeffreys argues, Ellis's ideas made women more vulnerable to abuse, popularizing notions which had been "staple motifs of men's pornography for centuries."[38]

Freud

In 1895, Emma Goldman was first introduced to the work of Sigmund Freud in Vienna, prior to his visit and subsequent publication in America.[39] A number of years after Emma Goldman's attendance at Freud's lecture in Vienna, America hosted his visit. In 1909, Sigmund Freud introduced his ideas to an audience of American intellectuals and professionals at Clark University in Worcester, Massachusetts.[40] Goldman also attended this lecture. Shortly after, Freud was translated and published in America.

His writings on sexuality, and its social significance, made a lasting impression on Goldman. The significance of "instinct," to which Goldman became acquainted through attending Freud's lecture, became an organizing principle of Goldman's conception of anarchism. Freud's usage of the concept was psychosexually derived, while Goldman used the concept in a characteristically less precise and more generic manner.

In Freud's view, the sexual instinct was "plastic and labile";[41] the "sexual instinct" and the "sexual object" were not conceptualized as inextricably connected, or in Freud's words "merely soldered together," but rather independent of one another. Freud argued that it "seems probably that the sexual instinct is in the first instance independent of its object; nor is its origin likely to be due to its object's attraction."[42]

In 1910, Freud added a footnote to his speculations regarding the independence of the sexual instinct, suggesting that a major difference existed between the "erotic life of antiquity" and that of contemporary times. He suggested that the ancients laid less stress on the object, emphasizing the instinct itself. In contemporary times, Freud notes, "we despise the instinct itself, and find excuses for it only in the merits of the object."[43]

Freud also discussed sexual instinct in terms of its perversions and gender-related propensities, claiming an element of aggressiveness in males. Freud also claimed that sexual instinct was different for men and women.

In the case of bisexuality, Freud connected the opposites—masculinity and femininity—calling the connection one which often has to be replaced in psychoanalysis by that between "activity and passivity."[44] The human instinct, then, was "gender-typed" by Freud's theory of psychoanalysis, setting in place assumptions about passivity and activity and their assignment to a particular gender.

Freud's definition of instinct possessed the dynamic of the "unconscious," which Jeffrey Weeks considers Freud's "major object of study and greatest discovery."[45] In his seminal work *Three Essays on the Theory of Sexuality* (1905), Freud states that the sexual drive can be provisionally "understood as the physical representation of an endosomatic, continuously flowing source of stimulation....The concept of instinct is thus one of those lying on the frontier between the mental and the physical."[46] In Jeffrey Weeks' interpretation, "...what is repressed in the formations of the unconscious is not biological instinct but wishes/desires, mental representations relating to physical possibilities."[47]

While the complexities of Freud's theories were accessible to those who might be interested in pursuing them, the "abridged" and more easily digested version of his ideas was being popularized by the mass media.[48] As D'Emilio and Freedman suggest, the complexities and subtleties of Freud's theories "took a backseat to the

concepts that infiltrated the middle-class imagination: the notion of
infantile sexuality, the drama of sexual conflict in the family, the case
histories of female patients who seemed to suffer from the denials of
their sexual desires, the idea that the sexual instinct permeated
human life and might change the course of civilization."[49] D'Emilio
and Freedman state that most importantly "Americans absorbed a
version of Freudianism that presented the impulse as an insistent
force demanding expression."[50]

In that period, Freudianism was being interpreted by jour-
nalists in a popularized and abridged form, sending the American
public the message that sexual impulses are "normal" and require
appropriate expression. One such message, found in *Good
Housekeeping*, conveyed the idea of the centrality of sex to human
existence:

> The urge is there and whether the individual desires or
> not, it always manifests itself....If it gets its yearning it is
> as contented as a nursing infant. If it does not, beware! It
> will never be stopped except with satisfaction.[51]

Many erroneous interpretations were drawn from Freud's
work,[52] the most important being that, Freud, the sex liberator,
believed society could be changed by the freeing of the sexual impulse. Instead, as Linda Gordon argues, Freud's work on civilization
suggests that human society's evolution will have a repressive effect
on sexuality; there will be a growing opposition between "civilization" and the free expression of sexual instincts.[53] As Steven Marcus
argues, Freud expressed the relationship as an inverse relation between "civilization and the free development of sexuality, of which
the consequences can be followed far into the structure of our existence."[54] Freud proposed that as a society undergoes what he called a
"process of human cultural development," each individual recapitu-
lates this development in his or her "evolution." As sex becomes the
"weak spot" in civilized societies, it often remains the "weak spot"
for individuals who have gone through the individual counterpart
to human cultural development. Freud wrote:

But many people are abnormal in their sexual life who in every other respect approximate to the average, and have, along with the rest, passed through the process of human cultural development, in which sexuality remains the weak spot.[55]

Shortly after 1909, Freud was viewed as the popularizer of the notion of infantile and childhood sexuality in North America.[56] His concept of "sexual instinct" applied to the adults of the society but, also, to those who had been deemed "pure" by virtue of their alleged asexuality. Freud begins his essay "Infantile Sexuality" by arguing that "not a single author has clearly recognized the regular existence of a sexual instinct in childhood."[57] The Victorian vision of the innocence and purity of childhood was grounded largely in the belief in the asexuality of children. Children, supposedly lacking the bodily drives which characterized the "basic" components of adult life, were portrayed in art, music, and literature as inhabitants of a sacred preserve of innocence.

According to Freud, the evolution of the human species was analogous to the evolution of an individual life. In Freud's conceptualization of evolution, the primeval period of the species and the childhood of the individual were paralleled. The evolution of infantile sexuality would produce the possible outcomes of perversion, neurosis or normal sexual life.[58] Freud found healthy manifestations of infantile sexuality in such behaviour as nursing and thumb-sucking:

We found it a regrettable thing that the existence of the sexual instinct in childhood has been denied and that the sexual manifestations not infrequently to be observed in children have been described as irregularities. It seemed to us on the contrary that children bring germs of sexual activity with them into the world, that they already enjoy sexual satisfaction when they begin to take nourishment and that they persistently seek to repeat the experience in the familiar activity of "thumb-sucking."[59]

Freud brought out of the closet, for public scrutiny, the troublesome manifestations of the sexual instinct which he called "the sexual aberrations." Close to, yet distinct from his work on the aberrations, Freud wrote an essay on "the Sexual Instinct in Neurotics" in which he outlined the damaging effects of mental repression on mental and physical health. The common diagnosis of hysteria, applied to Goldman along with hundreds of other women, was characterized by Freud as a condition in which an individual is considered "excessively civilized." Hysterics exhibit an "intensification of resistance against the sexual instinct" which co-exists with an "exaggerated sexual craving,"[60] eventually falling ill:

> Between the pressure of the instinct and his antagonism
> to sexuality, illness offers him a way to escape. It does not
> solve his conflict, but seeks to evade it by transforming
> his libidinal impulses into symptoms.[61]

Freud's so-called provocative, anti-establishment and "anti-puritan" claims were received by Goldman as a legitimization and explanation of her view of sexuality as well as a source of political justification for the inclusion of "instinct" in anarchist theory.[62]

The Influence of the Sexologists on Goldman

In a 1923 letter to the homosexual rights activist, Magnus Hirschfeld, Goldman chronicled her intellectual appreciation of the sexologists specifically naming Ellis, as well as Richard Krafft-Ebing and Edward Carpenter.[63] Goldman confessed that before becoming acquainted with the works of the sexologists, she knew little about "sexual psychology."

Goldman stated her travels in Europe in 1895 provided a more "intellectual" appreciation of sexuality:

> Later I came to Europe, where I became acquainted with
> the works of Havelock Ellis, Krafft-Ebing and Carpenter
> and some others, which made me fully aware of the crime

which has been perpetrated on Oscar Wilde and his kind. From then on I defended in the spoken and written word those whose entire nature is different in regard to sexual feelings and needs.[64]

Goldman's initial reaction to the work of Ellis, Krafft-Ebing and Carpenter was not unlike that she exhibited toward Freud. In her autobiography, Goldman recalls having been awed by Sigmund Freud, and feeling that he had led her out of a dark cellar into broad daylight.[65] The notion of sex repression had a great impact on Goldman who praised Freud for helping her understand the significance of her own sexual needs:

He helped me to understand myself, my own needs; and I also realized that only people of depraved minds could impugn the motives or find impure so great and fine a personality as Freud.[66]

Not until Goldman's return from Russia in 1921 did she have the opportunity to meet face-to-face with the British sexologists Ellis and Carpenter.[67] Jeffrey Weeks, in *Sex, Politics and Society*, noted that Edward Carpenter and Havelock Ellis were the first two people Goldman chose to see after her arrival in England. The British feminists, whom Weeks' labels the "respectable suffragists," were not attracted to the two sexologists. British women reformers such as Millicent Fawcett, who were "models of late-Victorian rectitude with regard to sexual mores," did not cultivate the company of the sex radicals, rejecting particularly, but not solely, their views on homosexuality.[68]

With awe and the utmost admiration, Emma Goldman recalls her meetings with Havelock Ellis and Edward Carpenter, which, in Goldman's words, "stood out as the fulfilment of a wish cherished for a quarter of a century."[69] This meant Goldman had been reading Ellis and Carpenter since 1899. As if to protect herself from charges of hero-worship or superficiality, Goldman commented that: "Not that I learned to know them [the sexologists] better through our

fleeting personal contact than I had through their works."[70]
Goldman wanted to make it clear that she was a critical student of
sexology, not just an admirer of its key personalities. Of her meeting
with Havelock Ellis, Emma recalled:

> If I had lived near him for years, I should not have real-
> ized better the oneness of the man with life's labours, so
> expressive of his unique personality and lofty vision was
> every line that had spoken to me out of the pages of his
> liberating work.[71]

Goldman's recollections of her meeting with Carpenter were
equally glowing, as she suggested her sexologist idol possessed "the
wisdom of the sage":

> My visit with Edward Carpenter lasted the greater part of
> an afternoon in his modest cottage at Guildford. He was
> nearly eighty, frail and feeble…. I attempted to tell him
> how much his books meant to me—*Towards Democracy,
> Angel Wings, Walt Whitman*. He stopped me, gently put-
> ting his hand over mine. Instead I should rather tell him
> about Alexander Berkman, he said.[72]

Affectionately and admiringly, Goldman reflects upon her summer of 1924: "Havelock Ellis and Edward Carpenter! My summer
was indeed enriched by these two grand seigneurs of intellect and
heart."[73]

In a society in which people exhibited, in Goldman's words,
"moral spasms" at the mere mention of sex, the courageous acts of
the sexologists publicly not only drew Goldman's attention but also
solidified her support and admiration. Freud, Ellis, and Carpenter
not only provided Goldman with "evidence" that her own passion
and desires were significant and acceptable, but also helped shape
her view of anarchism—a view which in many instances clashed
with those of her fellow anarchists because of her inclusion of the
"sex question" as essential. Goldman clearly viewed Freud, Ellis and

Carpenter as kindred spirits, intellectual mentors, and potential messiahs to the about-to-be-awakened sexual public.

Jeffreys maintains that despite the perceived liberatory message of the sexologists' work, their ideas were directly at variance with those of the feminists involved in the campaign to "challenge the construction of male sexuality."[74] Goldman was not among this group of feminists who sought to "challenge the construction of male sexuality." Although highly critical of the *results* of male sexuality, as manifested for example in frequent and unwanted pregnancies, Goldman did not blame men for this. Rather, she blamed a culture which she considered "puritanical" and repressive in its outlook towards sexuality—a culture that would not recognize sexuality's centrality to human well-being and did not provide the support and climate necessary for its free expression. As Goldman's feminism was subsumed within her anarchism, and not the reverse, feminist considerations, if not consistent with her anarchist considerations, often appear to receive secondary attention. Her position on the struggle for birth control, for example, produced the admission that her primary commitment was to the anarchist cause, and *not* to the birth control campaign.[75]

D'Emilio and Freedman state that the "significance of Freud, Ellis and other twentieth-century theorists involved more than their advocacy of sexual expression. The shift from a philosophy of continence to one that encouraged indulgence was but one aspect of a larger reorientation that was investing sexuality with a profoundly new importance."[76] Sexuality was being transferred from the realm of the ultraprivate to the realm of the social where its significance had been redefined.

The "pansexualist vision" held by the sexologists to a great extent shaped Goldman's vision of sexuality. The undeconstructed, undemarcated, all-encompassing, non-specific use of the concept "instinct" marks, in Goldman's work, her fluid and unconfined vision of the forces of sexuality. The pansexualist vision, as mentioned in the preceding chapter, is one in which the significance of "the instinct" is so pervasive that all social phenomena gain their definition and their potential for change through sexual means. For example, Goldman viewed "puritanism" and religion as forces which repressed and constrained sexuality. Recognizing the legitimacy and acceptability of sexuality would result in a transformation of those institutions which had previously denied free expression of "the instinct." When Goldman philosophizes "true emancipation...begins in Woman's Soul," the soul represents a component of her pansexualist vision, rather than a compartmentalized unit whose focus is strictly spiritual rather than sexual or physical. The pansexualist conception of sexuality influenced the shape of Goldman's theory of anarchism, in which she amalgamates the economic and structural components (i.e., Kropotkin's vision of mutual aid) and the psychological components in which sex plays an integral role. The eventual publication and popularization of the sexologists' work in America were most probably of great satisfaction to Goldman because she had been engaged for years in serious discussions and disagreements with her fellow anarchists over the importance of the "sex question." Kropotkin, as stated in chapter one, found Goldman "too loose" and too keen to include matters of sexual importance in her anarchist framework.[77]

Goldman's fellow anarchists, most of whom were male, failed to see how sexuality fit into a theory which was primarily a "political" one; they failed to see why sexuality, independent or dependent of the theory of anarchism, should be granted such an elevated level of significance.[78] Some of her fellow male anarchists felt sex was a private activity; to make it a public issue was not only unnecessary but politically detrimental. Other American "radicals" did much to publicize the work of the sexologists. D'Emilio and Freedman attribute the "bohemian radicals"—a category which included individuals such as Goldman, Margaret Sanger, Hutchins Hapgood, Floyd Dell, Gladys Oaks, Bill Haywood, John Reed, and Alexander Berkman—as playing a critical role in "pulling America into a modern sexual era."[79] D'Emilio and Freedman explain:

> They were few in number, but their work as novelists, playwrights, poets and journalists guaranteed that in some form the ideas they espoused—of Ellis, Freud, Key

and Carpenter—would reach a larger audience. If Americans were not quite ready to abandon marriage, many were prepared to accept revised notions of female sexuality and to reassess the place that sexual expression held in a happy life.[80]

Summary

Goldman refused to separate the personal from the political; sexual freedom was essential to her theory of anarchism. The sexologists' message inspired her, shaped her beliefs in the legitimacy of sexuality as a central component of anarchism, and validated her own sexual desires.

In her enthusiasm for the message of the sexologists, Goldman "bought into" their sexist, phallocentric assumptions. While the sexologists, and Goldman under their influence, attempted to advance the cause of sexual freedom, they paradoxically tightened "the grip of the system,"[81] pathologizing, as will be discussed in the next chapter, behaviours such as female homosexuality. Jeffrey Weeks explains:

> The founders of sexology…constructed a unitary model of sexuality from which it has been difficult to escape. On the one hand, we are offered a norm of behaviour, which is heterosexual, procreative and largely male…. On the other hand, there is an ever-growing catalogue of perversions, deviations, paraphilias…which inevitably marginalizes and in the last resort pathologizes other sexualities.[82]

NOTES

1. Jeffrey Weeks, *Sexuality and Its Discontents* (London: Routledge and Kegan Paul, 1985), p. 83.
2. Ibid.
3. Ibid. The pansexualist vision was one which took sex far beyond a procreation framework to one in which sex explained individual and social well-being.

4. John D'Emilio and Estelle Freedman, *Intimate Matters: A History of Sexuality in America* (New York: Harper and Row, 1988), p. 221.
5. Phyllis Grosskurth, *Havelock Ellis: A Biography* (New York: Alfred A. Knopf, 1980), p. xv.
6. Jeffrey Weeks, *Sexuality and Its Discontents*, p.142.
7. Sheila Jeffreys, *The Spinster and Her Enemies: Feminism and Sexuality 1880-1930* (London: Pandora, 1985), p. 129.
8. Ellis was noted primarily for his six-volume work, *Studies in the Psychology of Sex.*, published between 1897 and 1910. The volumes included: *The Evolution of Modesty, The Phenomena of Sexual Periodicity and Auto-eroticism; Sexual Inversion; Analysis of the Sexual Impulse; Sexual Selection in Man; Erotic Symbolism; The Mechanism of Detumescence; The Psychic State of Pregnancy;* and *Sex in Relation to Society.*
9. Havelock Ellis, *Studies in the Psychology of Sex*, Vol. VI: *Sex in Relation to Society* (London: Heinemann, 1910), p. vi.
10. D'Emilio and Freedman, *Intimate Matters: A History of Sexuality in America*, p. 224.
11. Jeffrey Weeks, *Sex, Politics and Society*, 2nd ed. (New York: Longman, 1989), p. 151.
12. Ibid.
13. Ibid.
14. Ellis, *Studies in the Psychology of Sex*, Vol. VI: *Sex in Relation to Society*, p. iii.
15. Ibid.
16. Ibid., p. 44.
17. Ibid., pp. 44-45.
18. Ibid., p. 46.
19. Weeks, *Sexuality and Its Discontents*, p. 95.
20. Havelock Ellis, *Studies in the Psychology of Sex*, Vol. III: *Love and Pain* (Philadelphia: F. A. Davis Company, 1903), p. 20.
21. Ibid., p. 93.
22. Ibid., p. 226.
23. Jeffreys, *The Spinster and Her Enemies*, p. 134.
24. Ellis, in Jeffreys, *The Spinster and Her Enemies: Feminism and Sexuality 1880-1930*, p. 129.
25. Ellis, *The Task of Social Hygiene*, p. 46.
26. Jeffreys, *The Spinster and Her Enemies*, p. 135.
27. Ellis, *The Task of Social Hygiene*, p. 63.
28. Ibid.
29. Ibid.
30. Jeffreys, *The Spinster and Her Enemies*, p. 135.
31. Ibid.
32. Ellen Key, *The Woman Movement*, trans. by Mamah Bouton Borthwick (New York: G.P. Putnam's Sons; London: The Knickerbocker Press, 1912), p. 218.
33. Havelock Ellis, *Sex in Relation to Society; Studies in the Psychology of Sex*, p. 247.
34. Ellis, *The Task of Social Hygiene*, p. 310.
35. Havelock Ellis, *Man and Woman: A Study of Secondary and Tertiary Sexual Characters*, p. 310.
36. Weeks, *Sexuality and Its Discontents*, p. 64.
37. Grosskurth, *Havelock Ellis: A Biography*, p. xv.
38. Jeffreys, *The Spinster and Her Enemies*, p. 129.
39. Freud's major psychoanalytic efforts were in the areas of hysteria, neurasthenia, neuro-psychoses, childhood sexuality, dreams, and sexuality and the etiology of neuroses. Freud acknowledged, in his early work on homosexuality entitled "The Sexual Aberrations" (1905), that his views on the subject were largely derivative of those of Havelock Ellis, Richard Krafft-Ebing, Albert Moll, Karl Moebius, Caspar Schrenck-Notzing, Viktor Lowenfeld, Albert Eulenburg, Iwan Bloch and Magnus Hirschfeld.
40. D'Emilio and Freedman, *Intimate Matters: A History of Sexuality in America*, p. 223.

41. Steven Marcus, in the introduction to Freud's *Three Essays on the Theory of Sexuality* (New York: Basic Books, 1975), p. xxviii.
42. Ibid.
43. Ibid.
44. Ibid., p. xxix.
45. Freud, in Weeks, *Sex, Politics and Society,* p. 153.
46. Ibid.
47. Ibid.
48. D'Emilio and Freedman, *Intimate Matters: A History of Sexuality in America,* p. 223.
49. Ibid.
50. Ibid.
51. Nathan Hale, *Freud and the Americans: The Beginnings of Psychoanalysis in the United States 1896-1917* (New York: Oxford University Press, 1971), pp. 342, 405.
52. Linda Gordon, *Woman's Body, Woman's Right: A Social History of Birth Control in America* (New York: Penguin Books, 1977), p. 186.
53. Ibid., p. 187
54. Marcus, in introduction to Freud's *Three Essays on the Theory of Sexuality,* p. xxiv.
55. Freud, *Three Essays on the Theory of Sexuality,* p. 15.
56. D'Emilio and Freedman, *Intimate Matters: A History of Sexuality in America,* p. 223.
57. Freud, *Three Essays on the Theory of Sexuality,* p. 39.
58. Ibid., p. 3.
59. Ibid., p. 98.
60. Ibid. pp. 30-31.
61. Ibid., p. 31.
62. Emma Goldman, *Living My Life,* p. 173.
63. Jonathan Katz, *Gay American History* (New York: Thomas Y. Cromwell Company, 1976), pp. 337-380.
64. Ibid.
65. Goldman, *Living My Life,* p. 173.
66. Ibid.
67. I have chosen not to analyze Carpenter's thought in the same way I have Ellis and Freud's because, when compared to the impact and influence of the latter sexologists, Carpenter's thought would not have been as influential.
68. Weeks, *Sex, Politics and Society,* p. 161.
69. Goldman, *Living My Life,* p. 173.
70. Ibid.
71. Ibid.
72. Ibid.
73. Ibid., p. 980.
74. Jeffreys, *The Spinster and Her Enemies,* p. 128.
75. Goldman, *Living My Life.*
76. D'Emilio and Freedman, *Intimate Matters: A History of Sexuality in America,* p. 225.
77. Goldman, *Living My Life,* p. 253.
78. Alice Wexler, *Emma Goldman: An Intimate Life* (New York: Pantheon Books, 1984), p. 102.
79. D'Emilio and Freedman, *Intimate Matters: A History of Sexuality in America,* p. 230.
80. Ibid., pp. 230-231.
81. Ann Snitow, Christine Stansell and Sharon Thompson, in introduction to *Powers of Desire* (New York: Monthly Review Press), p. 9.
82. Weeks, *Sexuality* (London and New York: Tavistock Publications, 1986), pp. 74-75.

CHAPTER 6

Emancipation, Feminism and Same-Sex Relationships: Goldman and the Interconnections

This chapter will locate Goldman in relation to the sex war(s) of her day, as well as in relation to contemporary feminist sex debates. Goldman's libertarian approach to sexuality will be examined in light of these debates over sexuality's inherent pleasures versus its inherent dangers. Integral to this discussion will be Goldman's treatment of same-sex relationships as a possible source of women's emancipation.

Reviewing the nineteenth-century feminist discourse, Ann Snitow, Christine Stansell and Sharon Thompson conclude that none of the discussion, implicitly or explicitly, dealt with lesbianism. The reasons for this exclusion of same-sex relationships "are not yet altogether clear; certainly there was a divergence between discourse and behaviour, since, as a number of historians have shown, the cultural gap between men and women allowed, even encouraged, middle-class women to cultivate sensual and at times erotic relations with each other."[1] Curiously, despite Goldman's extensive critique of the contemporary "tragedy" of women's emancipation, a critique which focused on the expression of "instinct" as a requisite for women's emancipation, she made no reference to the possibility of same-sex relationships. The "profound emotional impulses and complementaries drawing women toward women,"[2] about which contemporary feminists have written, were not presented by Goldman as emancipatory possibilities for women. Her rejection of human-made institutions on the grounds that they impede personal growth and the unfettered expression of instinct did not include a critique of perhaps the most basic "man-made" arrangement—compulsory heterosexuality.[3] Explicitly, Goldman's argument speaks to the desirability of compulsory heterosexuality (e.g., the love of a man and childbirth) and, implicitly, to the undesirability of social arrangements which divert woman's attention away from expressing her "natural" heterosexual impulses.

Goldman argued that the women's rights movement in her time diverted women *away* from "true" emancipation and male partnership. She criticized the narrowness of a vision that "banished man, as a disturber and doubtful character," out of women's emotional lives.[4] Goldman labelled the vision of man presented by her opponents "puritanical":

> Man was not to be tolerated at any price, except perhaps as father of a child, since a child could not very well come to life without a father. Fortunately, the most rigid Puritans never will be strong enough to kill the innate craving for motherhood.[5]

Ironically, Goldman's own vision limited sexual expression to heterosexual relationships, thereby rejecting the possibility of emancipation in same-sex relationships.

Mainstream feminists during Goldman's time were concerned that the sexualization of women would limit the opportunities for women and would expose them to additional abuse at the hands of men.[6] They saw Goldman's advocacy of freedom of sexual expression as benefitting men far more than women. British feminists, such as Francis Swiney and Elizabeth Wolstenholme Elmy, advocated psychic love and continence. Believing that sexualization would increase the burden on and abuse of women, these women reformers found ideas, such as those espoused by Goldman, deplorable and reprehensible.[7]

Adrienne Rich, representing a contemporary perspective on lesbianism, states that despite "profound emotional impulses and complementarities drawing women toward women," feminist positions predicated on the *reform* of compulsory heterosexuality assume a "mystical/biological inclination, a 'preference' or 'choice' that draws women towards men."[8] States Rich:

The lie keeps numberless women psychologically
trapped, trying to fit mind, spirit, and sexuality into a
prescribed script because they cannot look beyond the
parameters of the acceptable.... The lie is many-layered.
In Western tradition, one layer—the romantic—asserts
that women are inevitably, even if rashly and tragically
drawn to men; that even when the attractions are
suicidal...it is still an organic imperative.[9]

Rich poses questions about sexual expression and the direction
of "emotional and erotic energies" which never appear to have been
considered by Goldman—questions such as, does not the search for
tenderness and love in both sexes originally lead toward women?
Why wouldn't women redirect that search? Why are species-sur-
vival, impregnation, and erotic/emotional relationships so closely
identified with one another? Why are social strictures necessary to
enforce women's emotional and erotic loyalty to men?[10] The mother-
daughter bond in nineteenth-century America, for example, was
characterized, according to Smith-Rosenberg, by intensity and identification and "served as a model for subsequent relations with other
women."[11] Her research suggests "an intricate weaving together of
psychosexual and social-structural forces" which created the world
of nineteenth-century female intimacy.[12] In this world, mother and
daughters

...often slept with one another throughout the
daughters' adolescence, wept unashamedly at separation, and rejoiced at reunions.[13]

Goldman's seemingly intransigent endorsement of female
heterosexuality reflects the more profound political struggle between Goldman and the women reformers of the social purity and
suffrage movements. After 1900, the women reformers who had
campaigned on a social purity platform became integrated into the
platform of the female suffrage campaign. Sheila Jeffreys states:

It is possible that feminists were able to pursue their aims of an equal moral standard and the control of male sexuality for the protection of women, through their pursuit of the vote, which was seen as a symbolic achievement through which women's other wrongs might be righted.[14]

In America, the social purity movement, in its effort to "purify" all men and boys, adopted a "White Cross Pledge" card upon which a boy or man would have his name inscribed. The pledge card contained the following principles:

1. To treat all women with respect, and endeavour to protect them from all wrong and degradation.
2. To endeavour to put down all indecent langauge and coarse jests.
3. To maintain the law of purity as equally binding upon men and women.
4. To endeavour to spread these principles among my companions and to try and help my younger brothers.
5. To use every possible means to fulfil the command 'Keep Thyself Pure.'[15]

Admitting that while the women reformers had "broken down many old fetters," Goldman argued that they had, at the same time, forged many new ones. She was particularly critical of the social purity movement's vision of women as pure and uncorrupt doers of social good and institutional reform, a view which projected, according to historian, Judith Walkowitz, a rejection of male partnerships as well as a passionless and desexualized view of women.[16]

Writing of the degree to which heterosexuality limited women's options, Walkowitz explains that "desexualization could empower women to attack the customary prerogatives of men; it could also validate a new social role for women outside of the heterosexual family."[17] Carroll Smith-Rosenberg also notes that the "new woman" of the late nineteenth century forfeited her sexual identity to achieve social and economic autonomy or perceived equality. For Goldman, the forfeiting of sexual identity and activity was an outrageous price to pay for such perceived gains. As sexual expression, in Goldman's view, was the core of each human personality, to reject male sexual partnership as mentioned above in chapter five, was to reject, "life's greatest treasure, love for a man."[18] In this way, as Jeffreys argues, the issues of sex and suffrage became inextricably connected in the women's movement of the time. Gaining the vote meant, to the women reformers, gaining greater influence and power over the sexual behaviour of men. The women reformers of Goldman's time "were shocked by her advocacy of a full sexual life for women."[19] The debate's intensity and focus is made evident throughout Goldman's essay "The Tragedy of Woman's Emancipation" in which Goldman, as if countering the claims in an oral debate, defends her vision of emancipation while rejecting the claims of the social purity campaigners and suffragists. Because Goldman's essay is so closely focused on refuting what she perceived to be their anti-male bias, she fails to explore the possibilities for "true emancipation" outside the confines of the conventional pattern of heterosexuality. In her side of the argument she contrasted "married" life with a male partner to sexually unemancipated unmarried life. Goldman states:

> And yet we find many emancipated women who prefer marriage, with all its deficiencies, to the narrowness of an unmarried life: narrow and unendurable because of the chains of moral and social prejudice that cramp and bind her nature.[20]

Goldman does not, however, elaborate on the possible configurations beyond these two options.

Reinforcing the principles of social purity with Christian dogma, the women reformers, according to Jeffreys, "were free to fight the forms of male sexual behaviour they found oppressive and to name men as the perpetrators of sexual injustice against women."[21] The banner of social purity allowed women to express their discontent with men in a "legitimate setting."[22]

Goldman's opposition to the women reformers was inextricably intertwined with her overall theory of anarchism in which she perceived "puritanism" to be one of the great oppressors of the human spirit. Since anarchism was a theory of freedom, Goldman argued that it must include the most fundamental freedom—sexual expression. She, therefore, opposed those who advocated (or who were perceived to advocate) desexualization. Ironically, Goldman's view of sexual "freedom" as an integral component of anarchism, was limited and confined to gender-bound constructions. What emerges from Goldman's writing is an apparent inconsistency in advocating heterosexuality as the ideal and defending freedom of sexual expression of all kinds.

It may be postulated that Goldman viewed the political necessity to refute the women reformers' view of female emancipation as such a grave one, that she became intransigent and inflexible in her public position on sexual preference, for fear that she might be conceding some ground to her opposition. To take the position that Goldman *was* privately intransigent and inflexible in her sexual prescription for emancipation is dubious given the closeness between Goldman and a number of women in her life. For example, Goldman had great emotional attachment to her sister Helena and her niece Stella. Goldman's emotional and physical closeness to Louise Michel and her letter to Magnus Hirschfeld of 1923, in which she defended the alleged homosexuality of Michel,[23] are inconsistent with her public advocacy of heterosexuality as an ideal.

Goldman viewed the women reformers' platform of social purity, which attracted "a broad range of socially-minded people, from Protestant moral reformers to suffragists,"[24] as a repressive one; one which could potentially do great harm to sexual expressiveness and the movement, in other sectors, toward sexual openness. During a period when sexuality was working its way out of the closet through the work of Freud, Edward Carpenter and Havelock Ellis, Goldman viewed the social purity campaigners as a threat to the movement of sexual openness, birth control, and sex education.

In the opinion of some contemporary feminist historians, Goldman's apprehensions of the damaging effects of the social purity movement proved to be well-founded as, in the words of Snitow, the "principle of male and State protectionism that underlay the feminists' adherence to the image of the female innocent allowed anti-feminist forces to gain control of the movement and ultimately to strip it of feminist content."[25]

A damaging and anti-feminist result of the social purity reform, for example, was the implementation (1873) in the United States of the Comstock Law which prohibited the dissemination of birth control information through the U.S. mail. Goldman fought vehemently against the Comstock Law and was eventually arrested and imprisoned for its violation.

However, Goldman's libertarian approach had potentially unintended and damaging implications for women in general. Weeks' general observation on libertarianism, discussed above in chapter four, could be applied to Goldman's approach to sexuality:

> Its weakness [libertarianism in general] is that, like other approaches, it relies entirely on a fundamentalist [essentialist] view of sexuality whose truth it seeks to express. As a result its celebration of sex can easily become a glorification of all manifestations of desire.[26]

Weeks continues his assessment of the weaknesses of libertarianism with particular reference to women and feminist objections to this approach—objections which were strikingly similar to those presented to Goldman by her female reform opponents. Weeks states:

> The effect of this, as feminists have pointed out, can be to impose a view that sexual expression is not only pleasurable, but necessary—often at the expense of women. The real problems, of defining alternatives and constructing new forms of relating, are ignored. The difficulty, and the danger, of simple libertarianism is that

unfortunately sex does not unproblematically speak its own truth.[27]

There are similarities between the debate over sexuality raging in Goldman's day and the debate over sexuality raging in our day.

In Goldman's day, the debate was between libertarian feminists such as Goldman, Margaret Sanger, Crystal Eastman and Louise Bryant, who argued that the key to lifting women's oppression was to free them sexually, and those feminists whose concern was protecting women from the dangers of heterosexuality. Sexual freedom, the former group argued, could take the form of sexual varietism (i.e., heterosexual varietism), unmarried sexual relationships, motherhood without marriage, and sex for pleasure rather than reproduction. While the "pro-sex" side of the debate argued on behalf of sexuality's pleasures and liberatory potential, it failed to counterbalance sexuality's pleasures with its attendant problems or dangers. According to this group, to be pro-sex was to be pro-heterosexual. To be pro-sex, heterosexual, and a woman, in Goldman's day, presented potential dangers—dangers such as unwanted pregnancies, unsafe abortions, venereal disease and sexual abuse at the hands of men. The pro-sex side of the debate, however, glorified sex's emancipatory capabilities while ignoring or minimalizing women's vulnerability. Goldman's opponents in the debate represented what Ellen Carol DuBois and Linda Gordon call the social purity feminists whose protectionist ideals reflected their view of the victimization of women. Based on a limited vision for women, the social purity feminists fought to protect them from, what they perceived to be, the dangers of heterosexuality.

In our day, the debate over sexuality's pleasures versus its dangers for women is somewhat similar to that of Goldman's day. On the pro-sex side of the debate we find feminists such as Alice Echols and Aritha van Herk who argue that, in spite of the dangers, women should strive for greater pleasure and self-expansion through sexuality. As van Herk argues, "I refuse to be colonized out of my genuine pleasure by politics...this refusing must also refuse to be a discourse of denial—become a discourse beyond consent, through to initiative."[28]

On the other side of the contemporary debate over sexuality are feminists, such as Ellen DuBois and Linda Gordon, as well as social constructionist, Jeffrey Weeks, who argue that greater access to sex should not simply or necessarily be equated with greater truth or freedom for women. This side of the debate represents the view that as long as power relations favour men, greater sexual expression runs the risk of being at the expense of women. Women, therefore, must not only be aware of sexuality's inherent pleasures, but also of its embeddedness in relations of power and the attendant problems and dangers.

While Goldman viewed the expression of sexual impulses to be at the core of personal health and well-being, she failed explicitly to balance her argument with cases where an atmosphere of unfettered sexual expression was problematic for women, causing damage to health and well-being (e.g., venereal disease, unwanted pregnancy).

The charges against Goldman of being a "man's woman" bear particular relevance as Goldman was perceived to be advocating "free love," the consequences of which would be much graver for women than men. The loosening of sexual mores and the lifting of sexual constraints, while possibly emancipatory and cathartic for some, most certainly would be experienced differently depending upon one's gender, race and class. The proposed sexual liberation would result in man becoming the unequivocal winner and woman as one who, attempting to rid herself of inhibition and restraint and to enjoy a new-found freedom, must bear the responsibility of sexuality's consequences. Since women are more vulnerable in reproduction matters, they have much more to lose when contraception proves ineffective or when they become pregnant accidentally. As Weeks has noted, "sex does not *unproblematically* [italics mine] speak its own truth."[29]

In *Living My Life* Goldman recalls presenting a lecture on "woman's inhumanity to man" in which she argued the side of the "underdog"—man:

I resented my sex's placing every evil at the door of the male. I pointed out that if he were really a sinner as he is being painted by the ladies, women shared the responsibility with him …the inconsistencies of my sex keep the poor male dangling between the idol and the brute, the darling and the beast, the helpless child and the conqueror of worlds. It is really women's inhumanity to man that makes him what he is.[30]

In her autobiography, Goldman recalled holding up men as models for women's emancipation, urging women to emulate men's self-centredness, determination, and courage:

When she has learned to be as self-centred and as determined as he, when she gains the courage to delve into life as he does and pay the price for it, she will achieve her liberation, and incidentally also help him become free.[31]

The mutuality of sexual liberation was a view which Goldman championed. Instead of blaming the conditions of patriarchy (and men themselves) for women's condition, Goldman placed responsibility on women themselves. If women gained courage, self-directedness and determinism, as modelled after male behaviour, they in turn, could help men gain their freedom. According to Goldman, her female audiences, after hearing Goldman's thesis on "man as underdog," would rise up and protest: "You're a man's woman and not one of us."[32] The view of men as the enemy, allegedly espoused by Goldman's opponents, is still held by contemporary feminists such as Dale Spender. Spender argues that for centuries women have perceived men as the enemy and have been told this is not a "nice" or "useful" thing to do.[33] In cases of racism or class struggle, Spender argues, the oppressor is called the enemy. According to Spender, there is no good reason for making an exception in the cases of sex.

Perhaps Goldman perceived the aspiration of the women reformers to be so objectionable and potentially dangerous that she felt compelled to adopt an antithetical position. However, it is more likely that, due to Goldman's essentialist and libertarian view of gender and sexuality, her "construction" of womanhood (and manhood) differed sharply from that of her opponents. Goldman's essentialism created fixed notions of female and male nature and her libertarianism caused her to defend sexual freedom. However, due to Goldman's essentialist view of the sexes, sexual "freedom" was only permitted within rigidly demarcated gender roles.

While Smith-Rosenberg discusses the extent to which the "new woman"[34] prevailed during the years of Goldman's political activism, there is little recognition, on the part of Goldman, of "other" forms of female psychosexual expression. The "new woman" of late nineteenth-century and early twentieth-century in America, as described by Smith-Rosenberg, constructed her world around female principles and preferences. Women's colleges and settlement houses provided institutional settings within which women could study, teach, and live in an all-female environment. These institutional environments provided the opportunity for female networks and friendships of various intensities to flourish, with few complications from the outside world of male domination. In Smith-Rosenberg's analysis, between the 1890s and the First World War, the embracing of radical causes and loving female friendships gave the New Women a new power base: "loving and living with other women...the New Women amassed greater political power and visibility than any other group in American experience."[35] If Smith-Rosenberg's assessment is the correct one and, in fact, women "loving and living with other women" formed one of the options available to women of her day, why did Goldman not explicitly attend to the issue of female homosexuality, as one option, in a range of options, which could conceivably bring about psychic and sexual emancipation?

The Social Context of Goldman's Lack of Endorsement of Female Homosexuality

The medical labelling of same-sex intimacy as perverse conflated an entire range of relationships and stigmatized all of them as a single, sexually deviant personal identity. Same-sex relationships thus lost the innocence they had enjoyed during most of the nineteenth century. Nonetheless, these unions had expanded the opportunities for intimacy and sexuality apart from reproduction and the family.[36]

The visibility of same-sex associations was heightened in the early twentieth century, as the "new woman"—educated, professional and unmarried—was not encumbered by husband and children.[37] These associations included professionally prominent couples, such as Katharine Comaxe and Katharine Lee Bates, Mary Woolley and Jeannette Marks, Jane Admas and Mary Rozet Smith, and Florence Converse and Vida Scudder.[38]

These associations were ones which lacked the restrictiveness of same-sex relationships in the previous century, when married women attended to the needs of their husbands and children while having a variety of their own needs met through their associations with other women. As D'Emilio and Freedman note, this world of female passion and love was different from that of the mid-nineteenth century "in that its participants were freed from the bonds of matrimony, able to live and work independent from men."[39] Vida Scudder, who enjoyed a long-standing association with writer Florence Converse, commented that "a woman's life in which sex interests have never visited, is a life neither dull nor empty nor devoid of romance."[40] Scudder continued to make a case for romance without sex and without male contact when she wrote that "the absence of [the sex] factor need not mean death of romance, or even intensely emotionally significant personal relationships. Of these, I have had more than I care to dwell upon."[41]

For Goldman, "intensely emotionally significant personal relationships" must possess a heterosexual element, despite the apparent contradiction of her own relationship with fellow anarchist, Louise Michel, which she described as "soul-expanding."[42] As a proponent of sexual openness, and sexual varietism, and the lifting of sexual repression, why did Goldman, who said "I knew from my own experience that sex expression is as vital a factor in human life as food and air,"[43] exclude female homosexuality and autoeroticism from her discussion on "true" emancipation? If emancipation enabled one to recognize and express one's most primitive and instinctive desires, did Goldman think that women would (and should) express their desires in a homogeneous fashion?

I argue that Goldman was part of what Blanche Wiesen Cook refers to as the "historical denial of lesbianism."[44] In fact, Goldman's denial of the possibility that women's love of women could be erotic and sexually pleasurable, independent of the quality of previous male contact, reflected the sex-gender ideology of her day. Blanche Wiesen Cook explains:

> The historical denial of lesbianism accompanies the persistent refusal to acknowledge the variety and intensity of women's emotional and erotic experiences. That denial involves the notion so prevalent in 19th century medical textbooks that physical love between women was experimental masturbation, studious preparation for marriage. It involves the notion that women without men are lonely asexual spinsters and that erotic and sexual pleasure without male penetration is not erotic or sexual pleasure.[45]

Goldman not only denied what Cook refers to as the "reality," "diversity," and "vast range of perfectly pleasurable relations between women,"[46] but was less than open about her own relationship with companion Almeda Sperry and, to a lesser extent, Louise Michel. Ellen Carol DuBois and Linda Gordon's "Seeking Ecstasy on the Battlefield: Danger and Pleasure in Nineteenth-century Feminist Sexual Thought" addresses the issue of homosexuality among the feminists who took up the cause of sexual liberation. Mentioning Goldman among others, who "asserted woman's right to be sexual,"[47] DuBois and Gordon note that some of these feminists slept with a variety of lovers, did not marry, and became single mothers.[48] Some of these "sex-radicals," DuBois and Gordon observe, "had explicitly sexual relationships with other women, although a subsequent repression of evidence, along with their own silences about homosexuality, make it hard to uncover this aspect of their sexual lives."[49]

Goldman's seemingly myopic view of the "reality," "diversity," and "vast range of pleasurable relations between women,"[50] and her repression of that reality, reflects her support of what she perceived to be the "enlightened" theories of the sexologists. Goldman's adherence to sexology's "truths" may explain her lack of forthrightness about her own same-sex relationships. Lillian Faderman's *Surpassing the Love of Men* addresses the impact that the sexologists' message on inversion had on many women including, perhaps, Goldman. Faderman writes:

> Considering the models of inversion that Krafft-Ebing, Havelock Ellis, and their disciples presented (e.g., Alice Mitchell, the "typical invert" who cut her lover's throat), it was inevitable that many women fled into heterosexual marriage [in Goldman's case heterosexual varietism] or developed great self-loathing or self-pity if they accepted the label of "invert."[51]

Goldman, like many other women, reacted to "inversion" through the ideological screen of the sexologists—a screen which was greatly influential in the identification of love between women with "disease, insanity, and tragedy."[52] Havelock Ellis who, along with Freud and Carpenter, contributed to a corpus of work on human sexuality during this period, was considered to be "an enemy of Victorian repression and hypocrisy."[53] Holding "a place of honour in our pantheon of sexual liberators,"[54] Ellis defended male homosexuals, citing the major contributions many had made to society. Ellis's treatment of the female homosexual differed markedly from his treatment of her male counterpart. As Lillian Faderman has suggested in *Surpassing the Love of Men*, the sexologists, whose work was perceived by libertarians such as Goldman to be emancipatory and enlightened, actually had the oppressive effect of discouraging female friendship and unmarried life through the "diagnosis" or "label" of invert. For those who did not want to adopt the label of "invert" or have the label involuntarily applied, female friendships of various forms and intensities were avoided. Women who had intense friendships with other women, after becoming aware of the sexologists' "assessment," often hurried into marriage to avoid the application of and identification with the label.

Havelock Ellis, although not the first to create a stereotype of lesbians, made a significant contribution to the so-called "science of sexology" in which a classic "case" of the female homosexual or "invert" was presented. In his essay entitled, "Sexual Inversion in Women," Ellis stereotypes the female invert as a cigarette-smoking, confident, direct-speaking individual who nearly always possesses a disdain for "the petty feminine articles of the toilet."[55] In greater detail, Ellis's female "invert" is modelled in the following manner:

> When they still retain female garments, those usually show some traits of masculine simplicity, and there is nearly always a disdain for the petty feminine artifices of the toilet. Even when this is not obvious, there are all sorts of instinctive gestures and habits which may suggest to female acquaintances the remark that such a person ought to have been a man'. The brusque energetic movements, the attitude of the arms, the direct speech, the inflexions of the voice, the masculine straightforwardness and sense of humour, and especially the attitude towards men, free from any suggestion either of shyness or audacity, will often suggest the underlying psychic abnormality to a keen observer.[56]

Goldman appeared to have adopted a view of homosexuality similar to that of the sexologists, particularly to that of Ellis. The sexologists' view was gender-specific, as the aetiology and nature of female and male homosexuality was seen to be separate, just as the spheres of men and women were to be kept separate. Smith-Rosenberg reports that "the male sexologist who most directly broke into this female world of love and intimacy, defining it as both actively sexual and as sexually perverted, was Havelock Ellis."[57]

Ellis's work on inversion had a substantial influence on Freud's early work. In *Theories of Sexuality* (1895), Freud credits Ellis, Albert Moll, Richard Krafft-Ebing and others as having contributed to his theory of homosexuality. Thus, Ellis, not withstanding his iconoclastic and liberal reputation, "provided the theoretical underpinning for conservative attacks upon the new woman as sexually perverted and socially dangerous."[58] While Ellis was noted for his unrelenting defence of homosexuality, it should be underscored that his defence was on behalf of men, not women. The trial of Oscar Wilde, for example, sparked Ellis and others to become politically active, speaking out in defence of male inverts. Ellis defined male homosexuality, or inversion, as a congenital anomaly. In his theory of congenital, degenerative homosexuality, Ellis explains that at conception each organism is provided with fifty percent female "germs" and fifty percent male "germs" and, as these germs develop, either the female camp or the male camp gains the upper hand. In some individuals this process does not proceed normally and the sexual impulse becomes "organically twisted" into an inverted form. Ellis continued to argue that the seed of homosexual suggestion is sown in various soils in which it may thrive or die, depending on the difference in the soil (e.g., environmental differences).

The notion of the "difference in soil" or, less metaphorically, the influence of environment, contributed to Ellis's conservative treatment of female inversion, as he argued less about "congenital" influences and more about environmental influences. Although Ellis insisted that inversion was hereditary, biological and irreversible,[59] he argued in the case of lesbianism that very few women were true inverts. Ellis made a distinction between those women with genetic anomalies (the "congenital invert") and those women who were not genetically inverted but who were genetically predisposed to the advances of other women (the "homosexual"). Provided the homosexual woman was kept in a heterosexual environment where her heterosexual impulses could prevail, she could live a typically "normal" existence. If, however, she became entrenched in a same-sex environment such as a boarding school, women's club, college, or settlement house, (or prison) she may be susceptible to the advances of the (a) "congenital invert." This genetic distinction between "the congenital invert" and "the homosexual" caused Ellis to view the congenital invert as a dangerous and corrupting force in society, seducing other women away from their biological destination of heterosexuality and motherhood. Smith-Rosenberg interprets Ellis's trepidation over lesbianism in the following manner:

> By dichotomizing lesbians into "true inverts" and poten-
> tial heterosexuals, Ellis depicted the female invert not as a
> genetic anomaly and a helpless victim but as a woman on
> the make, sexually and radically dangerous. Seeking a
> more feminine partner, she sexually rivalled men.[60]

Ellis's biologically determined frame of reference, male-centred-ness, and his complementary view of the role of women vis-à-vis men, led him to reject lesbianism as a phenomenon in its own right. Ellis insisted that lesbianism be viewed in the context of male/female relationships—as perhaps an option by default. For example, in his 1895 essay "Sexual Inversion in Women," Ellis states that women who attract or are attracted by true inverts are "the pick of the women whom the average man would pass by."[61]

Because of the suspicion with which Ellis viewed the female congenital invert and the corrupting potential he ascribed to her, he was also suspicious of feminism, which drew women together in an environment void of male influence. Ellis's metaphor of sowing seeds in ground for the growth of lesbianism reflected his reservations about women's "modern movements of emancipa-tion":

> I do not say that these questionable influences of
> modern movements can directly cause sexual inversion,
> though they may indirectly, in so far as they promote
> hereditary neurosis—but they develop the germs of it,
> and they probably cause a spurious imitation. This
> spurious imitation is due to the fact that the congenital
> anomaly occurs with special frequency in women of

high intelligence who, voluntarily or involuntarily, influence others.[62]

Ellis's belief in a link between lesbianism and feminism was shared by his fellow male sexologist Iwan Bloch. Bloch, Ellis and August Forel, who were given the label of "fathers of sexology" at the 1929 Sex Reform Congress in London, held similar views about the feminism/lesbianism connection. What Ellis called the "homosexual," Bloch called the "pseudo-homosexual"; what Ellis labelled the "true invert," Bloch labelled the homosexual. Despite the difference in terminology, Bloch shared Ellis's apprehensions concerning feminism's potential as a fertile breeding ground for lesbianism. Bloch states:

> There is no doubt that in the women's movement—that is, in the movement directed toward the acquirement by women of all the attainments of masculine culture—homosexual women have played a notable part. Indeed, according to one author, the "Women's Question" is mainly the question regarding the destiny of virile homosexual women.... For the diffusion of pseudo-homosexuality the Women's Movement is of great importance...[63]

The Influence of Edward Carpenter on the Gender Bias

Edward Carpenter, the English sexologist and male homosexual emancipationist, also suggested a connection—in terms of cause and effect—between feminism and lesbianism. Although Carpenter himself was homosexual and a member of socialist organizations advocating homosexual rights, his description of the feminist/lesbian link implies that lesbianism is a reaction to unfair and unequal treatment of women by men. Speaking of his own "homogenic passion," Carpenter wrote, "Women are beautiful; but, to some, there is that which passes the love of women";[64] his explanation of female "homogenic passion" is sharply different:

...The movement among women for their own liberation and emancipation, which is taking place all over the civilized world, has been accompanied by a marked development of the homogenic passion among the female sex. It may be said that a certain strain in relations between the opposite sexes which has become owing to a growing consciousness among women that they have been oppressed and unfairly treated by men, and a growing unwillingness to ally themselves unequally in marriage—that this strain has caused womankind to draw more closely together and to cement alliances of their own...[65]

Although Carpenter suggests that male homosexuality may involve a love that "passes the love of women," female homogenic passion is that which *results* from unsatisfactory association with men. In other words, female homosexuality is a rejection of woman's first choice or inclination—heterosexuality. Their common dissatisfaction with heterosexual marriage, in Carpenter's words, "caused womankind to draw more closely together and to cement alliances of their own."[66] Nowhere does Carpenter suggest as he does in the case of male homosexuality, that this may be an independent choice on the part of women reformers; nowhere does Carpenter suggest that "men are beautiful; but to some, there is that which passes the love of men."

Carpenter's assessment of the composition of the women's movement, or what he called "the new movement," suggested that the supporters of the movement are not true representatives of their sex. Carpenter maintained that those women who do not direct their sexual impulses toward men and who do not desire children are on a false course of emancipation. The women of the "new movement" include, according to Edward Carpenter, categories such as those lacking a "maternal instinct," those lacking a sex drive, those who are "mannish in temperament," those who are "homogenic," those to whom children are a bore, those who are "ultra-rationalising and brain-cultured" and those who see men's sexual advances as "mere impertinence."[67]

The Double Standard and Goldman's Treatment of Female Homosexuality

The double standard with which the sexologists measured female homosexuality vis-à-vis male homosexuality is evident in Goldman's treatment of the subject. It was the words of Havelock Ellis, Krafft-Ebing, Carpenter, and others who made Goldman "aware of the crime which had been perpetrated upon Oscar Wilde and his kind."[68] Although Goldman mentioned her common affection for male *and* female friends who are "uranian,"[69] her outspokenness and show of support on behalf of male homosexuals reflected the sexologists' bias and differential treatment of male and female homosexuality. Goldman appeared to have adopted the sexologists' position that male homosexuality is firmly a genetic predisposition, while female homosexuality is relative and conditional—relative to and conditional upon the quality of women's association with men. The conceptual difference between male and female homosexuality revolved around the concept of "choice"; while nature, not choice predominated in the discussion on male homosexuality, choice was factored into the discussion on female homosexuality—choice in relation to women's diversion from/or continuation on nature's "true" path. If relationships with men proved to be unsatisfactory, then women may *choose* the company of women. Unlike the expressions used when male homosexuality was discussed, women's same-sex relationships are viewed as dependent upon and as a result of the quality of their previous or current heterosexual encounters. Goldman expresses a similar position succinctly when she states that if men cannot offer understanding and comradeship, treating women as human beings and not sexual objects, women will turn to their sisters for satisfaction.[70] Goldman, then, like the sexologists, defined female sexuality as largely secondary, as being responsive to male sexuality. Goldman explained the phenomenon of female homosexuality in a way which suggests that if men cannot offer women what they want, a woman will *respond* by turning to other

women. The sexologists' model of female sexuality containing finite
boundaries of "womanly" expression is reflected in Goldman's writing. As Jeffrey Weeks explains, the sexologists offered:

> ...A norm of behaviour which is heterosexual, procrea-
> tive and largely male, in which female sexuality has al-
> most invariably been defined as secondary or responsive
> to the male's .... Female breaches with the norm are fitted
> into a dichotomized picture of male activity and female
> passivity. Not surprisingly...lesbianism ...has generally
> been speculated about in terms which derive entirely
> from the male.[71]

Same-Sex Relationships: Public and Private Variation

Blanche Wiesen Cook has observed that although Goldman
could not be considered "homophobic" in an intellectual or traditional sense, "she felt a profound ambivalence about lesbianism as
a lifestyle."[72] Goldman's failure to endorse lesbianism as a possible
source of emancipation is even more mystifying in light of her own
experiences in same-sex relationships. According to biographer
Alice Wexler, Goldman endorsed "homosexuality" as early as
1890.[73] According to Cook, she was the only woman in America to
defend homosexuality *in general* and Oscar Wilde in particular.[74] In
1900, writer and psychiatrist, Oskar Panizza, asked Goldman to
spend an evening with him, Dr. Eugene Schmidt and Oscar Wilde.
Due to previous commitments, Goldman declined the invitation.[75]
A number of days later Dr. Schmidt called on Goldman and the two
went for a walk, during which according to Goldman in her
autobiography written thirty years after the event, Goldman
defended Oscar Wilde against the charges of homosexuality and
slammed the "miserable hypocrites who had sent him to his
doom."[76] The doctor, according to Goldman, astonished at her
forthrightness, asked how she dared come out with such state-
ments such as this in "Puritan America."[77] In Goldman's version of
this event in *Living My Life*, for the remainder of the afternoon the

two "were engaged in a battle royal about inversion, perversion, and the question of sex variation."[78] Ironically, it is Goldman who accused Dr. Schmidt of not being "free in his approach" to these issues. Goldman recalls the events:

> He had given much thought to the matter, but he was not free in his approach, and I suspected that he was somewhat scandalized that I, a young woman, should speak without reservation on such tabooed subjects.[79]

The vocabulary used by Goldman during this conversation (i.e., inversion, perversion, sex variation) was that of the sexologists. While Goldman obviously felt she had been liberated by the sexologists, as witnessed by her willingness to talk openly about sexual matters, she was, at the same time, contributing to the sexologists' pathologization of sexuality by classifying sexual behaviours as perversions, inversion, etc.

In her autobiography, Goldman recalls that "censorship came from some of my own comrades because I was treating such 'unnatural' themes as homosexuality."[80] The pressure of censorship provided Goldman with additional resolve to speak out on behalf of those victims of "social wrong" or "moral prejudice."[81] In this context, Goldman recalls the reaction to her lectures by female and male homosexuals alike who confided to her "their anguish and their isolation."[82] She recalls, in particular, the reaction of one young woman, whose homosexuality had caused her extraordinary misery and self-hate:

> She had never met anyone, she told me, who suffered from a similar affliction, nor had she ever read books dealing with the subject. My lecture had set her free; I had given her back her self-respect.[83]

Through this woman's story and others, Goldman was made more fully aware of the dreadfulness of the life of the homosexual in a heterosexist society:

This woman was only one of the many who sought me
out. Their pitiful stories made the social ostracism of the
invert seem more dreadful than I had ever realized
before.[84]

Given the testimonials of suffering by female homosexuals, it seems
paradoxical that Goldman so strongly supported female heterosexuality and did not publicly endorse female homosexuality. Her
stance appears to be inconsistent with her general theory of anarchism and its liberatory effects upon human behaviour. In her
autobiography, Goldman restates her view of the essence of anarchism:

To me anarchism was not a mere theory for a distant future; it was a living influence to free us from inhibitions,
internal no less than external, and from the destructive
barriers that separate man from man.[85]

Despite Goldman's vision of anarchism she, herself, appeared
reticent to endorse with equanimity female homosexuality.

What makes Goldman's prescription for female heterosexuality
even more ironic is her own experience with same-sex relationships
and the richness she attributed to such relationships. One such
relationship occurred between Goldman and Louise Michel, a
charismatic French revolutionary, painted by the French press as
"La Vierge Rouge"[86] who died in 1905. Louise Michel's sexual
orientation was exposed to public scrutiny in an earlier essay published by Herr von Levetzow.[87] Autobiographically, Goldman's expressions of sentiment for Louise Michel comprise a brief yet
descriptive account of a relationship which possessed a rarefied
quality. Goldman's recollections of the quality of relationship she
and Michel shared bare a striking resemblance to Smith-
Rosenberg's accounts of the intense and captivating bonds which
characterized female friendship during this period. With poetic
elegance and romantic wistfulness Goldman describes Michel and
her association with her:

As I sat near her at our first meeting, I wondered how anyone could fail to find charm in her.... Her whole being was illuminated by an inner light. One quickly succumbed to the spell of her radiant personality, so compelling in its strength, so moving in its childlike simplicity. Her hand in mine, its tender pressure on my head, her words of endearment and close comradeship, made my soul expand, reach out towards the spheres of beauty where she dwelt.[88]

In 1923, Goldman authored a major article in response to Karl von Levetzow, which appeared in the *Yearbook for Sexual Intermediate Types*, issued by Germany's leading homosexual rights organization—the Scientific-Humanitarian Committee.[89] In it she defended Louise Michel and other great personalities who faced social ostracism and persecution because of their homosexuality. Addressing the article to Dr. Magnus Hirschfeld, head of the Scientific Humanitarism Committee, Goldman thanked Hirschfeld for the opportunity to respond to Herr von Levetzow's essay on Louise Michel and for his "brave and courageous stand in the service of enlightenment and humaneness in opposition to ignorance and hypocrisy."[90]

She called for greater tolerance and understanding of "the various gradations and variations of gender and their significance in life":

...I am in no way motivated by a prejudice against homosexuality itself or any antipathy towards homosexuality in general. Had Louise Michel ever manifested any type of sexual feelings in all those relationships with people whom she loved, and who were devoted to her, I would certainly be the last to cure her of the 'stigma.'[91]

In her defence of Louise Michel, Goldman acknowledged homosexuality and lamented society's lack of understanding of these possibilities:

It is a tragedy, I feel, that people of a different sexual type
are caught in a world which shows so little understanding for homosexuals, is so crassly indifferent to the
various gradations and variations of gender and their
great significance in life. Far be it for me to seek to
evaluate these people as inferior, less moral, or incapable
of higher feelings and actions.[92]

However, there are contradictions between Goldman's
defence of homosexuality, particularly in relation to the allega-
tions against Louise Michel, and her essay on women's emancipation written in 1906. While Goldman, in her 1923 letter to
Hirschfeld, claimed not to "evaluate" homosexual persons on
moral or emotional grounds, she does set in place a type of evaluative or hierarchical claim when arguing, in "The Tragedy of
Women's Emancipation," that life's *greatest* treasure is the love of a
man and woman's *most* glorious privilege is the right to give birth
to a child.[93] Goldman's use of superlatives such as "greatest" and
"most" in her assessment of heterosexuality and motherhood is
certainly evaluative and suggests that heterosexual relationships
are healthier.

While writing in defence of Louise Michel, Goldman does not
admit that she and Michel were "lovers." Despite Goldman's own
autobiographical testimony as to the strength and power of her attraction to another woman, her earlier construction was that *true*
emancipation occurred in the realms of heterosexual attraction.[94]
Even though Goldman called for women "to insist on unrestricted
freedom" and "to listen to the voice of their nature," she then
proceeded to straightjacket female emancipation and sexuality into
"love for a man" and "birth of a child."[95]

In her rebuttal of Herr von Levetzow's essay, Goldman states
that

...he [Herr von Levetzow] has an antiquated conception
of the essence of womanhood. He sees in woman a being
meant by nature solely to delight man with her attrac-

tiveness, bear his children, and otherwise figure as a domestic and general household slave. Any woman who fails to meet these shopworn requirements of womanhood is promptly taken as a Uranian by this writer.[96]

Conceding that Michel's deepest relationships *were* with women,[97] Goldman concluded that such relationships are often initiated because of dissatisfaction with male companionship. Through this admission Goldman seems to assume a hierarchy of female sexual preferences in which male partnership was the first choice. Although one can find in Goldman's defence of Louise Michel a partial endorsement of female same-sex relationships, this endorsement is presented as an option by default—an option to be partaken in when male partnership proves unsatisfactory. Goldman argues:

> Modern woman is no longer satisfied to be the beloved of a man; she looks for understanding, comradeship; she wants to be treated as a human being and not simply as an object for sexual gratification. And since man in many cases cannot offer her this, she turns to her sisters.[98]

Significant, of course, is Goldman's final statement in the preceding paragraph—"and since man in many cases cannot offer her this, she turns to her sisters"—as its inclusion makes Goldman's endorsement of female homosexuality fall short of being an independent and original choice which some women might immediately take. In defending Louise Michel, Goldman did not fail to add that she had several deep relationships with men.[99]

Goldman's letter to Magnus Hirschfeld is more a response to the way in which homosexuals, male and female, are prejudicially treated by a homophobic society than an unequivocal defence of female homosexuality as a legitimate expression of one's "tastes and desires." In stating that: "As an anarchist, my place has been on the side of the persecuted,"[100] Goldman's disapproval of the social ostracism and persecution visited on homosexuals is not predicated upon the belief that the expression of female homosexual behaviour is "the voice of her nature."[101] Instead, Goldman implied that failing her "natural" call to man and child, woman may, by default, find sexual satisfaction with a female partner. Goldman appears to be making an assumption of the universality of instinct, tastes and desires which is in direct contradiction to her anarchist principles of individuality and the value of individual instinct.

In a seemingly obtuse and uncharacteristically ambiguous manner, Goldman ends her defence of Louise Michel and her alleged homosexuality in the following way:

> In short, Louise Michel was a complete woman, free of all prejudices and traditions which for centuries held women in chains and degraded them to be household slaves and objects of sexual lust. The new women celebrated her resurrection in the figure of Louise, the woman capable of heroic deeds but one who remains a woman in her passion and in her love.[102]

Blanche Wiesen Cook interprets Goldman's final line of defence of Louise Michel as being indicative of her view that, while to be a lesbian "was an absolute right," "it was also to be rendered somehow less a woman."[103] Throughout Goldman's political life, her view of female same-sex relationships appears to have changed little. In 1928 while in exile, Goldman expressed concern over her friend Eleanor Fitzgerald's recently-established lesbian relationship. In a letter to Alexander Berkman, Goldman wrote:

> ...Really, the Lesbians are a crazy lot. Their antagonism to the male is almost a disease with them. I simply can't bear such narrowness...[104]

In explaining why Fitzgerald (Fritzie) would make such a choice (i.e., that of another woman) Goldman noted that, consistent with the arguments in her 1923 article on Louise Michel, the quality of Fritzie's previous heterosexual relationships had been poor.[105]

The letters from Goldman's companion Almeda Sperry suggest that Goldman and Sperry had an emotionally and passionately charged relationship which, according to Lillian Faderman and Blanche Wiesen Cook, could also be considered a "lesbian" association. According to Faderman's *Surpassing the Love of Men:*

> "Lesbian" describes a relationship in which two women's strongest emotions and affections are directed toward each other. Sexual contact may be part of the relationship to a greater or lesser degree, or it may be entirely absent.[106]

Defining what constitutes "lesbianism," in light of a particular discussion surrounding Jeannette Marks and Mary Wooley, Blanche Wiesen Cook writes:

> Even if they [Jeannette Marks and Mary Wooley] did renounce all physical contact we can still argue that they were lesbians: they chose each other and loved each other. Women who love women, who choose women to nurture and support and to form a living environment in which to work creatively and independently are lesbians. Genital "proofs" to confirm lesbianism are never required to confirm the heterosexuality of men and women who live together for 20 or 50 years.[107]

The ideas of Faderman and Cook represent one side of the contemporary debate over the definition of lesbianism. Arguing that genital contact or "proofs" may or may not be part of a lesbian relationship, Faderman and Cook define lesbianism as relationships in which women's primary emotional ties are with other women. The contemporary debate over the definition of lesbianism sets in opposition this view with one which stresses an explicitly erotic component.[108] As Jean Kennard argues, "only if we insist on the erotic nature of a lesbian bond can we consider the possibility of lesbianism as an innate aspect of sexual identity."[109]

Although Goldman curiously fails to mention Almeda Sperry in her autobiography, an extensive correspondence took place between the two women in 1912. Sperry was born in 1879 and was thirty-three years old when she wrote "I am a savage, Emma, a wild, wild savage."[110] Sperry's letters to Goldman, returned by Goldman after an unspecified period of time, were imbued with a "spirited, personal, deeply felt socialist-anarchist-feminist consciousness."[111] In one undated letter to Goldman, Sperry asserts:

> I have shown you the secret places of my soul thinking if I did so without reservation that it would help the cause along. I would not care if you told my story to the public or even use my name from the platform.[112]

The secret places of her soul, of which Almeda Sperry speaks and which her letters describe, contained expressions of passionate and sexual love for Emma Goldman. Jonathan Katz, author of *Gay American History*, states that "it is difficult to know exactly what occurred between Sperry and Goldman, but there is no doubt about the character and intensity of Sperry's feelings, so strongly and unambiguously expressed."[113]

Less clear, however, is the reciprocity of these feelings on the part of Goldman. Blanche Wiesen Cook writes that although there is evidence that Goldman "experimented" with a woman herself, there is "nothing simple about Goldman's attitude towards lesbianism."[114] Cook notes that Goldman never referred to Almeda Sperry and, therefore, it is impossible to know the "significance of this correspondence in her life."[115] Katz observed that "Goldman returned Sperry's affection, though with less passion and desperate need than Sperry felt."[116] Sperry, in an undated letter to Goldman, wrote:

> Never mind about not feeling as I do. I find restraint to be purifying. Realization is hell for it is satisfying and degenerating.[117]

If Goldman's feelings were *not* reciprocal, they were so by virtue of *degree* of sentiment and not *type* of sentiment. Goldman clearly had affection for Sperry and a desire to be near to her, as one is able to infer from Sperry's letter of August 24, 1912, in which she wrote:

> It is so very, very sweet of you to address me with endearing terms. I assure you that no one in the world appreciates such expressions of endearment more than myself, especially when they emanate from such a tower of strength as yourself.[118]

As well, Sperry's reply to a suggestion by Goldman that Almeda spend a week in the country with her, shows Goldman as the initiator. Sperry reveals her passionate intentions when she responds to Goldman's invitation:

> ...I, too, wish I could spend a week with you in the country .... Just before you sink into slumber, dear heart, I rest in your arms. I browse amongst the roots of your hair—I kiss your body with biting kisses—I inhale the sweet, pungent odour of you and you plead with me for relief.[119]

The proposed sojourn in the country where the two companions would be together did become a reality. In a letter to Goldman, dated September 23, 1912, Sperry reflects upon their time together. The letter alludes to the likelihood that Goldman did indeed reciprocate Sperry's affections, erotic and otherwise:

> Dearest: I have been flitting about from one thing to another today, in vain endeavour to quell my terrible longing for you.... I am instantly seized with a fire that races over my body in recurrent waves.... Dear, that day you were so kind to me and afterwards took me in your arms, your beautiful throat, that I kissed with a reverent tenderness.... How I wish I [was] with you on the farm!

You are so sweet in the mornings—your eyes are like
violets and you seem to forget, for a time, the sorrows of
the world. And your bosom—ah, your sweet bosom, unconfined. Lovingly, Almeda.[120]

Had Almeda Sperry's letters to Goldman not been signed they
could have been easily mistaken for Goldman's own letters written
to Ben Reitman in which Goldman alludes to her primitive and
savage nature. Sperry, with the same intensity and unbridled passion employed by Goldman in her correspondence to Reitman,
writes: "...It is the untamed part of me that loves you because you
don't want to put leading strings on it.... And it is the wild part of me
that would be unabashed in showing its love for you in front of a
multitude or in a crowded room."[121]

However the relationship between Sperry and Goldman
manifested itself, the association contained physical, erotic, emotional, as well as political elements. Admittedly, less intense than Sperry's,
Goldman's involvement in such same-sex relationships raises questions concerning the sex-preference exclusivity with which she once
described female emancipation—an exclusivity which failed to acknowledge the place of same-sex relationships as an expression of
"instinct" and, ultimately, as a source of emancipation.

Goldman's imprisonment in 1917 for advocating draft
avoidance during World War I first exposed her to lesbianism.[122]
Goldman credits her "understanding" of homosexuality, however, to
Freud through whom, in 1895, she had learned about the "inverted
phase." In 1929, she wrote to Alexander Berkman:

...In fact it was Freud who gave me my first understanding of homosexuality. I had known about it
through...my own imprisonment...but I knew nothing
about its inverted phase until I heard Freud in Vienna.[123]

During this period, Kate O'Hare, a socialist lecturer, who was
also imprisoned under the Espionage Act at the Missouri State
Penitentiary in 1917, and Goldman became companions.[124] The two

political prisoners developed a deep mutual affection. Admitting that the two would have been fierce opponents outside of the confines of prison, Goldman recalled that, in prison, their relationship was quite the contrary:

> In prison we soon found common ground and human interest in our daily association which proved more vital than our theoretical differences. I also discovered a very warm heart beneath Kate's outer coldness and found her a woman of simplicity and tender feeling. We quickly became friends, and my fondness for her increased in proportion as her personality unfolded itself to me.[125]

Goldman and O'Hare shared an emotional closeness but, in addition, a physical proximity. In *Living My Life* Goldman wrote:

> Soon we politicals—Kate, Ella [another young anarchist], and I—were nicknamed "the trinity." We spent much time together and became very neighbourly. Kate had the cell on my right, and Ella was next to her. We did not ignore our fellow-prisoners or deny ourselves to them, but intellectually Kate and Ella created a new world for me, and I basked in its interests, its friendships and affection.[126]

In 1920, Kate Richards O'Hare published *In Prison*, a detailed account of the treatment of female prisoners in Missouri State Penitentiary, in which she revealed the extent to which same-sex relationships permeated relations among and between incarcerated women. If O'Hare's observations were accurate, it is most probable that Goldman was also aware of the extent to which the "sex perversions"[127] dominated prison life. According to Jonathan Katz, O'Hare's account of prison lesbianism was "a rare and chilling document of prison life," conveying "the general barbarity of conditions and the oppressive context of the prison Lesbianism."[128] The barbaric and oppressive conditions of prison lesbianism were also a part of the outside world and its treatment of female inverts. Katz documents the plethora of "treatments" imposed upon these women to alter their sexual orientation—including abstinence, asexualization, aversion therapy, clitoridectomy, cold sitz baths, group therapy, hormone therapy, hypnotism, ovariectomy, and psychoanalysis. Based on the time she and Goldman spent cell-by-cell in prison, O'Hare concluded that:

> It is a stark, ugly fact that homosexuality exists in every prison and must ever be one of the sinister facts of our penal system. In the Missouri State Penitentiary it is, next to the task, the dominating feature in prison life and a regular source of revenue to favoured stool pigeons.... In fact, homosexuality was not only permitted by this trusty [stool pigeon], but indulgence was actively fostered by this coloured murderess, and, in the cases of young, helpless, and unprotected women, actually demanded and enforced.[129]

It is noteworthy that while O'Hare had a great deal to say about lesbianism, in this case in the prison context, Goldman's own account of the phenomenon is very brief: "Years ago...my sole acquaintance with homosexuals was limited to a few women I had met in prison..."[130]

Summary

Even though the male heterosexual definition of female sexuality at times contradicted her own sexual experiences and those of women around her, Goldman not only accepted the male and heterosexual model of sexuality but promoted it as well.[131] Typical of the "pioneers" of sexual liberation, Goldman and other women began to explore the sexual world but "did not imagine changing its overall boundaries."[132] Despite Goldman's view of the transcendent and emancipatory possibilities of sexuality, it "remained bound up with the structure of gender."[133]

It has been noted that Goldman felt a "profound ambivalence about lesbianism as a lifestyle."[134] Her view that female same-sex relationships were an option by default, represented Goldman's larger view that "pro-sex" meant "pro-heterosexual." In this way, Goldman felt that in order to enter the world of sex, she had to "travel alone and leave other women behind."[135] DuBois and Gordon explain this pattern exhibited by women of the "pro-sex" movement:

> This rejection of women occurred both because the dominant tradition of feminism was so antisexual, and because their own understanding of sex [that of the women of the "pro-sex" movement] was so heterosexual.[136]

Goldman's gender-bound, heterosexual, and male view of human relations caused her to adopt the socially-constructed view that women, not men, were women's major opponents. Despite Goldman's lifelong complaints of loneliness, longing for a friend of her own sex with whom she could share the thoughts and feelings she "could not express to men,"[137] Goldman's relations with other women were often characterized by competition and jealousy.[138] Goldman attributed her inability to find friendship among other women to "antagonism, petty envy and jealousy"[139] because men liked her. Goldman's emphasis upon the importance of male attention and attraction seemed to impede the development and sustenance of a community of female support. As a result, Emma Goldman relied predominantly on men for political and emotional support.[140] Goldman's political and personal competition with other women caused her to reject, in part, female ways, including female-centred and female-defined sexuality, being "part of a generation that branded intense female friendships as adolescent."[141] In adopting and endorsing the male, heterosexual construction of sexuality and human association, Goldman rejected a "community of women," leaving behind her feminist heritage.[142]

NOTES

1. Stansell, Christine, Ann Snitow, and Sharon Thompson, eds., in the introduction to *Powers of Desire: The Politics of Sexuality* (New York: Monthly Review Press, 1983), p. 23.
2. Adrienne Rich, "Compulsory Heterosexuality and Lesbian Experience," in *Powers of Desire: The Politics of Sexuality*, edited by Christine Stansell, Ann Snitow and Sharon Thompson (New York: Monthly Review Press, 1983), p. 182.
3. Compulsory heterosexuality is defined by Rich as a "prescribed script" which causes women to uncritically accept the boundaries of sexuality.
4. Emma Goldman, *Red Emma Speaks: Selected Writings and Speeches by Emma Goldman*, compiled and edited by Alix Kates Shulman (New York: Random House, 1972), p. 138.
5. Ibid., p. 138.
6. Sheila Jeffreys, *The Spinster and Her Enemies: Feminism and Sexuality 1880-1930* (London: Pandora, 1985), p. 40.
7. Ibid.
8. Rich, "Compulsory Heterosexuality and Lesbian Experience," p. 182.
9. Ibid., p. 200.
10. Ibid., p. 183.
11. Carroll Smith-Rosenberg, *Disorderly Conduct: Visions of Gender in America* (New York and Oxford: Oxford University Press, 1985), p. 32.
12. Ibid.
13. Ibid.
14. Sheila Jeffreys, *The Spinster and Her Enemies*, p. 26.
15. John D'Emilio, and Estelle B. Freedman, *Intimate Matters: A History of Sexuality in America* (New York: Harper and Row, 1988), p. 39.
16. Judith R. Walkowitz, "Male Vice and Female Virtue: Feminism and the Politics of Prostitution in Nineteenth-Century Britain," in *Powers of Desire: The Politics of Sexuality*, edited by Christine Stansell, Ann Snitow and Sharon Thompson (New York: Monthly Review Press, 1983), p. 429.
17. Ibid.
18. Emma Goldman, *Red Emma Speaks: Selected Writings and Speeches by Emma Goldman*, compiled and edited by Alix Kates Shulman (New York: Random House, 1972), p. 141.
19. Richard Drinnon, *Rebel in Paradise* (Chicago: University of Chicago Press, 1961), p. 153.
20. Goldman, *Red Emma Speaks: Selected Writings and Speeches by Emma Goldman*, p. 139.
21. Jeffreys, *The Spinster and Her Enemies*, p. 24.
22. Ibid.
23. Goldman in Jonathan Katz, *Gay American History* (New York: Thomas Y. Cromwell Company, 1976), p. 378.
24. Stansell, Snitow and Thompson, introduction to "Male Vice and Female Virtue: Feminism and the Politics of Prostitution in Nineteenth-Century Britain," in *Powers of Desire*, p. 419.
25. Ibid., p. 420.
26. Jeffrey Weeks, *Sexuality and Its Discontents* (London: Routledge Kegan Paul, 1985), pp. 55-56.
27. Ibid., p. 56.
28. Aritha van Herk, "Laying the Body on the Line," *Border Crossings*, 9 (Fall 1990), p. 86.
29. Weeks, *Sexuality and Its Discontents*, p. 56.
30. Goldman, *My Disillusionment in Russia*, pp. 556-57.
31. Ibid.

32. Ibid.
33. Dale Spender, *Women of Ideas and What Men Have Done to Them: From Aphra Behn to Adrienne Rich* (London: Ark Publications, 1983), p. 17.
34. Smith-Rosenberg defines the "new woman" as a "specific sociological and educational cohort born between the late 1850s and 1900s." These women, according to Smith-Rosenberg, rejected conventional female roles, fighting for the "rights and privileges commonly accorded bourgeois men." The key to identifying the "new woman" was not her high-profile visibility but rather, Smith-Rosenberg argues, her economically and socially autonomous life. For a fuller discussion of the "new woman," see Smith-Rosenberg's *Disorderly Conduct*, pp. 176-178.
35. Smith-Rosenberg, *Disorderly Conduct*, p. 256.
36. John D'Emilio, and Estelle B. Freedman, *Intimate Matters: A History of Sexuality in America* (New York: Harper and Row, 1988), p. 130.
37. Smith-Rosenberg, *Disorderly Conduct*, p. 190.
38. Ibid., pp. 190-191.
39. Ibid., p. 130.
40. Ibid., p. 192.
41. Ibid., pp. 192-193.
42. Goldman, *Living My Life*, p. 168.
43. Ibid., p. 225.
44. Blanche Weisen Cook, "The Historical Denial of Lesbianism," *Radical History Review*, 20 (Spring/Summer 1979), p. 60.
45. Ibid.
46. Ibid.
47. Linda Gordon and Ellen DuBois, "Seeking Ecstasy on the Battlefield: Danger and Pleasure in Nineteenth Century Feminist Thought," *Feminist Studies, 9* (Spring 1983), pp. 31-47.
48. Ibid., p. 41.
49. Ibid., p. 47.
50. Cook, "The Historical Denial of Lesbianism," *Radical History Review*, 20, p. 60.
51. Lillian Faderman, *Surpassing the Love of Men: Romantic Friendship and Love Between Women from the Renaissance to the Present* (London: Jaction Books, 1981), p. 252.
52. Ibid.
53. Smith-Rosenberg, *Disorderly Conduct*, p. 275.
54. Ibid.
55. Havelock Ellis, "Sexual Inversion in Women," *Alienist and Neurologist*, XVI, 1895, p. 25.
56. Ibid.
57. Smith-Rosenberg, *Disorderly Conduct*, p. 275.
58. Ibid.
59. Ibid., p. 276.
60. Ibid., p. 279.
61. Havelock Ellis, "Sexual Inversion in Women," *Alienist and Neurologist*, XVI, 1895, pp. 147-48.
62. Ibid., pp. 155-56.
63. Jeffreys, *The Spinster and Her Enemies*, p. 108.
64. Quoted in Jonathan Katz, *Gay American History* (New York: Thomas Y. Cromwell Company, 1976), p. 359.
65. Ibid., p. 363.
66. Ibid.
67. Edward Carpenter, *Love's Coming of Age* (Manchester: Labour Press, 1896), p. 131.
68. Goldman in Jonathan Katz, *Gay American History*, p. 379.
69. Goldman's use of the term "Uranian" was commonly used during her time as an ungendered label for homosexuals.
70. Golman, in Katz, *Gay American History*, p. 380.

71. Jeffrey Weeks, *Sexuality* (London and New York: Tavistock Publications, 1986), p. 74.
72. Cook, "The Historical Denial of Lesbianism," p. 56.
73. Alice Wexler, "Emma Goldman," lecture delivered at Harbourfront Authors Series, Toronto, October 15, 1989.
74. Cook, "The Historical Denial of Lesbianism," p. 56.
75. Goldman in Katz, *Gay American History*, p. 376.
76. Goldman, *Living My Life*, p. 269.
77. Ibid.
78. Ibid.
79. Ibid.
80. Ibid.
81. Ibid.
82. Ibid.
83. Ibid., p. 556.
84. Ibid.
85. Ibid.
86. Goldman, *Living My Life*, p. 167.
87. Katz, *Gay American History*, p. 167.
88. Goldman, *Living My Life*, p. 168.
89. Katz, *Gay American History*, p. 377.
90. Ibid., p. 378.
91. Ibid.
92. Ibid., pp. 378-379.
93. Emma Goldman, "Tragedy of Women's Emancipation," in *Anarchism and Other Essays* (New York: Mother Earth Publishing Association, 1910), p. 140.
94. Ibid.
95. Ibid.
96. Goldman in Katz, *Gay American History*, p. 380.
97. Ibid.
98. Ibid.
99. Ibid.
100. Ibid., p. 379.
101. Goldman, "The Tragedy of Women's Emancipation," in *Anarchism*, p. 140.
102. Goldman in Katz, *Gay American History*, p. 380.
103. Cook, "Female Support Networks and Political Activism: Lillian Wald, Crystal Eastman, Emma Goldman," *Chrysalis*, 3 (1977) p. 57.
104. Goldman, *Nowhere At Home: Letters from Exile of Emma Goldman and Alexander Berkman*, edited by Richard and Anna Marie Drinnon (New York: Schocken Books, 1975), p. 128.
105. Ibid., pp. 132-33. Goldman's use of the word "disease" in describing what she considered to be the lesbian attitude toward men was typical of the sexologists' construction of sexual deviance as pathology—a construction which greatly influenced Goldman.
106 Lillian Faderman, *Surpassing the Love of Men*, p. 64.
107. Cook, "The Historical Denial of Lesbianism," p. 64.
108. Martha Vicinis, "One Life to Stand Beside Me': Emotional Conflicts in First-Generation College Women in England," *Feminist Studies*, 8, no. 3 (Fall 1982): pp. 603-28.
109. Jean Kennard, "Ourself Behind Ourself: A Theory for Lesbian Readers," in *The Lesbian Issue*, edited by Estelle B. Freedman et al. (Chicago and London: The University of Chicago Press 1985), p. 154-155.
110. Katz, *Gay American History*, p. 527.
111. Ibid., p. 524.
112. Ibid.
113. Ibid., p. 523.
114. Cook, "Female Support Networks and Political Activism: Lillian Wald, Crystal Eastman, Emma Goldman," p. 57.
115. Ibid.

116. Katz, *Gay American History*, p. 523.
117. Ibid.
118. Ibid., p. 527.
119. Ibid., p. 528.
120. Ibid.
121. Ibid., p. 527.
122. Goldman, in Drinnon and Drinnon, *Nowhere At Home*, p. 146.
123. Ibid.
124. Goldman, *Living My Life*, p. 666.
125. Ibid., p. 667.
126. Ibid.
127. Kate Richard O'Hare, *In Prison, by...Sometime Federal Prisoner Number 1669* (New York: Knopf, 1923), p. 113.
128. Katz, *Gay American History*, p. 68.
129. O'Hare, *In Prison*, p. 113.
130. Goldman, in Katz, *Gay American History*, p. 379.
131. Ellen Carol DuBois and Linda Gordon, "Seeking Ecstasy on the Battlefield," p. 41.
132. Ibid.
133. Ibid.
134. Cook, "Female Support Networks and Political Activism," p. 56.
135. DuBois and Gordon, "Seeking Ecstasy on the Battlefield," p. 41.
136. Ibid.
137. Goldman, *Living My Life*, p. 160.
138. Ibid.
139. Ibid.
140. Cook, "Female Support Networks and Political Activism," p. 45.
141. DuBois and Gordon, "Seeking Ecstasy on the Battlefield," p. 41.
142. Ibid., pp. 41-42.

CHAPTER 7

Conclusion

Emma Goldman's contribution to anarchist thinking was the incorporation of feminism and sexuality into her theory of anarchism. Her theory rejected the long-standing bifurcation of private and public. By including feminism and sexuality, Goldman altered a tradition of androcentric theory-construction among anarchists—an exclusionary tradition which neglected issues related to women and sexuality on the grounds that they were "private," and therefore outside the scope of "public" theory.

While Goldman's theory of anarchism integrated so-called "private" experience and "public" theory, dichotomous thinking, nevertheless, does persist within it. Goldman dichotomized the following principles, creating the impression that each was the binary opposite of the other:

Gemeinschaft (community)	*Gesellschaft (society or "State")*
individuality	*individualism*
difference between men and women	*equality of men and women*
nature, instinct or desire	*reason or intellect in the form of careers regulated by the State*
pleasure of sexual expression	*sexual repression by church, State and "puritan" values*

In Goldman's dichotomous construction of social life, she rejected activities carried out in the service of the State, under institutional control and at the expense of sexual and emotional expression; she endorsed the concept of Gemeinschaft (community) and rejected the concept of Gesellschaft (society); endorsed a notion of individuality and rejected a form of individualism as governed by social and economic laissez-faire; endorsed the view that women were different from men (i.e., women as mothers) and rejected the view of women's equality in the public sphere (i.e., women as "professional automatons," childless and single); endorsed the value of instinct and desire as a source of emancipation and rejected intellectual pursuits governed by the State; endorsed the pursuit of sexual pleasure and rejected the values of those institutions and individuals which she perceived to be "anti-sex." Despite Goldman's placement of many aspects of social life into these dichotomies, she rejected the view of separate spheres for men and women—a view popularly embraced during her time. Rejecting what she called "the dualism of the sexes," Goldman argued that men and women did not represent two antagonistic worlds and, therefore, should inhabit the same domain.

According to the taxonomy of theories of sexuality developed by social constructionist Jeffrey Weeks, Emma Goldman could be categorized as an essentialist and a libertarian. Goldman's essentialist view of sexuality was one that assumed a unitary drive—biologically-determined and instinct-driven—undifferentiated by social conditions such as class, culture, ethnicity and history. Goldman's essentialism, coupled with libertarianism, shaped a view of sexuality as a positive, healthy instinct worthy of free and unfettered expression. Greatly influenced by the ideas of Freud and the discourse of sexology, Goldman constructed an unambiguous view of sexuality that was gender-bound, male-centred, phallocentric, and heterosexual. While it was Goldman's stated desire to liberate sexual "instinct" from the social forces that confined it, she constructed her own confined categories of behaviour, to which she assigned differing degrees of moral value. Female same-sex relationships were viewed by Goldman as an option by default, to be engaged in only when heterosexual relations proved unsatisfactory. Goldman's views on sexuality, therefore, could be perceived as having the effect of tightening "the grip of the system,"[1] as the ambiguities, complexities and ambivalence of sexuality were overlooked in favour of an essentialist construction, containing absolute truths. Under the influence of sexology, Goldman substituted a new sexual morality containing new "truths," for an old one, accepting such labels as "inversion" and "perversion." Goldman simply recast sexuality in a different mould rather than freeing it from *a priori* definitions and labels.

Goldman's libertarian view equating women's sexuality with emancipation is relevant to the sex debates of the second wave of feminism—debates over sexuality's inherent pleasures versus its inherent dangers. These contemporary debates also focus on whether or not "sexual liberation" in a male-dominated culture can be equated with "women's liberation." Goldman promoted women's sexual freedom using ideas such as free love, voluntary motherhood, sexual varietism, a rejection of female chastity, sex education for girls and young women, and the separation of sexuality and reproduction through accessible birth control. Goldman romanticized sexual liberation, ignoring, in the words of her most recent biographer, "the ways in which 'free love' has often been used by men to rationalize the sexual exploitation of women."[2] Goldman's "pro-sex" position encompassed an uncritical treatment of the male sex "drive" or "instinct."

Arguing against the "pro-sex" position and for one that acknowledges the inherent dangers of sexuality, contemporary feminist Sheila Jeffreys contends "...that this so-called 'drive' or 'urge' is a social construct and that male sexuality need not be uncontrollable, aggressive and exploitative, must be the basis of a feminist perspective on sexuality."[3] Gender-bound and phallocentric, Goldman's view of sexual liberation suggests that women's sexual expression be cast in a mould of heterosexuality and motherhood, *in response* to the urges of their male counterparts. Goldman's pro-sex position assumed the essential male "urge" to be "good and necessary and women and girls of any age cannot be justified in resisting its demands."[4]

Contemporary feminist Elizabeth Fox-Genovese's assessment that "no politics remains innocent of that which it contests,"[5] is relevant to the sexual politics of Emma Goldman. While Goldman vehemently rejected the forces that confined and limited women's lives, her own politics engendered the potentiality for female confinement and limitation. Goldman spoke of the issue of women's sexual freedom or "free love" as if the expression of sexual instinct "unproblematically speaks its own truth";[6] as if the lifting of sexual repression from women's lives represented the ultimate emancipatory accomplishment, offering the final resolution of women's "problems." The unproblematical manner with which Goldman treats sexual liberation creates the impression that women's sexuality (in the midst of male-dominated sexuality) is safe, healthy and on an equal footing with that of men. In failing to recognize the heightened vulnerability that "sexual liberation" would present to women and that in the area of sexuality, "more than any other area of human social life, the inequality of power between men and women is most clearly expressed,"[7] Goldman's politics were vulnerable to that which they contested—female subjugation.

Social constructionist feminists Ann Snitow, Christine Stansell and Sharon Thompson argue that, "women have been particularly burned by the simplified freedoms, the cynical psychological shortcuts of the sexual revolution."[8] The authors express their suspicion "of the sexual license of a self-proclaimed liberal culture insensitive to women's sexual vulnerability."[9] Taking a position against libertarianism in contemporary sex debates, Snitow, Stansell and Thompson pose the question: "At what point does libertarianism shade into a laissez-faire position that posits a theoretical choice with which abstractly equal individuals bargain and contract in the sexual marketplace? Do we gain more autonomy from saying 'yes' or saying 'no' in a grossly unequal world?"[10]

Goldman's emphasis on what Snitow, Stansell, and Thompson might consider to be a "psychological shortcut" to sexual revolution—the "emancipation of the soul"—leaves unattended the unequal status of men and women. Goldman dismissed the claim made by her liberal reformer sisters that men and women represent two antagonistic worlds, as if to suggest that such an observation is anti-male and anti-sex and, therefore, anti-emancipatory. By stressing sexual freedom for women (on male terms), Goldman neglected to attend to other forms of freedom—freedom of safety and security enabling women to walk alone at night or to feel safe in the confines of their own homes. Goldman's equating of women's liberation with sexual liberation assumes that sexual revolution will be symmetrically experienced by both men and women. In the real world, however, men's freedom has frequently been achieved, not in conjunction with, but at the expense of women.

Some contemporary radical feminists, such as Alice Echols, also link women's liberation with sexual liberation. However, unlike Goldman, Echols recognizes that power inheres in sexuality rather than withering away in supposed egalitarian relationships.[11] Echols argues that "we might achieve more equality were we to negotiate rather than deny power."[12]

Social constructionist feminist Sheila Jeffreys, taking the position that "sexuality (on male terms) presents inherent dangers for women,"[13] argues that analyses of sexuality must begin with an assumption of a power relationship (i.e., economic and/or political) between the sexes; those analyses which do not, according to Jeffreys, are "doomed to failure."[14]

Goldman dismissed the socially constructed inequality between men and women. In her attempt to persuade women that they must discard the "ridiculous" notion that men and women represent two antagonistic worlds, she refused to acknowledge that men and women *do* represent two antagonistic worlds as they relate to the possession of power. As a result, she failed to articulate how the inequality of power between the sexes would be played out in the real world. How could sexuality be liberatory for women given the inherent power imbalances between the sexes?

Goldman's belief in the inherent pleasures of women's sexuality was linked to her anarchist vision. In this vision, men and women would inhabit the same domain; there would not be a sharp divide between private and public life. Goldman's sexual politics, therefore, were not based on the real world but on an envisioned world, in which the power of the State would be replaced by the free association of a community of sexually "free" and equal individuals.

Contemporary social constructionist feminists Ellen Carol Du-Bois and Linda Gordon, maintain that women today must not make the same mistake as early twentieth-century sexual libertarians such as Goldman. They argue that today, unlike the early twentieth-century sexual libertarians, we must "analyze how male supremacy and other forms of domination shape what we think of as 'free' sexuality."[15]

Goldman's failure to construct a view of sexuality on the basis of power relations between the sexes is largely due to her unitary and simplistic view of power. Power, for Goldman, was that which the State possessed, resulting in its domination, control and oppression of the individual. However, as social constructionist theorists have argued, power is not something which resides in a single thing; it is, as Weeks suggests, a concept "created in the relationships which sustain it."[16] For Goldman, power residing in the State represented the ultimate threat to the free expression of "instincts" and "desires," while power which resided in sexual relationships went unaddressed. Goldman's unitary view of power, contained in the bureaucratic/legislative realm and to be eliminated by the anarchist community, fails to recognize the omnipresence of power residing in the habits, customs, traditions of the anarchist community, as well as how this power would adhere to sexual relations. The informal power inherent in the so-called habits, customs, and traditions of patriarchy in Goldman's envisioned anarchist community, may have been of equal threat to women's freedom (sexual and otherwise) as was and is the formal power of the State in capitalist society.

In summary, Goldman's ideas on the liberatory potential of women's sexuality are relevant to the current feminist debates on sexuality's pleasures versus its dangers. Goldman emphasized sexuality's pleasures, rather than its dangers, equating women's freedom with sexual freedom, as do some contemporary feminists. I would argue that today, as was true of Goldman's day (although not recognized by Goldman), sexuality's pleasures are seldom realized in the absence of its dangers. In the current sexual climate where AIDS makes sex a potentially life-threatening act, where sexual harassment of working women occurs daily, where female homicide is most frequently caused by a male lover or spouse, where one women in ten is battered by her male lover or spouse, sexuality cannot be associated wholly with pleasure or freedom. Sexuality *does* have the potential to also cause pain and oppression. Goldman failed to recognize that sexuality may not always be pleasurable or emancipatory, perhaps because of her lifelong attempts to create a perfect sexual/emotional union from which she could gain unconditional love and exclusive affection. Contemporary feminists on the "pro-sex" or "pro-pleasure" side of the argument must not make the same mistake as Goldman; they must recognize that cautious awareness of sexuality's dangers need not be "anti-sex" or "anti-emancipatory," but rather a realistic view of the state of sex-gender relations.

Also, Goldman's ideas are significant for contemporary feminism and social reform because of their relevance to the difference versus equality debates. Rejecting a truncated view of womanhood in which women are single, childless professionals, sacrificing their emotional and sexual expression in service to the State, Goldman affirmed women's specificity while, at the same time, sought women's freedom to develop their full human potential. According to Goldman, however, the development of women's potential would not and could not occur within the public State-dominated realm, as contemporary feminists on the equality side of the debate would argue. The realm of the public "State," for Goldman, was a source of domination, oppression and control for both women and men. In contrast to contemporary feminist conceptions of "integrative feminism," which aim at transcending the private/public, difference/equality divide, Goldman's form of "integrative feminism" is unique. While contemporary conceptions of "integrative feminism" employ the affirmation of women's specificity in their "revisioning" of the world in such a way as to seek its extension into the public realm or State, Goldman does not. Instead, Goldman's "integrative feminism" involves a revisioning of the public realm according to the tastes, instincts and desires of individual women (and men). In other words, the public realm must be reconstructed in harmony, according to the preferences of the women and men who inhabit it, rather than simply "improved" through the injection of women.

Like Goldman, I believe that the public State-dominated realm will not necessarily be "purified" or "improved" by women's entry to it. Also, like Goldman, I believe that women's freedom to develop their full human potential does not necessarily occur through their attainment of State-dominated careers and professions. The current number of women earning substantially less than their male counterparts, encountering a "glass ceiling" when it comes to promotion, and/or working "double shifts" (i.e., in the home and in the paid labour force) under the guise of women's "liberation," reinforces this belief.

The value which Goldman placed on individual instincts, tastes, and desires (or what she called "internal" factors) has implications, not only for feminist theory, but also political action and education. Goldman's message is that we should construct our "external" or public lives in harmony with our most basic internal desires, rather than in opposition and/or denial of these desires. The "external" organizations of the public realm must be reconstructed in *response* to human instincts, tastes and desires, rather than through an attempt to revision the unresponsive State, and the institutions under its purview, through the injection of new values and/or new voices.

NOTES

1. Ann Snitow, Christine Stansell and Sharon Thompson, in the introduction to *Powers of Desire* (New York: Monthly Review Press, 1983), p. 9.
2. Alice Wexler, *Emma Goldman: An Intimate Life* (New York: Pantheon Books, 1984), p. 278.
3. Sheila Jeffreys, *The Spinster and Her Enemies* (London, Boston and Henly: Pandora, 1985), p. 196.
4. Ibid.
5. Elizabeth Fox-Genovese, "The Personal Is Not Political Enough," *Marxist Perspectives*, 2 (Winter 1979/80), p. 94.
6. Jeffrey Weeks, *Sexuality and Its Discontents* (London: Routledge and Kegan Paul, 1985), p. 56.
7. Jeffreys, *The Spinster and Her Enemies*, p. 196.
8. Snitow, Stansell and Thompson, *Powers of Desire*, p. 12.
9. Ibid.
10. Ibid., p. 13.

11. Alice Echols, "The Taming of the Id: Feminist Sexual Politics, 1968-83," in *Pleasure and Danger: Exploring Female Sexuality,* edited by Carol S. Vance (Boston and London: Routledge and Kegan Paul, 1984), p. 66.
12. Ibid.
13. Jeffreys, *The Spinster and Her Enemies,* p. 196.
14. Ibid.
15. Ellen Carol DuBois and Linda Gordon, "Seeking Ecstasy on the Battlefield," in *Pleasure and Danger,* edited by Carol S. Vance (Boston and London: Routledge and Kegan Paul, 1984), p. 43.
16. Weeks, *Sex, Politics and Society,* p. 7.

Bibliography

Anderson, Margaret. *My Thirty Years' War.* London: Alfred A. Knopf, 1930.

Anderson, Margaret. "The Immutable." *The Little Review* 1 (November 1914): 19-22.

Avrich, Paul. *An American Anarchist: The Life of Voltairine de Cleyre.* Princeton, N.J.: Princeton University Press, 1978.

Avrich, Paul. "Bakunin and the United States." *International Review of Social History* 24 (1979): 320-40.

Avrich, Paul. "Kropotkin in America." *International Review of Social History* 25 (1980): 1-34.

Avrich, Paul. *The Modern School Movement: Anarchism and Education in the United States.* Princeton, N.J.: Princeton University Press, 1980.

Avrich, Paul. *The Russian Anarchists.* Princeton, N.J.: Princeton University Press, 1967.

Barko, Naomi. "The Emma Goldman You'll Never See in the Movies." *MS,* March 1982.

Berkin, Carol Ruth. "Private Woman, Public Woman: The Contradictions of Charlotte Perkins Gilman." In *Women of America: A History,* edited by Ruth Berkin and Mary Beth Norton. Boston: Houghton Mifflin Company, 1979.

Berkman, Alexander. *Prison Memoirs of an Anarchist.* 1912 Reprint. Pittsburgh, Pa.: Frontier Press, 1970.

Berkman, Alexander. *The Bolshevik Myth.* New York: Boni & Liveright, 1925.

Berkman, Alexander. *Now and After: The ABC of Communist Anarchism.* New York: Vanguard Press, 1929.

Berelson, Bernard. "Population Policy: Personal Notes." *Population Studies* 25 (July 1971): 173-192.

Berman, Paul, ed. *Quotations from the Anarchists.* New York: Praeger Publishers, 1972.

Buhle, Mari Jo. *Women and American Socialism, 1870-1920.* Urbana: University of Illinois Press, 1981.

Callahan, Raymond B. *Education and the Cult of Efficiency.* Chicago: University of Chicago Press, 1962.

Canadian Broadcasting Corporation. "Emma Goldman: A Life of Anarchy." Toronto, 1983.

Carpenter, Edward. *Love's Coming of Age.* Manchester: Labour Press, 1896.

Chevigny, Bell Gale. "Daughters Writing: Toward a Theory of Women's Biography." *Feminist Studies* 9 (Spring 1983): 79-102.

Chodorow, Nancy. *The Reproduction of Mothering: Psychoanalysis and the Sociology of Gender.* Berkeley: University of California Press, 1978.

Clark, Lorenne M. G., and Lange, Lynda, ed. *The Sexism of Social and Political Theory: Women and Reproduction From Plato To Nietzsche.* Toronto: University of Toronto Press, 1979.

Cook, Blanche Wiesen. "Female Support Networks and Political Activism: Lillian Wald, Crystal Eastman, Emma Goldman." In *A Heritage of Her Own: Towards a New Social History of Women,* edited by Nancy F. Cott and Elizabeth H. Pleck. New York: Simon & Schuster, 1979.

Cook, Blanche Wiesen. "The Historical Denial of Lesbianism." *Radical History Review* 20 (1979): 60-65.

Cook, Blanche Wiesen. "Female Support Networks and Political Activism: Lillian Wald, Crystal Eastman, Emma Goldman." *Chrysalis* 3 (1977): 43-61.

Coward, Rosalind. *Female Desire. Women's Sexuality Today.* London: Paladin, 1984.

Coward, Rosalind. *Patriarchal Precedents: Sexuality and Social Relations.* London: Routledge and Kegan Paul, 1983.

David, Henry. *A History of the Haymarket Affair.* New York: Farrar & Rinehart, 1936.

D'Emilio, John, and Freedman, Estelle B. *Intimate Matters: A History of Sexuality in America.* New York: Harper and Row, 1988.

Dell, Floyd. *Women as World Builders.* Chicago: Forbes and Co., 1913.

Demerath, Nicholas J. *Birth Control and Foreign Policy.* New York: Harper and Row, 1976.

Dinnerstein, Dorothy. *The Mermaid and the Minotaur.* New York: Harper/Colophon, 1977.

Drinnon, Richard. "Emma Goldman: A Study in American Radicalism." Ph.D. dissertation, University of Minnesota, 1957.

Drinnon, Richard. *Rebel in Paradise.* Chicago: University of Chicago Press, 1982.

Dubois, Ellen Carol and Gordon, Linda. "Seeking Ecstasy on the Battlefield: Danger and Pleasure in Nineteenth Century Feminist Thought." *Feminist Studies* 9 (Spring 1983): 31-49.

Durkheim, E. *Suicide.* London: Routledge and Kegan Paul, 1952.

Durkheim, Emile. *Education and Sociology.* London: Gencoe, 1956.

Durkheim, Emile. *The Division of Labour in Society.* Translated by George Simpson. Glencoe Illinois: Free Press, 1964.

Dyer, Richard. "Male Sexuality in the Media." In *The Sexuality of Men,* edited by Andy Metcalf and Martin Humphries. London: Pluto Press, 1985.

Echols, Alice. "The Taming of the Id: Feminist Sexual Politics, 1968-83." In *Pleasure and Danger: exploring female sexuality,* edited by Carole S. Vance. Boston and London: Routledge and Kegan Paul, 1984, pp. 50-72.

Ehrenreich, Barbara and English, Deirdre. *For Her Own Good.* Garden City N.Y.: Doubleday Anchor, 1979.

Eichler, Margrit. *Nonsexist Research Methods: A Practical Guide.* Boston: Allen and Irwin Inc., 1988.

Ellis, Havelock. *Man and Woman: A Study of Secondary and Tertiary Sexual Characters.* London: Heinemann, 1934, first published in 1894.

Ellis, Havelock. *The Psychology of Sex.* London: William Heinemann, 1946, first published in 1933.

Ellis, Havelock, *Sex in Relation to Society.* Vol. VI of *Studies in the Psychology of Sex.* London: Heineman, 1946, first published in 1910.

Ellis, Havelock. *Sexual Inversion.k Vol. II of Studies in the Psychology of Sex.* Philadelphia: F.A. Davis Company, 1927, first published in 1897.

Ellis, Havelock. *Analysis of the Sexual l Impulse, Love and Pain, the Sexual Impulse in Women.* Vol. III of *Studies in the Psychology of Sex.* Philadelphia: F.A. Davis, 1913, first published in 1903.

Ellis, Havelock. *Sexual Selection in Man.* Vol. IV of *Studies in the Psychology of Sex.* Philadelphia: F. A. Davis Company, 1906.

Ellis, Havelock. "Sexual Inversion in Women." *Alienist and Neurologist* XVI, 1895.

Ellis, Havelock. *The Task of Social Hygiene.* London: Constable, 1913.

Elshtain, Jean Bethke. *Public Man, Private Women.* Princeton, N.J.: Princeton University Press, 1981.

Faderman, Lillian. *Surpassing the Love of Men-Romantic Friendship and Love Between Women from the Renaissance to the Present.* London: Jaction Books, 1981.

Falk, Candace. *Love, Anarchy and Emma Goldman.* New York: Holt, Rinehart and Winston, 1984.

Fine, Sidney. "Anarchism and the Assassination of McKinley." *American Historical Review* 60 (1955): 777-99.

Fishbein, Leslie. *Rebels in Bohemia: The Radicals of the Masses, 1911- 1917.* Chapel Hill: University of North Carolina Press, 1982.

Foucault, Michel. *The History of Sexuality.* Translated by Robert Hurley. London: Allen Lane, 1979.

Fox-Genovese, Elizabeth. "The Personal Is Not Political Enough." *Marxist Perspectives* 2 (Winter 1979/80): 94-113.

Frazer, Winifred, L.E.G., and E.G.O.: *Emma Goldman and "The Iceman Cometh."* Gainesville: University of Florida Press, 1974.

French, Marilyn. *Beyond Power: On Women, Men and Morals.* London: Abacus, 1986.

Freud, Sigmund. *Three Essays on the Theory of Sexuality.* Introduction by S. Marcus. New York: Basic Books, 1975.

Gagnon, J.H., and Simon, William. *Sexual Conduct: The Social Sources of Sexuality.* London: Hutchinson, 1973.

Geddes, Patrick, and Thomson, J.A. *Sex.* London: Contemporary Science Series, 1914.

Goldberg, Harold J. "Goldman and Berkman View the Bolshevik Regime." *Slavonic and East European Review* 34 (April 1975): 272-76.

Goldman, Emma. *Anarchism and Other Essays.* New York: Mother Earth Publishing Association, 1910.

Goldman, Emma. *Anarchism on Trial: Speeches of Alexander Berkman and Emma Goldman Before the United States District Court in the City of New York, July 1917.* New York: Mother Earth Publishing Association, 1917.

Goldman, Emma. "Johann Most." *American Mercury,* June 1926.

Goldman, Emma. *Living My Life.* 2 Vols. New York: Alfred A. Knopf, 1931. Reprint. New York: Dover Publications, 1970.

Goldman, Emma. *My Disillusionment in Russia,* 1922. Reprint. New York: Thomas Y. Crowell, 1970.

Goldman, Emma. *Nowhere At Home: Letters from Exile of Emma Goldman and Alexander Berkman.* Edited by Richard Drinnon and Anna Maria Drinnon. New York: Schocken Books, 1975.

Goldman, Emma. *Red Emma Speaks: Selected Writings and Speeches by Emma Goldman.* Compiled and edited by Alix Kates Shulman. New York: Random House, 1972.

Goldman, Emma. *The Social Significance of the Modern Drama.* Boston: Richard G. Badger, 1914.

Goldman, Emma. *The Social Significance of the Modern Drama* Introduction by Harry G. Carlson; preface by Ericka Munk. New York: Applause Theatre Book Publishers, 1987.

Gordon, Linda. *Woman's Body, Woman's Right: A Social History of Brith Control in America.* New York: Penguin Books, 1977.

Grosskurth, Phyllis. *Havelock Ellis: A Biography.* New York: Alfred A. Knopf, 1980.

Guerin, Daniel. *Anarchism: From Theory to Practice.* New York: Monthly Review Press, 1970.

Gutman, Herbert, *Work, Culture and Society in Industrializing America.* New York: Alfred A. Knopf, 1976.

Hale, Nathan G. Jr. *Freud and the Americans: The Beginnings of Psychoanalysis in the United States, 1896-1917.* New York: Oxford University Press, 1971.

Hapgood, Hutchins. *A Victorian in the Modern World.* New York: Harcourt Brace, 1939.

Hartman, C.R., and Burgess, A.W. "Sexual Abuse of Children: Causes and Consequences." In *Child Maltreatment,* edited by Dante Cicchetti and Vicki Carlson. Cambridge: Cambridge University Press, 1989, pp. 95-128.

Hawthorn, Geoffrey. *The Sociology of Fertility.* London: Collier-MacMillian Limited, 1970.

Himes, Norman. *Medical History of Contraception.* New York: Gamot Press, 1963.

Howells, Kevin. "Adult Sexual Interest in Children: Considerations Relevant to Theories and Actiology." In *Adult Sexual Interest in Children,* edited by Mark Cook and Devin Howells. London: Academic Press, 1981, pp. 55-98.

Hughes, Patricia. "Fighting the Good Fight: Separation or Integration." In *Feminism in Canada,* edited by Angela Finn and Geraldine Miles. Montreal: Black Rose Books, 1982.

Ignatieff, Michael. *The Needs of Strangers.* London: Chatto and Windus, 1984.

Jeffreys, Sheila. *The Spinster and Her Enemies: Feminism and Sexuality 1880-1930.* London: Pandora, 1985.

Joll, James. *The Anarchists.* London: Eyre & Spottiswoode, 1964.

Jordanova, Ludmilla. "Natural Facts: a historical perspective on science and reality." In *Nature, Culture and Gender,* edited by Carol MacCormack and Marilyn Strathern. Cambridge University Press, 1980.

Katz, Jonathan, ed. *Gay American History: Lesbians and Gay Men in the U.S.A.* New York: Thomas Y. Cromwell Company, 1976.

Kennard, Jean E. "Ourself Behind Ourself: A theory for Lesbian Readers." In *The Lesbian Issue,* edited by Estelle B. Freedman et al. Chicago and London: The University of Chicago Press, 1985.

Key, Ellen, *The Woman Movement,* trans. by Mamah Bouton Borthwick. New York: G. P. Putnam's Sons; London: The Knickerbocker Press, 1912.

Kirchwey, Freda. "Emma Goldman." *The Nation,* 2 December 1931.

Kennedy, David. *Birth Control in America: The Career of Margaret Sanger.* New Haven: Yale University Press, 1970.

Kollontai, Alexandra. *The Social Basis of the Woman Question*. Edited by Alix Holt. *Selected Writings of Alexandra Kollantai*. New York: W.W. Norton, 1971.

Kropotkin, Peter. *The Conquest of Bread*. London: Chapman and Hall, 1906.

Kropotkin, Peter. *Kropotkin's Revolutionary Pamphlets*. Edited by Roger Baldwin. New York: Benjamin Blom, 1927.

Kropotkin, Peter. *Memoirs of a Revolutionist*. Boston: Houghton Mifflin Co., 1899.

Kropotkin, Peter. *Mutual Aid*. London: William Heinemann, 1903.

Lacan, Jacques. *The Ego and Freud's Theory in the Technique of Psychoanalysis 1954-1955*. New York: W. W. Norton, 1988.

Lasch, Christopher. *The New Radicalism in America 1889-1920*. Philadelphia: Temple University Press, 1981.

Leehan, James, and Wilson, Laura Pistone. *Grown-Up Abused Children*. Springfield: Charles C. Thomas, 1985.

Lenz, Elinor, and Myerhoff, Barbara. *The Feminization of America*. Los Angeles: Jeremy P. Tarcher Inc., 1985.

Malinowski, Bronislaw. *Sex, Culture and Myth*. London: Rupert-Hart-Davis, 1963.

Marchak, M. Patricia. *Ideological Perspectives on Canada*. 3d edition. Toronto: McGraw-Hill Ryerson, 1987.

Marsh, Margaret. *Anarchist Women, 1870-1920*. Philadelphia: Temple University Press, 1981.

Miles, Angela. "Ideological Hegemony in Political Discourse: Women's Specificity and Equality." In *Feminism in Canada*, edited by Angela Miles and Geraldine Finn. Montreal: Black Rose Books, 1982.

Miller, Martin A. *Kropotkin*. Chicago: University of Chicago Press, 1976.

Mitchell, Juliet. *Feminism and Psychoanalysis*. New York: Random House/Vintage, 1974.

Nisbet, Robert A. *The Present Age: Progress and Anarchy in Modern America*. New York: Olvol, 1988.

Nisbet, Robert A. *The Sociological Tradition*. New York: Basic Books, 1966.

O'Hare, Kate Richards. *In Prision, by...Sometime Federal Prisioner, Number z1669*. New York: Knopf, 1923.

Osofsky, Stephen. *Peter Kropotkin*. Boston: Twayne Publishers, 1979.

Overbeek, J. *History of Population Theories*. Rotterdam University Press, 1974.

Padgug, Robert. "Sexual Matters: on conceptualizing sexuality in history." *Radical History Review* 20 (Spring/Summer 1979): 8-13.

Perrow Charles. *Complex Organizations*. New York: Random House, 1979.

Pierson, Ruth Roach. "Ellen Key: Maternalism and Pacifism." In *Delivering Motherhood: Maternal Ideologies and Practices in the 19th and 20th Centuries*, edited by Katherine Arnup, Andrée Lévesque, and Ruth Roach Pierson. London and New York: Routledge, 1990.

Plummer, Kenneth. "Sexual Diversity: a sociological perspective." In *Sexual Diversity*, edited by Kevin Howells. Oxford: Blackwell, 1984.

Poirier, Suzanne. "Emma Goldman, Ben Reitman, and Reitman's Wives: A Study in Relationships." *Women's Studies* 14 (Summer 1988): 227- 298.

Poovey, Mary. *Uneven Developments: The Ideological Work of Gender in Mid-Victorian England*. Chicago: University of Chicago Press, 1988.

Prentice A., and Pierson, R. "Feminism and the Writing and Teaching of History." In Angela Miles and Geraldine Finn, ed. Feminism: *From Pressure to Politics.* Montreal: Black Rose Books, 1989.

Preston, William, Jr. *Aliens and Dissenters: Federal Suppression of Radicals, 1903-1933.* New York: Harper and Row, 1963.

Proceedings and Addresses of the National Education Association of the United States 1890-1930.

Reich, Wilhelm. *The Function of the Orgasm. Sex-Economic Problems of Biological Energy.* London: Panther Books, 1972.

Reichert, William W. *Partisans of Freedom: A Study of American Anarchism.* Bowling Green, Ohio: Bowling Green University Press, 1976.

Rich, Adrienne. "Compulsory Heterosexuality and Lesbian Experience." In *Powers of Desire: The Politics of Sexuality,* edited by Christine Stansell, Ann Snitow and Sharon Thompson. New York: Monthly Review Press, 1983.

Rich, Adrienne. *Of Woman Born.* New York: Bantam Books, 1976.

Rosenberg, Karen. "The 'Autumnal Love' of Red Emma." *Harvard Magazine,* January-February 1984.

Ross, Ellen, and Rapp, Rayna. "Sex and Society: A research Note from Social History and Anthropology." In *Powers of Desire: The Politics of Sexuality,* edited by Christine Stansell, Ann Snitow and Sharon Thompson. New York: Monthly Review Press, 1983.

Rowbotham, Sheila, and Weeks, Jeffrey. *Socialism and the New Life.* London: Pluto Press, 1977.

Rubin, Gayle. "The Traffic in Women: Notes on the 'Political Economy' of Sex." In *Toward on Anthropology of Women,* edited by Rayna R. Reiter. New York: Monthly Review Press, 1975.

Scheman, Naomi. "From Hamlet to Maggie-Verver, The History and Politics of the Knowing Subject." *Poetics* 18 (4-5, 1989): 449-469.

Scott, Joan Wallach. *Gender and the Politics of History.* New York: Columbia University Press, 1988.

Sears, Hal D. *The Sex Radicals: Free Love in High Victorian America.* Lawrence: Regents Press of Kansas, 1977.

Segal, Lynne. "Sensual Uncertainty, or why the clitoris is not enough." In *Sex and Love: New Thoughts on Old Contradictions,* edited by Sue Cartledge and Joanna Ryan. London: The Women's Press, 1983.

Shulman, Alix Kates. "Emma Goldman: Anarchist Queen." In *Feminist Theorists,* edited by Dale Spender. London: The Women's Press, 1983

Shulman, Alix Kates. *To the Barricades: The Anarchist Life of Emma Goldman.* New York: Thomas Y. Crowell, 1971.

Shulman, Alix Kates. "Dancing in the Revolution: Emma Goldman's Feminism." *Socialist Review* 10 (March-April 1982): 31-44.

Shulman, Alix Kates, ed. *Red Emma Speaks: An Emma Goldman Reader.* New York: Schocken Books, 1983.

Smith, Bernard. *Forces in American Criticism: A Study in the History of American Thought.* New York: Harcourt Brace, 1939.

Smith, Dorothy E. "The Social Construction of Documentary Reality." *Sociological Inquiry* 44 no. 4 (1974): 257-268.

Smith-Rosenberg, Carroll. *Disorderly Conduct: Visions of Gender in America.* Toronto: Oxford University Press, 1986.

Smith-Rosenberg, Carroll, and Rosenburg, Charles. "The Female Animal: Medical and Biological Views of Woman and Her Role in Nineteenth Century America." *The Journal of American History* 60 (March 1974): 332-356.

Snitow, Ann. "A Gender Diary." In *Conflicts in Feminism*, edited by Marianne Hirsch and Evelyn Fox Keller. Sterling, Virginia: World Composition Services, 1990.

Solomon, Martha. *Emma Goldman.* Boston: G.K. Hall, 1987.

Spacks, Patricia Meyer. "Selves in Hiding." In *Women's Autobiography: Essays in Criticism*, edited by Estelle C. Jelinek. Bloomington: Indiana University Press, 1980.

Spender, Dale. *Women of Ideas and What Men Have Done to Them; From Aphra Behn to Adrienne Rich.* London: Ark Paperbacks, 1983.

Stansell, Christine; Snitow, Ann; and Thompson, Sharon. eds. *Powers of Desire: The Politics of Sexuality.* New York: Monthly Review Press, 1983.

Stites, Richard. *The Women's Liberation Movement in Russia: Feminism, Nihilism, and Bolshevism, 1860-1930.* Princeton, N.J.: Princeton University Press, 1978.

Sydie, R.A. *Natural Women, Cultured Men: A Feminist Perspective on Sociological Theory.* Toronto: Methuen, 1987.

Sydie, R.A. "The Value of Reproduction: A Partial Re-examination of Tönnies' Gemeinschaft and Gesellschaft" *Atlantis* 13 (Fall 1987): 137-147.

Tax, Meredith. *The Rising of the Women: Feminist Solidarity and Class Conflict, 1880-1917.* New York: Monthly Review Press, 1980.

Taylor, Frederick. *The Principles of Scientific Management.* New York: Harper and Brothers, 1915.

Tönnies, Ferdinand. *Gemeinschaft und Gesellschaft.* Translated and edited by Charles P. Loomis. New York: Harper and Row, 1965.

Unger, Roberto. *Knowledge and Politics.* New York: Free Press, 1975.

van Herk, Aritha. "Laying the Body on the Line." *Border Crossings* 9 (Fall 1990): 86-88.

Vance, Carole S. "Gender Systems, Ideology, and Sex Research." In *Powers of Desire: The Politics of Sexuality*, edited by Christine Stansell, Ann Snitow and Sharon Thompson. New York: Monthly Review Press, 1983.

Vance, Carole S. "Pleasure and Danger: toward a politics of sexuality." In *Pleasure and Danger. Exploring Female Sexuality*, edited by Carole S. Vance. Boston and London: Routledge and Kegan Paul, 1984.

Vance, Carole S., ed. *Pleasure and Danger: Exploring Female Sexuality.* Boston and London: Routledge and Kegan Paul, 1984.

Vesey, Laurence. *The Communal Experience: Anarchist and Mystical Counter-Cultures in America.* New York: Harper and Row, 1973.

Vicinus, Martha. "Sexuality and Power: A Review of Current Work in the History of Sexuality." *Feminist Studies* 8, no. 1 (Spring 1982): 134-56.

Vicinus, Martha. "One Life to Stand Beside Me: Emotional conflicts in First-Generation College Women in England." *Feminist Studies* 8 (Fall 1982): 603-28.

Walkowitz, Judith R. "Male Vice and Female Virtue: Feminism and the Politics of Prostitution in Nineteenth-Century Britain." In *Powers of Desire: The Politics of Sexuality*, edited by Christine Stansell, Ann

Snitow and Sharon Thompson. New York: Monthly Review Press, 1983.

Weber, Max. *Economy and Society.* New York: Bedminster Press, 1968.

Weeks, Jeffrey. *Sex, Politics and Society: The Regulation of Sexuality Since 1800.* London and New York: Longman, 1981.

Weeks, Jeffrey. *Sex, Politics and Society: The Regulation of Sexuality Since 1800.* 2nd ed., New York: Longman, 1989.

Weeks, Jeffrey. *Sexuality.* London and New York: Tavistock Publications, 1986.

Weeks, Jeffrey. *Sexuality and Its Discontents.* London: Routledge and Kegan Paul, 1985.

Weibe, Robert. *The Search for Order.* New York: Hill and Wang, 1967.

Wexler, Alice. *Emma Goldman: An Intimate Life.* New York: Pantheon Books, 1984.

Wexler, Alice. "Emma Goldman." Harbourfront Authors Series, Toronto: (October 1989).

Wexler, Alice. *Emma Goldman in Exile: From the Russian Revolution to the Spanish Civil War.* Boston: Beacon Press, 1989.

Wexler, Alice. "Emma Goldman on Mary Wollstonecraft." *Feminist Studies* 7 (Spring 1981): 113-33.

Wexler, Alice. "Emma Goldman in Love." *Raritan: A Quarterly Review* 1 (Summer 1982): 116-45.

Wexler, Alice. "The Early Life of Emma Goldman." *The Psychohistory Review* 8 (Spring 1980): 7-21.

Wolff, Kurt H., ed. *Emile Durkheim et al.: Essays on Sociology and Philosophy.* New York: Harper and Row, 1960.

Woodcock, George. *Anarchism: A History of Libertarian Ideas and Movements.* New York: World Publishing Co., 1962.

Woolf, Virginia. *Three Guineas.* London: The Hogarth Press, 1951.

Index

abortion, 80
American National Education
    Association (1910), 93
anarchism
    Goldman's commitment to, xi
    Goldman's theoretical
    contributions to, 1-3, 5, 7, 22
Anarchist Congress (of 1907), 7-8

Baginsky, Max, 7-8
Berkin, Carol Ruth, xvi
Berkman, Alexander, xi, 42, 44-45
biological determinism, 67-69
birth control, xii
    and religion, 75-76
    and status of women, 72-73
Bloch, Iwan, 161
bureaucracy, 87-92

Carpenter, Edward, 108, 137, 138,
    139
    on feminist/lesbian link, 162
    on lesbianism, 161-163
Carter, Angela, 110
Chodorow, Nancy, 34
Cleyre, Voltairine de, xv
Converse, Florence, 155
Cook, Blanche Weisen, 156, 164,
    170, 171, 172

Darwin, Charles, 83
D'Emilio, John, 124, 139, 140
Dinnerstein, Dorothy, 34
Drinnon, Richard, x, xviii, 14, 25,
    26
DuBois, Ellen Carol, 114, 119,
    156, 187
Durkheim, Emile, 26, 101, 102
    and the "needs of the organ-
    ism," 68

Echols, Alice, 119-120, 186
Ehrenreich, Barbara, 34
Ellis, Havelock, 41, 57, 100, 110,
    137, 138
    and eugenics, 129-131
    and female homosexuality, 157,
    158-161
    and female modesty, 125-126
    on feminist/lesbian link, 160-161
    and male aggression, 126-127
    and male homosexuality, 125
    and masturbation, 124
    and marriage, 125
    and misogyny, 126-128
    and philosophy of separate
    spheres, 131
    and women's emancipation,
    129-131
    contribution to sexual liberalism,
    124
Elmy, Elizabeth Wolstenholme,
    145
Elshtain, Jean Bethke, 3, 33
English, Deirdre, 34
eugenics, 77-78, 84

Falk, Candace, xvii, 61, 81, 88
Faderman, Lillian, 157, 171
Fawcett, Millicent, 137
feminism
    and positions on sexuality,
    118-120
    debates on sexuality pleasures
    versus dangers, 151-152
    "pro-sex" positions, 119
Fitzgerald ("Fritzie"), Eleanor, 170
Ford, Henry, 90
Forel, August, 161
Foucault, Michel, 105
    and relations of power, 114, 117
Fournier, Charles, 108
Fox-Genovese, Elizabeth, 184
Freedman, Estelle, 124, 139, 140
French, Marilyn, 34, 35, 117
Freud, Sigmund, 57, 106
    and homosexuality, 159
    on sexual instinct, 132-133,
    135-136
    popularization of theories, 133
Frick, Henry Clay, xi

Gagnon, J.H., 105
gender, 113
    and sexuality, 113-114
Gilman, Charlotte Perkins, xvi
Goldman, Abraham, ix
Goldman, Emma,
    and birth control, xiii, 71-72, 74
    and "difference" versus
    "equality" debates, vii-viii
    and education, 92, 93

and eugenics, 81, 82
and female heterosexuality, 146, 148
and female homosexuality, 154-158
and individuality, 83
and influence of Freud, 132, 137
and "integrative feminism," 56, 188
and libertarian position on sexuality, 150
and "maternal" feminists, 57
and nature/culture dichotomy, 30-32
and opponent women reformers, 148-151
and "puritanism," 79, 140
and "sex debates" of second-wave feminism, xviii, xx
and sexual liberation, 140, 153
and significance of sex repression, 57
and the State, 35-40, 87-88, 90-91, 95-96
and theory construction, 2-3, 5
and Tonnies' view of Gemeinschaft, 26-28
and the vote for women, 36-37
and "tragedy" of women's emancipation, 144, 145, 148
and women's "nature", xix, 40-46
and women's place in the "private and public" realms, 46-52
and women's same-sex relationships, xx
biographical sketch, ix-xvi
conflict between private and public life, xiv-xv
dichotomous thinking, 30-32, 182-183
early life, ix-x
first introduction to Freud, 132
first meeting of sexologists, 137
libertarian view of sexuality, 183-184
rejection of sexual dualism, 52-59
relationships with women, 177
treatment of female homosexuality 163-177
view of power, 187
view of sexologists, 123

view of sexuality, 117-118, 120
Goldman, Taube, ix
Gordon, Linda, ix, 71, 73, 74-75, 77, 86, 114, 119, 156, 187
on Freud, 134
Grosskurth, Phyllis, 124

Harris, Frank, 45
Havel, Hippolyte, 67
Haymarket anarchists, x, xiii
Hirschfeld, Magnus, 136, 149, 167, 168, 169
Hughes, Patricia, 34

Ibsen, Henrik, xix
and feminism, 18-20
influence on Goldman, 5-6, 16-22
on liberty and individuality, 20-21
Ignatieff, Michael, 112
individualism, 82, 83
and women, 84-87

Jeffreys, Sheila, 124, 148, 184, 186
on Havelock Ellis, 127, 132
Jordanova, L.J., 29-30

Katz, Jonathan, 172, 175
Kennard, Jean, 171
Kennedy, David, 75
Kersner, Jacob, x
Key, Ellen, 40-41, 130-131
Kollontai, Alexandra, 42-43
Kosmak, George, 71
Krafft-Ebing, Richard, 136, 159
Kropotkin, Peter, 84, 87
influence on Goldman, 5-6, 8-16

Lasch, Christopher, 25
Lenz, Elinor, 53
lesbianism, 144
Levetzow, Karl von, 167, 168
liberalism, 82, 83

Marchak, M. Patricia, 82
Marcus, Steven, 134
Marcuse, Herbert, 108
Malinowski, Bronislaw, 100, 101, 102
Mannheim, Karl, 26
Marks, Jeannette, 171
McKinley, William, xii
Mead, Margaret, 103
Michel, Louise, 149, 155, 156
relationship with Goldman, 166-170

Miles, Angela, 55, 56
Mill, J.S., 109
Mitchell, Juliet, 106
Moll, Albert, 159
Mother Earth, xii, xxi, 7
Myerhoff, Barbara, 53

nature/culture dichotomy, 28-30
    feminist criticism of, 32-35
Neill, A.S., 108
Nettlau, Max, 43
"New Woman," 154, 155

O'Hare, Kate, 174
    relationship with Goldman,
    174-176

Parsons, Lucy, xv
Pierson, Ruth, 38-40
Plummer, Kenneth, 100, 105
Poovey, Mary, 68
Prentice, Alison, 38-40

race-suicide debate, 77, 78, 81, 82
Rapp, Rayna, 48, 103, 104, 111
Reich, Wilhelm, 102-103, 108
Reitman, Ben, xii, xvii, 174
reproduction
    theoretical perspectives on,
    115-117
Rich, Adrienne, 145-146
Roosevelt, Theodore, 78, 81
Ross, Ellen, 48, 103, 104, 111
Rubin, Gayle, 113

Sanger, Margaret, xv, 76, 77, 81
Scheman, Naomi, 84
Schmalhausen, Samuel, 45
Schmidt, Eugene, 164, 165
Scott, Joan Wallach, 40
Scudder, Vida, 155
Segal, Lynne, 119
sexologists
    influence upon Goldman,
    136-141
sexology, xx
sexuality
    definition of, xxi
    liberal-pluralist approaches to
    the regulation of, 109
    libertarian approaches to the
    regulation of, 108-109
    moral absolutist approaches to
    the regulation of, 106-108

radical-pluralist approaches to
    the regulation of, 111
    social organization of, 112-115
Shulman, Alix Kates, xvii, 15, 66,
    67
Simmel, Georg, 26
Simon, William, 105
Smith, Dorothy, 4
Smith-Rosenberg, Carroll, 41,
    147, 154, 166
Snitow, Ann, 144, 150, 185
social constructionism, xxi
Soloman, Martha, ix, xviii
Spencer, Herbert, 83
Spender, Dale, 153
Sperry, Almeda, 171
    relationship with Goldman,
    172-174
Stansell, Christine, 144, 185
Swiney, Francis, 145
Sydie, Rosalind, 35

Taylor, Federick W., 89-90
Thompson, Sharon, 144, 185
Tonnies, Ferdinand, 26-28, 35

Unger, Roberto, 4, 30

Vance, Carol, 104, 114
Victorian medical model, 68-69
    and birth control, 69-70
Van Herk, Aritha, 51

Walkowitz, Judith, 147
Weber, Max, 26, 89
Weeks, Jeffrey, xx, 123, 137, 141,
    150, 152
    on essentialist approaches,
    99-103
    on non-essentialist approaches,
    103-106
    on sex/society dichotomy, 28-29
    on theoretical approaches to
    the regulation of sexuality,
    106-112
    on theoretical taxonomy of
    sexuality, xx, 99-112
Wexler, Alice, ix, xiv, xvi, 61, 164
Wiebe, Robert, 88, 94
Wilde, Oscar, 159, 163, 164
Woodcock, George, 5, 14
Wooley, Mary, 171
Woolf, Virginia, 32-33, 60

THE GEOGRAPHY OF FREEDOM
The Odyssey of Elisée Reclus
by Marie Fleming
Introduction by George Woodcock

A celebrated geographer turns to political philosophy. Elisée Reclus was a 19th-century French geographer and anarchist whose fascinating life and original ideas are undergoing a well deserved revival of interest. He had a passionate curiousity about the interaction between humans and their environment, and his 19-volume *Nouvelle Géographie universelle*, celebrated in its time, is still a classic of human geography.

One of the revealing and fundamental themes of this examination is that Reclus's anarchist theory was the product of an interaction of utopian reflection and science, two strands of thought taken to be mutually exclusive. This work is the only English-language analysis of Reclus's political ideas.

Marie Fleming teaches political science at the University of Western Ontario, London.

A solid addition to the resurgence of anarchist scholarship...for upper-division students and all political theory collections.
Choice

Many of the issues and problems dealt with in the book are not simply of historical significance, but will be seen as relevant today by those who are concerned about moral values in our social life.
Canadian Journal of Political Science

Fleming has contributed to our understanding of nineteenth-century anarchist theory by exploring the life of a figure largely unknown to historians of political thought.
American Political Science Review

246 pages, bibliography, photographs
Paperback ISBN: 0-921689-16-0 $16.95
Hardcover ISBN: 0-921689-17-9 $36.95
Biography/Politics

THE ANARCHIST COLLECTIVES
Workers' Self-Management in Spain 1936-39
edited by Sam Dolgoff

Sam Dolgoff, editor of the best anthology of Bakunin's writings, has now produced an excellent documentary history of the anarchist collectives in Spain. Although there is a vast literature on the Spanish Civil War, this is the first book in English that is devoted to the experiments in workers' self-management, both urban and rural, which constituted one of the most remarkable social revolutions in modern history.
Paul Avrich

The eyewitness reports and commentary presented in this highly important study reveal a very different understanding of the nature of socialism and the means for achieving it.
Noam Chomsky

195 pages, illustrated
Paperback ISBN: 0-919618-74-X   **$14.95**
Hardcover ISBN: 0-919618-73-1   **$29.95**
History/Politics/Philosophy

DURRUTI
The People Armed
by Abel Paz
translated by Nancy MacDonald

An exhaustive biography of the legendary Spanish revolutionary Buenaventura Durruti, who died at age forty in 1936. Durruti was an uncompromising anarchist who knew battle, exile, imprisonment, strikes, insurrections, and life underground. This man, who started life as a rebellious young worker and who at his death was mourned by millions, acted always on the conviction that freedom and revolution are inseparable, refusing all honours, awards and bureaucratic positions.

Wherever you go it's Durruti and Durruti again, whom you hear spoken of as a wonder man.
Toronto Daily star

323 pages, illustrated
Paperback ISBN: 0-919618-74-X   **$14.95**
Hardcover ISBN: 0-919618-73-1   **$29.95**
Biography/History/Politics